THE MARK

A War Correspondent's Memoir of Vietnam and Cambodia

THE MARK

A War Correspondent's Memoir of Vietnam and Cambodia

by Jacques Leslie

Four Walls Eight Windows, New York/London

Published in the United States by:
Four Walls Eight Windows
39 West 14th Street, room 503
New York, N.Y., 10011

U.K. Offices:
Four Walls Eight Windows/Turnaround
27 Horsell Road
London, NL1 XL, England

First printing April 1995.

Library of Congress Cataloging-in-Publication Data:
Leslie, Jacques, 1947-.
The Mark: a War Correspondent's Memoir of Vietnam and Cambodia/by Jacques Leslie.
p. cm.
ISBN: 1-56858-024-X
1. Vietnamese Conflict, 1961-1975 -- Personal narratives, American. 2. Vietnamese Conflict, 1961-1975 -- Journalists. 3. Leslie, Jacques, 1947 -. I. Title
DS559.5.L48   1995
959.704'38 -- dc20   94-38062
                                                    CIP

Printed in the United States
10 9 8 7 6 5 4 3 2 1

For Leslie, Tristan, Kadie, and Sarah

Table of Contents

There is an old proverb that a girl may sleep with one man without being a trollop, but let a man cover one little war and he is a war correspondent.

— A.J. Liebling

And where we had thought to find an abomination, we shall find a god; where we had thought to slay another, we shall slay ourselves; where we had thought to travel outward, we shall come to the center of our own existence; where we had thought to be alone, we shall be with all the world.

— Joseph Campbell

PROLOGUE

It was Nick Proffitt who coined the phrase. On the evening in 1972 when I first heard it, I was at his villa in Saigon, sitting on the big veranda that overlooked a bigger garden that in the moonlight looked mysterious, possibly mined, whence emanated the plaintive calls of geckos, nocturnal lizards, saying "uh-oh" over and over again. I was a fledgling war correspondent, aged 24, and Nick, a colleague, was my first friend in Vietnam. On many nights I'd stay at his house past the eleven o'clock curfew, when the city was silent and disquietude rose from the empty streets, and we'd sit enclosed in the humidity talking endlessly about the war. We thought we knew a secret nobody in the States knew, and burned with our frustration in communicating it. As soon as Nick mentioned the mark, I knew I had it, I knew we both did. Having the mark meant being addicted to Vietnam, being used to intrigue and pumping adrenalin and layer after layer of lie, truth, lie, truth, until the two were indistinguishable; the mark was the perverse and frightened expression of our love. People with the mark shared a yearning they suspected Vietnam of being able to satisfy, and while they hated the war (for wars are meant to be hated), they loved it even more, and hated themselves for loving it.

The mark was alchemical. It transformed sordid objects into things of wonder, even beauty; it made fear tolerable. Under its spell I'd leave Nick' s villa at midnight or so, nodding good-bye to him as he closed the hulking metal gate behind me, and then I'd be alone on the street, exposed. It was at that spot that Nick's terrified successor, Lloyd Norman, once was held up by a man who put his hand inside his jacket pocket and made it look like a pistol, and by doing so managed to relieve Lloyd of his wallet and watch; in a country distinguished by the scope of its violence, the thief struck me as quaintly pacific, nearly gentlemanly. I'd stride down the street, stunned that the moon could shine so brightly over such benighted ground: it gave everything a silver outline, like Jesus in a medieval painting. I'd see the silhouette of the Vietnamese soldier who manned the outpost on the corner, and I'd try to show him by my pace and stature that I was an American, before he lifted his rifle and looked through the crosshairs. Usually he didn't even acknowledge me: I learned to feel relieved when my presence failed to evoke the slightest movement in him. I'd walk past the Catholic cathedral where the daughter of South Vietnam's president would get married within days of the climax of nearly five years of peace negotiations, and fancy cars would line up outside as if their high-ranking occupants were filled with the joy of matrimony instead of the trepidation that everyone knew gripped the city. I'd pass by the park where lovers gathered on their motorcycles in the early evening and then raced home to beat the curfew, and I'd feel the longing and desperation of their romances — it was like a haze they'd left to settle over the park after they'd gone home. Down the street was the Presidential palace itself, the very seat of foreboding, wreathed in shadows, nearly invisible, ringed by layers of barricades; I'd imagine President Thieu, as stolid and graceless as the edifice he inhabited, sitting at its core, endlessly calculating the logarithms of killing, and I'd shudder as the sinister emanations passed through me. As I walked, I'd hear the outgoing artillery in the distance, either deadly or futile, no one ever knew which. At last I'd reach my courtyard and unlock the metal door and walk up the circular staircase to my villa, through the living room with its checkerboard floor and its bar adorned with rice straw, and I'd take one last look through the lattice windows at the park and the palace and the cathedral. It took only five minutes from Nick's house to mine, but by the time I reached home I could feel my heart pumping, and I'd know that I never wanted to live in any place where evening walks offered less drama. In Vietnam I'd found my universe of darkness and light, the font of all my feeling. My mark was deep.

So deep was my mark, in fact, that it outlived the war by a decade and a half. At first it felt like a blessing, then a curse, and finally a blessing again: at last I understood that the mark was my destiny, my path, and that in following the path to its end I had solved the mystery of my life. Then I looked back at my experiences in Indochina and for the first time saw their harmony.

TAXIING
Chapter

1

    I did not realize until years after the event that it was the pivotal one, the one that turned me from the profession I thought I loved. I had been covering Vietnam for 14 months, and I had just begun to develop a reputation for writing startling war stories. A month earlier, as a ceasefire went fitfully into effect across South Vietnam, I had sauntered into Viet Cong territory, until that time a land as menacing to most Americans as an exploding star, and I'd emerged with what struck some of my colleagues and me as the story of the war. "'WE ARE FRIENDS,' VIET CONG TELL VISITING U.S. NEWSMAN," said the headline across the top of my newspaper, the Los Angeles *Times*. I loved that headline, not least for its uncommon blackness and even including its use of the quaint term "newsman," but most of all because it affirmed my membership in the international fraternity of foreign correspondents in whose ranks I had until then doubted I belonged.

    A month later, however, a tiny doubt lodged itself inside my subconsciousness, roiling the tranquil sea of my ambition. The decisive event began with an anonymous phone call: a Vietnamese-accented voice said I should go to a certain hospital room in Cholon, the city abutting Saigon, at a certain time the next day. In truth, I was not altogether ignorant about the purpose of the call, for a week earlier I'd been told it might come, in connection with a story I was trying to write about the treatment of political detainees inside South Vietnam's prisons. Still, I did-n't know whom I'd be meeting, and the idea of being summoned by an anonymous caller added a frisson of titillation to the encounter. Wasn't that how reporters in old movies were always getting their most important stories?

I savored the intrigue right up to the moment I opened the door to the hospital ward, and espied 13 Vietnamese men sit-ting strangely inert upon the floor. Apparently apprized of my identity as a reporter, they hailed me with an enthusiasm I found disconcerting, if for no other reason than that it belied the grotesque condition of their bodies. They were sideshow speci-mens who refused to play the part, acting instead as if they were stars of the high wire. None of the men could walk. They'd all worn shackles in prison for periods ranging from five to ten years, and as a result their leg muscles were atrophied, virtually non-existent. In addition, their bodies were covered with scars, testament to the beatings administered to them. Despite all this, it was not their appearance that unsettled me: I'd already seen my share of mangled corpses, so a few live bodies, no matter how misshapen, could not easily puncture my composure. What gave me pause was their serenity, their lack of distress at their deformation. They not only insisted on displaying their fleshless legs, but they were always smiling, as if pain had no purchase. Without being asked, they rolled their hospital pajamas to the knee and lined up side by side — they wanted me to document their legs' disfigurement with photographs. One of them noted merrily that my forearms were thicker than his calves, and it was all I could do to smile back wanly. Then they beckoned me to pose with them. When they reached out to put their arms around my shoulders, I flinched — I didn't want the barrier of touch bro-ken, I didn't want them that close.

Why did they keep smiling? Their tales were so horrific I thought surely hell could be no worse. Over the next few hours they explained that they'd all been kept inside the "tiger cages" in South Vietnam's Con Son Island prison. The tiger cages were the most notorious cells in the Saigon regime's most notorious penal institution; they were six-by-ten foot cubicles whose only opening was a metal grill in place of a ceiling. The men said they were beaten with clubs, sprayed with lime that caused them to vomit and sneeze — their jailers even dumped excrement and boiling water on them. Sometimes the men were given so little water that they prized the few drops left after rinsing bowls containing their excretions; sometimes they drank their own urine. They'd been so hungry that when they were let out of the cages, they feigned collapse so that they could grab a few mouthfuls of grass; after their jailers caught on, the grass was kept short, and when the prisoners tried to eat it, the jailers pried it out of their mouths. Altogether, they said, half their fellow inmates died.

Yet far from being consumed by anger, these men alluded to hatred only once, when they told of a prisoner who'd been given a mysterious injection and then died; his last words, they said, were a diatribe against his jailers. Instead, they spoke of their solidarity, their mutual love, as if their rice bowls contained lotuses instead of fly-covered fish paste, as if the prison floor were a half-inch thick in rose petals instead of lime. The men passed time staring at the beads of water that formed on the walls of the cells, and composed and recited poems to one another. Poems! One man wrote out a copy of a poem and presented it to me, "our patient and beloved correspondent." Later that day I had it translated. The poem's narrator describes picking vegetables in the prison garden while exulting in the breeze that "blows in rhythm with the movement of our hands." Then he recalls a fellow inmate who died a year earlier, shackled and hollow-eyed, and regrets that the dead man was not given medicine, water, and vegetables from the garden, for then

> He would still be living today,
> Sitting beside us, sharing his joy with us.

That's right: joy. I knew as soon as I read the poem that the men had plumbed life's riddle: somehow they'd faced death and come out the other side. Deprived of everything but their lives, they had learned how to take pleasure in simple existence: they were the first free men I'd ever met. What I was not prepared to embrace was the corollary: if they, though unable to walk, embodied freedom, then I, shackled in less obvious ways, did not. It was as if they cast an unwelcome shadow across my chosen course, beckoning me to alter it; years passed before I realized the significance of the intersection. They were at the heart of the puzzle I didn't yet know I was trying to solve.

Perhaps it's in the nature of a maze that its explorers are not aware of choosing it, but rather stumble into it, seemingly by chance, long before they realize that the forbidding walls on either side comprise a conundrum. That would begin to explain my first trip to Vietnam, when I dropped in to Saigon as if it were a tourist stop like Bali or Bangkok, and then didn't stay long enough to find out anything more than that it terrified me. I was two years out of Yale, having just completed a post-graduate stint of teaching English and studying Chinese at a Hong Kong university; I'd taken the fellowship to get a taste of life abroad before settling down to what I assumed would be a journalism career in the United States. I visited Saigon during a kind of "Farewell Southeast Asia" vacation swing, trusting a restless impulse that was magnified the longer I lolled in the conventional tourist meccas. The trip to Saigon was uneventful, but I felt suffused with a low-grade dread I couldn't shake as long as I was there. Everything was drearier than I'd imagined; nobody wore crisp white suits like Marlon Brando in "The Ugly American." The buildings were all functional gray and depressing, as mournful in their way as the daily downpour that emptied the sidewalks and filled me with foreboding. Suddenly I was the only person on the streets; I didn't want to be alone like that, not in Saigon. One night I went to a movie at an American base. The theater was outdoors, and I was distracted by illumination flares floating earthward on the horizon. It was the sort of movie you'd watch only because sedatives weren't available.

The only time the GIs showed the slightest sign of life was when a character in the movie said, "Everybody's got a right to be a sucker once in his life." They cheered.

I stayed with a few acquaintances who worked for International Volunteer Services, a Peace Corps-like outfit most of whose employees were in their early 20s, as I was. Saigon was boring, they said; the real action was in the countryside; I should go there. *No thanks*, I thought to myself. Instead, a day or two after I saw the movie, I realized I couldn't take another day in Vietnam. With a burgeoning sense of urgency I packed, scribbled a note announcing my departure, and rushed to the airport, as if my survival depended on boarding the next plane out. I wasn't ready for Vietnam yet, and didn't think I'd ever have to be.

Yet I was back in just a year and a few months, primed. I'd returned to the United States, set myself up as a freelance journalist in Washington, D.C., and thought constantly of the vibrant continent I'd so recently departed. I hired a tutor in Chinese, which I'd studied in Hong Kong, and for a short time I possessed a Burmese girlfriend, but what I chiefly did was languish. Uncertain how long I wished to remain in Washington, I took a furnished apartment that looked as if it had been decorated by a specialist in kitsch, and tried not to notice. Each day I sat at a rickety formica-topped table that doubled as my desk and dining board. In nine months I sold three magazine pieces, one of which was about Washington's Chinatown. I subscribed to two papers, three on Sundays, and wondered what it must be like to work for one of them.

Then a man died, and a door mysteriously opened. Months before, the Los Angeles *Times*' foreign editor, Robert Gibson, had searched for a young Chinese speaker with journalistic ambitions. Himself hired by the United Press and sent to cover the Korean War at the age of 22, Gibson wanted to give a similar opportunity to someone else: he was looking for a budding journalist to train in Vietnam for eventual assignment in

China. To me this sounded like putting a rookie in the World Series to prepare him for the regular season, not that I would have complained, far from it; the problem was that before I'd even heard of the job, Gibson had filled it. Gibson's choice was Frank Aller, a China specialist fresh from a Rhodes scholarship at Oxford (where he'd been future President Bill Clinton's roommate). Aller also happened to be a draft-dodger; he'd gone to England thinking he probably wouldn't be able to return to the United States without facing a prison sentence. Gibson persuaded Aller's draft board to grant Aller the right to reenter the country without penalty; then, once Aller returned, Gibson stationed him on the *Times'* foreign desk for a few months so that he'd be familiar with the paper's operations. By then I'd heard of Aller's hiring from a mutual friend, and regretted that I hadn't had a chance to apply for the job myself. In ensuing months I heard rumors that Aller harbored misgivings about going to Vietnam, that he was a kind of tortured soul, and I secretly hoped he'd decide not to go after all. Then the mutual friend somberly informed me that three days before Aller was scheduled to go to Saigon, he'd shot himself to death. I understood my friend's grief but, not knowing Aller, I could hardly replicate it; instead, I hurriedly sent my clippings to Gibson. After a three-week tryout I was hired.

I spent three months on the *Times'* foreign desk, aching to leave. I gathered that I baffled some of the other reporters; they thought going to Vietnam as a journalist was not much different from being drafted, and wondered what depravity kept me from opting for the Southern California Good Life, which despite what evidence I could see they claimed to enjoy. Once I was venturing down the hall towards the snack machine when I encountered the metropolitan editor, a pear-shaped throwback to "The Front Page" whose intellectual curiosity extended as far as the Los Angeles Rams and the Los Angeles Dodgers. I was carrying around a thick tome called *Two Vietnams*, and I mentioned that I was struggling through it. "Looks like a yawner to me," he said, and ambled off.

I was on a mission, of course; I was shocked nobody could see that. The war, after all, had been the leitmotif of my college experience, from which I was now only three years removed. I'd graduated in 1968, when turmoil seemed to define the country. Melancholy most of the time, I assumed that my distress and America's were intertwined. What plagued me, I thought, were poverty, racial discrimination, police brutality, and above all the war in Vietnam; the only way I could make myself happy was to make the entire nation, the entire world happy. I took course after course in the social sciences, trying to find the country's deliverance and my own, but all the news was bad. I picked up the paper one morning and cried: it contained the first day's accounts of the Tet Offensive. Vietnam became the lens through which I saw the world: I knew the aftereffects of childhood polio would keep me from being drafted, yet I was as preoccupied by the war as anyone in danger of participating in it. Something about Vietnam touched me so deeply that without having been there, I felt I knew the place. In a column I wrote for the Yale *Daily News* I said that Vietnam possessed so many layers of stimulation that anyone going there risked being constantly overwhelmed. I couldn't explain how I knew that, but when I lived there, I confirmed it.

Now, held back from the grand arena by mere editors, I sensed my opportunity to act nobly. The dread I'd experienced during my first trip to Vietnam had vanished as soon as the title "foreign correspondent" was conferred on me; now I'd be linked to a home office, I'd be linked to the world. My life had purpose: I was going to make a nation grateful for newspapers, for I was going to explain why the war was evil. Not that I talked about that: almost every other word out of the mouth of Gibson was "objectivity," which as he defined it sounded like my idea of "hawkishness." Gibson didn't fit my fantasy of a foreign editor, suave and wise; he looked like a worn sofa, with too much stuffing around his mid-section and not enough on top of his head,

where carefully placed strands of hair did not quite conceal
his baldness. He acted as if he wanted me to consider him
my patron and mentor, which in a sense he was, but I could-
n't summon the necessary awe. For one thing his model of
objective reporting was George McArthur, about to be my
Saigon bureau chief, who, like Gibson, dated back to the
Korean War, *their* formative war. McArthur's stories suggested he still thought he was in Korea. He looked at
Vietnam and saw good guys (Americans) and bad guys
(North Vietnamese and Viet Cong); he even wrote a story
mocking Communist cows. I thought my ride in Vietnam
might not be smooth.

Of course, I understood that McArthur wasn't the
most significant obstacle I faced. I didn't know whether I
was capable of war reporting, or any kind of reporting for
that matter. I was painfully aware, however, that my existence in Washington had been threadbare, bereft of chal-
lenge and emotional sustenance; now at least I could step
out of that gray world into one full of color. I knew I was
gambling my life, but I thought the risk was justifiable. I told
myself that I learned most when, disregarding fear, I cast
myself into unfamiliar worlds; now I'd grow or die. I was all
potential energy, like a rock on top of a mountain; I was
ready to roll down it, I was ready to live.

A few days before my departure, Gibson arranged a
farewell luncheon in the executive dining room. The participants were Frank Haven, the managing editor; Gibson; my
father; and me. Painfully aware of the gap between their
ages and mine, I felt outnumbered. I sat at the table, watching, while they exchanged polite repartee. I suspected
Haven of disapproving of my being hired, Gibson of supporting the war, and my father of general oppression of
sons. I just wanted to go to Vietnam.

I arrived in Saigon on New Year's Day, 1972. It was

late in the war, but nobody knew that then: part of what gave this war its particular aura was that no one could imagine its ending. McArthur met me at the airport. A native of rural Georgia, he cultivated a yokel's pose: he wore more grease in his hair than I'd seen in four years at Yale, and his favorite expression was "He doesn't know whether to wind his ass or scratch his watch." I'd met him in Los Angeles, where he appeared shopworn, out-of-date, but he looked now as if Saigon refreshed him, as if Vietnam were a more satisfying version of Hawaii. In L.A., I realized, he'd been holding his breath, a captive of the homeland, but now he breathed out and was breezy; his manner exuded a certain country exhilaration, as if Saigon of all places possessed much of what was still hearty in the world. I didn't know enough to recognize the symptoms. McArthur was addicted to Vietnam. He had the mark.

The long drive from Tan Son Nhut, the Saigon airport, was eventful enough to convince many Americans to turn around and get back on their planes, having had their fill of foul smells, loud motorcycles, barriers demarcated by barbed wire, drivers who preferred the wrong side of the street because it had less traffic — but I'd absorbed that stuff a year and a half earlier, and no longer felt intimidated. This time I thought the road glittered with promise. McArthur didn't even notice the surroundings; he drove in sweeping arcs, disregarding lanes like everybody else, and plied me with advice, such as that I should never ignore a Saigon policeman's command to stop, as a friend of his once had and the policeman shot out his eye.

McArthur deposited me at the Caravelle Hotel, a bland bandbox in the center of town that Americans considered Saigon's best hotel, apparently because it was the only one to exude no local color. I ate dinner alone in the restaurant on the hotel's top floor, notorious for having been a swank observation point for journalists during the 1968 Tet Offensive, and then I returned to my room, but I was too restless to go to bed. A voice inside me whispered: *You are about to begin your real life. No more drabness, no more loneliness. Everything from now on will be dramat-*

ic, romantic, intense. I tried to think of someone to visit, and came up with Kevin Buckley, a *Newsweek* reporter I'd known when he was stationed in Hong Kong. I called him, and he told me to come right over.

In the inflated parlance of Saigon, all expensive apartments were called villas, but Kevin's was one of the few that deserved the appellation; as *Newsweek*'s Saigon bureau chief, he lived in a house permanently rented by the magazine. A white-frocked maid let me in through a vast swinging gate that appeared designed to block out the ugly reality outside. I was led to a spacious veranda where Kevin and his companion, a *New Yorker* writer named Frankie Fitzgerald, greeted me. For an hour or so they regaled me with the Saigon version of wit, such as that for Kevin's birthday a colleague gave him a gas mask. They also offered me a few wry story ideas. My favorite was "American officials' most frequently used clichés," of which the couple provided a sampling: "It's safer in Saigon than it is in Washington, D.C." "There's corruption here, but there's corruption in Cook County, too." "If there's ever peace in this country, it will make a great resort area." American officials were laughable; I'd only been in the country a few hours and I knew that.

Kevin and Frankie wanted to go to bed, but I was still restless; the talk hadn't calmed me at all. I knew right away what I'd do. As I left the villa, the heat from the departed day rose up from the sidewalk, through my sandals, up my calves, and I experienced the energy as sexual. I wasn't a sexual neophyte exactly, but I suffered from a kind of perpetual sexual hunger. If that didn't distinguish me from other American males my age, this did: I suspected Vietnam of being able to slake my appetite.

Now I strode through Saigon's red light district, hoping to be lured. No such luck. Bar girls, happy faces painted on top of sad ones, leaned out of their gloomy dens, beckoning, "Hey you GI you come see me you numbah one!" I wanted no part of any transaction that began that way. For half an hour I paced back and forth, finding reasons to reject all appeals; none of the bar girls matched any fantasy of mine. Now it was getting late;

I'd have to hurry or the sexual tension would fade. In desperation I decided on a massage and arbitrarily picked a parlor. The place was dirty, and only one ceiling fan worked. The masseuse looked aloof, contemptuous. It was near closing time, she said. I'd have to settle for an abbreviated massage at the full rate; "special massages" — she made an up-and-down motion with her closed fist — cost more. I was losing interest. I stripped and got a straight massage, given indifferently, as if the masseuse were squeezing a snake. I left the parlor smelling of talcum powder, and, restless still, went to bed.

The next day I ventured out of the Caravelle for a walk. The hotel abutted Saigon's main street, known to old-timers by its euphonic old French name, Rue Catinat, and to newcomers like me by its droll government-bequeathed Vietnamese name, Tu Do, or Freedom Street. A few steps out of the Caravelle, I was embarked on a voyage of potential drama, past pickpockets and beggars and black market money changers, past fat GIs and draft-dodging Vietnamese "cowboys" in tight pants who stole watches off Americans' wrists (I lost two that way) and angry one-legged ex-ARVN soldiers who wielded their crutches like bayonets. At one end of the street, toward the murky Saigon River, was the red light district where I'd wandered the previous evening. Now I headed in the other direction, passing the old French opera house that had been transformed into the South Vietnamese Assembly — from opera to comic opera, I thought.

I crossed the street to reach a wacky rendition of a public square, dominated by a huge, ugly statue of two soldiers, one seeming to shove the other into combat. For a small fee a man with a big box camera offered to take my picture in front of it; I was amazed by the GIs who took the photographer up, and stood with their Vietnamese "dates" issuing cheesy smiles as if they were at Yellowstone or Niagara Falls. The photographer didn't tempt me as much as the items for sale at the outdoor crafts market in one corner of the square. What a testament to free enterprise! How about a fluorescent nude (presumably a Vietnamese woman, but no Vietnamese had breasts *that* big) painted on black velvet, or a leather jacket embroidered with this legend on the back: "When I die I'll go to heaven because I've spent my time in hell — Saigon, Vietnam"? Surely here was proof of foreign occupation: Saigon's cultural expression was governed by the tastes of American GIs.

I went back across the street for a cold drink at the once-elegant Continental Hotel, the next building after the Opera. The open-air bar on the ground floor was known as the "Continental Shelf" in honor of the clientele that typically washed up there. Among its patrons were all manner of prostitutes, including deaf ones and some in drag; pimps; vendors of cigarettes, drugs, nude photographs, and artifacts made of brass artillery casings; American soldiers; diplomats; and journalists. A demented ex-ARVN general sat alone in one corner, alternately screaming and singing to the wall. The deaf whores propositioned Westerners with gestures more eloquent than words. Car fumes wafted through the room, mixing sweetly with the *citrons pressés*, and engine noises drowned out conversation. Just in witnessing the scene, I felt a party to its zany egalitarianism.

Saigon didn't feel like home, but something better: the place I had to come to when I left home. I'd visited Paris, London, Amsterdam, Copenhagen, but I preferred Saigon: it was extreme, like a Hieronymus Bosch painting. Twenty years earlier it had been the terrain of Graham Greene and Lucien Bodard, all undercurrents and evocations, gracious despite its decadence. Now it was blatant, vulgarized, a pie in the face of every sentimentalist. In Saigon I felt alive.

I must have been the greenest reporter who ever set foot in Vietnam. I was 24, and I had almost no experience as a newspaper reporter. I didn't know whether lieutenants or captains were higher ranked, whether battalions or companies were larger. I was terrified that I would never understand the Vietnamese-

English-army-bureaucracy-pidgin patois that overwhelmed the language I knew. What were VNAF and HES and CORDS and especially COMUSMACV? Why was the South Vietnamese army called ARVN, for Army of the Republic of Vietnam, while the regime itself was labeled not the RVN but the GVN, for Government of Vietnam? Where was Go Cong, which Americans pronounced as if it were a cheer for the Communists? Why did the briefer point to Military Region One and say Eye-core? Now I see all the acronyms as war debris, as inert as the mountains of used helmets or shell casings or fragments of army installations I later saw despoiling the Vietnamese landscape, but at the time the acronyms were scary, the code words of a fraternity I wanted desperately to join. I felt gullible and skeptical at the same time; I was afraid to believe anything I was told and afraid not to. I was reluctant to ask questions because they might reveal me as a novice: what if I confused an AK-47 with an M-16, or addressed an officer by the wrong rank? I confessed my ignorance of military matters to McArthur and he just muttered "Jesus." He must have been worried: how could he abide a kid who didn't know whether to wind his ass or scratch his watch?

It hadn't been McArthur's idea to teach foreign reporting to a neophyte. He'd told me in L.A. he wasn't pleased to be my mentor, but now he appeared resigned to doing his duty, or at least a minimal version of it. Together we made courtesy calls on several American officials who dealt with the press. McArthur's more valued sources, the C.I.A. agents, army officers, and embassy officials who constantly fed information to him and only one or two other reliably hawkish reporters, he kept to himself. As for Vietnamese sources, he had none, unless you included his cook, whose opinions he guilelessly cited as reflecting "the Vietnamese point of view." At MACV, the U.S. armed forces installation near the airport that looked like a misplaced American suburb, he introduced me to the military spokesman, an unctuous colonel who joked about how little information he'd reveal, and, as the months passed, proved true to his word.

Back in town, McArthur took me to the Joint U.S. Public Affairs Office, or JUSPAO (the acronyms were clattering in my brain like spent bullets) to get accreditation. All the employees were standing outside the building, having just evacuated it. McArthur recognized an official, who said it was nothing unusual, just a bomb scare: someone had called in a threat. The official said he doubted the Viet Cong did it, that it was probably just a disgruntled colleague. I wasn't sure he was joking.

McArthur's grandest gesture was to arrange a chat with Ellsworth Bunker, the 77-year-old ambassador who lent his stolid patriarchal air to the execution of American policy. Bunker rarely spoke to journalists, so my meeting him was something of an event, perhaps a favor in return for McArthur's turning a sympathetic ear to the embassy's interpretations of events. McArthur told Bunker I was a Yale graduate. Bunker said he was in the Class of '16. We talked about Yale for a few minutes and then McArthur and I left. I never talked to Bunker again.

In his office McArthur showed me his scrapbook, in which he pasted the published versions of his stories; he advised me to keep a scrapbook of my own. He also showed me a clipboard with a chart comparing his journalistic output to that of the 18 other L.A. *Times* correspondents. Down the left-hand side of the page he listed all the reporters; across the top were columns with headings for total stories, front page stories, opinion pieces, and news briefs. He culled the statistics from a memo Gibson sent the foreign staff each week, in which our contributions were summarized. With a brashness fortified by four years at Yale, I held the chart in contempt, and was amazed that McArthur wasn't embarrassed about displaying it; what was more difficult to admit was that I wondered where I'd rank on it.

I wanted to learn everything as fast as I could. I was breathless for usable information, the sort of fact that would score a point in a newspaper story or at least a conversation. I collected opinions about Vietnam with the obsessive selectivity of a connoisseur and put them on display in my letters home; it was if Vietnam filled the holes I perceived in my character, as if Vietnam alone made me feel worthy. "I've been in Vietnam two days and already find myself beginning to be sucked into the intellectual whirlpool," I wrote a friend, and I was, willingly, happily. Among the things I informed my correspondents was that as long as the South Vietnamese regime survived, I was probably safe, but that if it collapsed, its soldiers might riot and kill all the Westerners they could find. The regime, I added melodramatically, was indeed slowly collapsing.

A week passed before I wrote my first story; I worried that I'd taken too long. The story wasn't earthshaking, it wasn't even news; it was just a collection of my impressions of Saigon. I knew nothing about its fate until four days later, when the paper came in the mail. There it was, right on the front page, just below the lead story, under a headline that read, "Anything Goes in Race For Buck With Saigon's Sidewalk Army." I was too grave to allow myself exultation, but I at least felt pleased: I was in the big leagues at last. Hoping to savor the enhancement that I assumed print imparted to words, I read through the piece, and was disturbed to detect some errors. Apparently some punctuation had been lost during cable transmission. Why didn't the foreign desk catch the omissions? I felt my professional reputation was at stake: a million, two million, three million people might have seen the piece. Did everyone in L.A. pick up the paper and say, "Who is this guy Leslie whose story is on the front page?" Did they think my writing was distinctive? Did the *Times'* news service distribute the story? Did the Washington *Post*, which had access to the piece, use it? Journalism was serious business — didn't the guys on the foreign desk know that?

I was ready for an outing, and McArthur happened to be able to supply one. Con Son Island, about 50 miles off the

South Vietnamese coast, was well-known as the site of the "tiger cages," where political prisoners were said to be routinely tortured and treated as animals. With its usual flair for tactlessness, the South Vietnamese government arranged a party on the island for American officials, diplomats, and journalists. McArthur was among the invited, but he considered junkets less important than golf, which he played almost daily, and suggested I go instead. When I told Gloria Emerson, the highly inflammable New York *Times* correspondent, about the trip, she replied that she had been invited on such expeditions "dozens of times" but always refused. She made clear that I should do the same: "I mean, if you want to know what Auschwitz looks like...." I had a different Nazi image in mind: it would be like witnessing Hitler cavorting with Eva Braun at Berchtesgaden, his Bavarian hideaway. I found that alluring: I would be a spy.

The trip seemed innocent enough. South Vietnamese economics minister Phan Kim Ngoc, who organized it, explained that its purpose was to show us Con Son's beauty, to counter its undeserved reputation for horror. Ngoc, a fidgety, urbane man with a thick veneer of earnestness, said this so matter-of-factly I thought he might believe it. Apparently the trip was considered a military priority, for Ngoc and his forty guests flew to the island on a South Vietnamese air force transport plane. We swam on the beach and ate barbecued food and more or less pretended to be in Malibu. I have a photograph taken that day showing me standing next to Hoang Duc Nha, President Thieu's twenty-nine-year-old nephew and cousin, whom some considered the second most powerful man in the country. Opponents of the war said that Nha was unspeakably odious, that he had blood on his hands, but his countenance was baby-faced, almost innocent, and I was non-plused. In the photograph Nha is smiling broadly, while I look cocksure — my head is wrapped in a towel to protect against the sun, making me look like an Arab in a burmoose. I was trying to convince myself that I wasn't afraid of Mr. Nha.

In the afternoon Ngoc took us on an island bus tour that

ended at a gift shop next to the prison. No ordinary tourist shop, it offered canes, chopsticks, scabbards, and Chinese chess sets, all made by prisoners. Though we never were shown inside the prison, I heard the manager of Bank of America's Saigon branch say the trip proved the prison was no concentration camp. "Yes," his wife said, "it's just a normal prison." Later one of Ngoc's deputies in the economics ministry told me that Con Son would make a great tourist resort after the war.

A week or two after I arrived in Saigon, I moved into a villa of my own. McArthur was its last tenant; he'd relocated to more luxurious quarters and reserved the old place for me. He left me some of his unwanted furniture, and I bought a few other necessities: a rattan chair, a wooden desk, a fluorescent lamp. My interests didn't extend to decor: the apartment's most prominent features were its stark white walls. A year after I moved in, I sent away for some art posters, but they arrived just before I left, and I ended up selling them to friends at bargain discounts.

The apartment was incongruously large for one person. It occupied the second floor of a stately old house where my landlady's family once lived. Pressed for money, she, her mother, daughter, and two foster children moved to a smaller house just behind the original one; my office looked into its living room. A staircase led up from the ground floor entrance to a second floor entry, where my kitchen, dining room, and living room merged. The walls rose to a point only a yard or so from the floor; above were swinging wooden shutters and metal lattices that extended almost to the ceiling. Most of the time I left the shutters open, hoping for a breeze to alleviate the heat, but air wasn't all that got through. Once, for example, a bat crept in, and terrorized me with careening sorties, while I terrorized it with a broom. Eventually we declared a truce, and the bat found a way to leave.

Part of the apartment was intended as a bar, and was fancifully decorated with rice straw, as if it were a thatched hut — here I was in Vietnam, and my residence reminded me of "South Pacific." The landlady was proud of the apartment's one remarkable artifact, the living room ceiling fan. It was barely functional, but utility wasn't the point. Manufactured in Hanoi, it must have predated the 1954 partition of Vietnam, for nothing except arms and soldiers had come south since. Unlike conventional fans, with three or four angled blades, it had two little fans which hung from the tips of poles protruding from the rotating hub. When it was on, it looked like a biplane in a tailspin. It generated more conversation than it did wind, and was outlandish enough to justify the tradeoff.

I spent most of my time in the apartment's office. Its floor was covered with dark green paint, evocative of a naval boiler room, but the paint had peeled in spots to reveal a disturbing pink layer underneath. The telephone, inherited from McArthur, was bright red: my hot line. Distributed around the room like numbers on a clock were my wicker easy chair; a wooden bookcase filled with Vietnam books, mostly unread; my desk; a green metal file cabinet; and a rattan bed covered with a shaggy white cloth, another of McArthur's hand-me-downs, a suitable setting for the sort of girlie center spread I saw adorning a thousand GI barracks. I thought the bed would be handy in case guests came, but none ever did. On the wall above the desk I posted a map showing South Vietnam's 44 provinces, each in a different color. Bare fluorescent tubes ran horizontally just beneath the ceiling. In their harsh glare I'd sit at the desk, composing a story, and occasionally look up at the map and count how many provinces I'd visited. I got up to 27.

The bedroom was sparse. One rickety cabinet was enough for all my clothes. I left my traveling gear — the flak jacket, helmet, poncho, and big green army boots — out on shelves, like trophies. A big window faced one of the bedrooms in my landlady's house, so I kept the curtains closed.

I needed a maid. McArthur told me there were two

kinds: those who slept with their employers and did a few chores and those who simply did chores. I knew enough not to entangle sex with housecleaning, and hired a middle-aged Chinese woman, Sinh, who'd worked for a departing American journalist and his wife. They spoke glowingly of her, but I found her taciturn and unsettling. She arrived each day in the late morning, cleaned and made lunch and dinner, and was gone by early evening. I'd hoped to practice my Chinese with her, but she rarely spoke, and mumbled when she did. At dinner I'd eat in the silence, self-consciously reading a magazine or *Stars & Stripes*, feeling her eyes on me.

My colleagues were an uneven crew, brash and insightful and blind and driven. There were journalists who never spent a night outside Saigon, and others who preferred the countryside with all its risk and discomfort. There were television reporters who'd started as disc jockeys and an Italian photographer who was once a male prostitute. There were ex-marines, ex-academics, ex-volunteer agricultural workers. Some journalists had never read a book about Vietnam; others had written them. Some slept with prostitutes night after night; others brought not just their wives but their children, and went about raising a family as if they lived in an American suburb. Not that their families necessarily thrived: some wives got divorces rather than stay in Saigon, while others formed consciousness-raising groups or launched affairs or did both. There were journalists who admired Richard Nixon and journalists who admired Ho Chi Minh; none, though, claimed to admire Nguyen Van Thieu, the South Vietnamese dictator. One journalist, Bob Shaplen of *The New Yorker*, wrote a piece every month or two; Larry Greene of the Chicago *Daily News* wrote up to four stories a day and wore sneakers as if they augmented his quickness. Addictions flourished, to alcohol, marijuana, opium, sex, and danger; on the other hand, some journalists were so unnerved they left Vietnam after a month, sometimes in pursuit of another profession. There were journalists like the L.A. *Times'* Bangkok correspondent, Jack Foisie, an occasional visitor to Saigon, so generous he'd offer colleagues a swig from his hip flask in the middle of battle, and there were journalists like the CBS correspondent who "accidentally" let a competitor's battle footage fall out of a helicopter. Some journalists went for swims at the American ambassador's residence and got their information from American officials; some followed grunts through the mud; a few just relied on the daily military briefings and endured their colleagues' contempt. Some American journalists spoke Vietnamese, French, or Chinese; some didn't even speak English very well. Over the course of the war the journalists took more casualties than some combat battalions; to me they were deviant heroes in whose reflected glory I hoped to shine.

Nick Proffitt, who succeeded Kevin Buckley as *Newsweek*'s Saigon bureau chief soon after I arrived, was my first friend in Vietnam. I liked him as soon as I met him. He was fat and wore loud shirts and was breathtakingly profane — he called his wife "Numb Nuts" and denounced his editors with consistent, cheerful relish. He was a few years older than I was, had risen to a relatively important position after only five years in the profession, and treated me as only slightly less wise than he was. He accepted my ignorance of the military as a remediable trifle and patiently explained the basics, beginning with the order of officers' ranks. He was a good teacher: once he had aspired to be a general, and possessed some insight into the way soldiers thought. He was obviously hooked on Vietnam: he'd even named his dog "COSVN," after the elusive Viet Cong jungle headquarters, the so-called Communist Office for South Vietnam. Nick's wife would station herself in front of the television in the living room of the *Newsweek* villa, watching reruns on the American armed forces station, while Nick and I sat on the veranda where I'd chatted with Kevin and Frankie on my first day in Saigon. We'd parse the war until we ran out of words, and then we'd play chess, the generals' game.

Beggars intrigued me. They were so calculating it was easy not to think of them as victims: they were small-time schemers in a country of schemes, their deformities their biggest assets. The most devious beggar I witnessed was a little girl who worked the sidewalk in front of the Continental Shelf. Tiny fingers, minus forearm and hand, extended from her elbow like matches from a matchbook; I didn't like to look. In her effort to extract donations from Western passersby — Vietnamese weren't worth the trouble — she at first smiled sweetly. If that didn't work, she turned hostile, defiantly waved her stump in front of the targeted person, and refused to leave him alone until, horrified and embarrassed, he gave her money. How angry she was, how well she understood the nature of charity and capitalized on it! Once two friends and I got into a car parked outside the Continental. The girl asked us for money. When we turned her down, she pressed her stump against the car window. The parking place was tight, and we hurried to get out of it, first driving forward, then reversing, our desire to escape that appalling limb intensifying. When we finally pulled away, she screamed at us and took a last swipe at the hood with the stump.

It didn't take long before the beggars were just part of the scenery, as commonplace as M-16s. After a while we treated them as jokes — it was our defense. Nick presided over a "Freak of the Month" contest in which the most appalling beggar anyone had seen was selected and given a nickname. "The Grape Arbor" had a growth protruding from her face that looked like grapes. "Smiling Jack," a leper, greeted Westerners as if they were long-lost friends, giving a broad smile and a wave of his bandaged, fingerless hands. I hated for Smiling Jack to wave at me; when he did I gave him money, or, more frequently, looked away.

Our favorite beggar was "the Crab," a kid who plied his trade in front of the main square, under the patriotic banner which said in Vietnamese, "The soldiers suffer, the people are grateful." The Crab was a polio victim. He sat in the dirt, wearing only shorts, one leg curled in front of him while the other, hideously twisted, pointed over his head, pincer-like. The Crab didn't use a hard sell; he didn't have to. One of my colleagues, a Washington *Post* reporter, even wrote a story about him, so filled with pathos that readers donated a wheelchair, a television, God knows how much money. Filled with pride in his good deed, the journalist turned over the gifts to the Crab's family, but the next day the Crab was back at his usual spot, as dirty and forlorn as ever, no wheelchair in sight. Nick and I took pleasure in our colleague's consternation: he should have understood that in Vietnam begging was a profession, not an act of desperation.

Why did the Crab get the best location in Saigon? Why didn't other beggars crowd in where Westerners were so numerous? Nick and I wondered whether the beggars were organized, like the Mafia; we imagined a head man, the King of the Beggars, who stationed them around the city according to their earning power and got a cut of the proceeds. Once several lepers took positions on Smiling Jack's block, but they disappeared after a few days. Did the King force them to leave? I liked the idea of him, real or apocryphal, because he symbolized what I could feel: something was always unforeseen in Vietnam, hidden beneath layers of complexity and deception.

I had so much to learn I hardly noticed nothing warlike was happening. American officials were predicting a monstrous Communist onslaught, as big as the Tet Offensive, but who knew if they were right? Meanwhile, the only combat was small-scale, hit-and-run, not the sort of thing editors cared about, hardly even the sort of thing journalists could find while it was still happening. I was fortunate: I had arrived during a lull.

My first excursion into the countryside was with Nick and Ron Moreau, another *Newsweek* reporter, into Tay Ninh, the province abutting Cambodia. Nick had heard that Cambodian troops had fled there to avoid possible combat on their side of the border. According to Nick's information, South Vietnamese soldiers stationed in the Cambodian town of Krek had suddenly withdrawn back into South Vietnam, apparently to fortify defenses there in anticipation of the offensive. The Cambodian officers at Krek, abandoned by their supposed allies and horror-stricken at the thought of being attacked by the Communists, followed the South Vietnamese on foot. It was a story of South Vietnamese contempt for the Cambodians and Cambodian military ineptitude.

We drove to Tay Ninh in two or three hours and found a few hundred Cambodian soldiers and their families camping along the road as Vietnamese hawkers moved among them selling food. The Cambodians possessed not only weaponry but their household goods; the hawkers had to be careful not to trip over live chickens, M-16s, pots, canteens, baskets of melons, rifle cartridges, tied shards of wood, and helmets. We got out of the car to ask the Cambodians some questions, but who could communicate with them? I volunteered to try, using my wobbly French. A Cambodian officer was willing to talk with me, and his French was probably no worse than mine, but he was obviously under duress: he looked terrified, and quivered slightly as he spoke. The object of his fear was a South Vietnamese officer standing next to him, who instructed him on how to answer each question. I asked why the Cambodians were in South Vietnam, and after a short conversation with the Vietnamese officer he answered that they had come to "study military courses." I recognized the moment as the first time I'd been lied to in Vietnam, but the lie was so transparent all I felt was pity for the man. We watched as trucks arrived to take the Cambodians back to Phnom Penh, bypassing the potential danger at Krek, and then we returned to Saigon. I had a story, albeit a marginal one, and my French had been a useful asset. It was just possible that I could do this job.

Vietnamese, Cambodian, American, it didn't matter—

everyone got tangled in the tentacles of the war's corruption, including journalists. That was the moral of the story Nick took delight in telling me one afternoon when I strolled into his office.

Like so many Vietnam stories, this one had sex at its core. Weeks earlier, a colleague had dropped by Nick's office to boast of an affair he'd launched with his Vietnamese secretary. Now, however, he'd come back, deflated, having learned the price of his liaison. One of the secretary's duties, he explained, was to pick up his mail at the JUSPAO building, where correspondents were allowed to use a U.S. Army post office branch. The privilege enabled us to bypass Vietnamese customs inspections of packages, a fact of more than passing interest to the secretary. That day our colleague happened to pick up his mail himself, and discovered to his amazement that 60 identical packages were waiting for him. He opened one and found a set of pool balls inside. Suddenly he understood why his secretary had warmed to him. Pool was becoming popular in South Vietnam, and she was using his mail privilege to smuggle pool balls into the country. He would have been justified in firing her instantly, but he was too entangled to do that; instead, the affair continued, and the precious cargo went out to pool halls throughout the country.

Of all the reporters in Saigon, I admired Gloria Emerson most. I noticed her articles while I was living in Washington, long before I became a Vietnam correspondent. She wrote exclusively about the war's social impact, about refugees, orphans, prostitutes, cripples. Her compassion and outrage were apparent, and struck me as appropriate responses to the war. I even liked her writing style: alone among the Vietnam journalists I'd read, she seemed to use words with care, even subtlety. I imagined her fierce, dedicated, and tender, and once I got to Vietnam, I wanted to emulate her.

I soon discovered that other journalists distrusted her reporting, accusing her of exaggeration and outright dishonesty.

McArthur couldn't stand her. I thought they were all just jealous. She was the center of attention wherever she went, a circumstance I believed justified by her talent. She was gawky, with long, flailing arms that suggested uncompleted wings, and walked stiffly, as if the burden of the war had made her brittle. A former Paris fashion reporter, she was 42 and looked physically unsuited to Vietnam. I couldn't imagine her, for instance, using the smelly latrines on army bases; she wasn't deterred, however, from visiting even the remotest outposts, and I thought her brave. In my mind she was a mournful Auntie Mame, a font of passionate, almost desperate vitality. She saw pain everywhere. Once, having just entered a colleague's apartment, she stopped to stare at a rivulet of water running down a crack in the living room wall. "The man upstairs must be crying," she solemnly announced.

Gloria sometimes referred to a few of the youngest American journalists in Saigon as her "children," which I interpreted to mean that she might provide me, the youngest of them all, a measure of support. I waited until I'd written a few stories and then asked her for a critique. To my surprise, she looked annoyed, but she agreed to read the stories. While I was out of town she left a note at my villa. It dismissed the stories as "not particularly distinguished or original," and concluded:

> *It seems obvious that you have no remarkable flair*
> *for writing, or describing, but that hasn't stopped*
> *most of the press corps and you should be miles*
> *ahead of them in another year or so.*

It seemed to me that in one sentence Gloria had written off the entire press corps, leaving me with the consoling notion that I might become the best of this dismal group. I wish I could report that I thought, "Screw Gloria," and put the matter out of my mind, but I was far from possessing that kind of self-assurance then. I felt wounded. I hated Gloria and wanted to prove her wrong, and at the same time I wondered how my heroine could possibly be mistaken.

Gloria's note was at least galvanizing; I was anxious now to prove myself by going "up-country" alone in search of stories. My first solo venture was to a firebase called Ben Het, a scraggly parcel of mud and dust protruding pimple-like from a verdant valley floor in the middle of Vietnam's Central Highlands. Ben Het was one of a string of bases designed to prevent North Vietnamese infiltration through the mountains. Its soldiers carried out their mission by firing round after round of artillery into the void, where North Vietnamese soldiers might or might not roam, in preparation for an offensive they might or might not launch. War was a confusing abstraction to me then: all I saw of "the enemy" was an empty fuel drum, on which American helicopters grandly expended 28 rockets. Considering the possibility of a Communist offensive, I thought nothing looked the way it should, not the sentry I found asleep at his position, nor the soldiers I saw lurching around the base after getting drunk on rice wine. Instead of preparing feverishly for an attack, Ben Het's two American advisers struggled to stave off boredom. One of them, a captain not much older than I, was taking a correspondence course in accounting, and, judging by his sober appearance, I suspected he'd found his metier. Except for the scar that ran down one cheek, I'd seen guys like him a thousand times, the sort who majored in business and married young and specialized in smart, conventional thinking. He spoke cautiously, not just to me but to everyone, as if his chief concern with words was that they could be used against him. The scar was what distinguished him. I didn't ask him how he got it — he could have cut his face on a pop bottle at age five — but it looked to me like a war wound. It alone said he knew something that couldn't be found in textbooks. It was enough.

Not so his comrade, a sergeant who reminded me of Ted Kluszewski over the hill, gawky and oversized, muscle gone to fat, betraying no hint of unusual activity upstairs. The sergeant professed to like fighting; he said he was looking forward to a Viet Cong attack. He showed me where he took rifle practice, and when I asked to try my hand with his M-16 — I'd never touched one before — he was glad to oblige. I hit a target, and he said, "I'd like to have you here when the VC attack." I didn't bother to tell him how profoundly our wishes differed.

At night I lay in a cot in an airless bunker, cringing when the artillery went off, wondering each time if the Offensive was underway. A B-52 strike against a distant promontory possessed an eerie radiance that violated my assumptions about the aesthetics of destruction: as the bombs struck the ground, they lit a part of the sky with purples and pinks that reminded me of a sunset through the L.A. smog. A B-52 strike filled a square mile of terrain with 72 tons of bombs, but it still was disturbingly pretty, like the soldiers' name for it: arclight. It was hard to imagine that someone could die because of it, that someone might be dying right now, out there where it was purple and pink.

Imagining, in fact, was as essential to the soldiering enterprise as weaponry: that was the lesson I learned at Ben Het. The advisers saw one empty fuel drum and wove it into an intricate reverie that encompassed tactics, strategy, and ideology, that incorporated the fuel drum's presumed construction in North Vietnam, its piece-by-piece transport south, and its re-assembly in the mountains, all in the service of a hypothetical military campaign which threatened not just the Saigon regime but somehow, urgently, the more rooted regime in Washington. I wasn't capable of that kind of imagining: the Viet Cong didn't fully inhabit my reality until a year later, when, astonishingly, I sat down to dinner with one of them in the middle of a moonlit rice field in the Mekong Delta. It was odd: I needed to see the Viet Cong in order to make them real, yet I was frightened of them. The advisers, on the other hand, could imagine the enemy effortlessly, yet they were not afraid. It wasn't until years later that I understood the choice we all faced, to imagine or to feel. The soldiers used imagination to benumb themselves; they killed abstractions.

I edged into combat by degrees; at first I wasn't even sure that what I was experiencing was combat. I couldn't visualize it any more than I could the Viet Cong. I walked around base perimeters, looking at the placement of claymore mines and inspecting bunkers' overhead cover, but the mechanics remained mysterious, as if I were learning baseball by examining a mound and a batting cage on an empty field. I couldn't see how it was all going to work. What made the men fight? What made one side win and the other lose? I asked Alex Shimkin, a part-time *Newsweek* reporter who was considered a military genius, and he just shrugged and said, "Nobody knows. You put the two sides together, but you can't predict what will happen." I'd hoped for a more clear-cut answer. I wanted to believe in my invincibility; I wanted to believe that if I filled my brain with enough germane information, I could be safe from the chaos of war, safe from death. I knew Alex was telling me that if I was near fighting, I wasn't safe.

The first time I thought I'd been shot at had nothing to do with combat at all. I was in the back seat of a car hurtling through the Mekong Delta, on a road bisecting land so flat that the roundness of the earth seemed an impossibility. Here the only conceivable danger came from traffic; rickety wooden houses lined the road, in fact, because their inhabitants had opted for the highway's security, despite its noise and dust, over the bombs and battles in the interior. I was staring at the scenery when our driver began crossing a bridge; neither of us noticed a stop sign just before it. By the time we were halfway across, a South Vietnamese sentry at the other end had leapt to his feet, pointed his rifle, and fired — he missed the car, though it seemed to me that he was aiming at it. As extreme as the sentry's reaction was, it produced the desired effect: the driver backed up, then waited for acknowledgment before proceeding across the bridge. Was it true that for the first time in my life I'd been shot at, even though I'd felt no fear and seen no enemy? I told

McArthur about the incident when I got back to Saigon, but he was scornful: the sentry, he said, couldn't have meant to harm us.

My next brush with danger was less ambiguous. David Elliott, a scholar and Vietnamese speaker who was acting as my interpreter, and I were in Cheo Reo, a backwater mountain town we'd chosen to visit precisely because it was remote — we wanted to see what impact the war made in such a strategically insignificant place. Cheo Reo was so calm, in fact, that it invited relaxation: the Viet Cong hadn't rocketed the place in eight months, and the whole country was enjoying a military lull anyway. We'd just said good night to Ed Sprague, an American economic development official who'd been showing us around Cheo Reo, and were undressing in a guest room adjoining his quarters in the province advisers' compound. Suddenly we heard explosions just outside our room. On instinct we dove to the floor. It sounded like shells, but we couldn't tell whether it was incoming or outgoing. Another round landed, audibly spraying gravel. No more doubt: incoming.

Dave and I ran out the door, looking for a bunker, but on the way we ran into Sprague, whose head was covered with blood. He said the wound was superficial; he was more concerned about his Vietnamese secretary, who'd been hit in the face. I was terrified now: I desperately wanted a bunker. Dave and I finally found one, but after rushing inside it, we were engulfed in smoke — it took us another minute or two before we realized that the building above us was in flames. In the haze and confusion I felt certain my life was in danger; it was the first time since I'd arrived in Vietnam that I fervently wished to be someplace else. Someone yelled, "We've got to escape!" My imagination took hold: this is the Offensive, the Viet Cong are launching a ground attack! Or were they? Were the Viet Cong about to overrun the compound, or did the man say "escape" when he really meant something less dramatic, like "leave"? Gradually I understood that he meant only that we should move to another bunker because this one was too smoky, and we departed.

Some Americans were running around the compound now, trying to put the fire out, but I still had premonitions of the Offensive. I wondered if the Viet Cong might soon launch a second barrage. I asked Dave, "Are shells visible before they land?" It was a wonderfully innocent question: I wanted to know if I could run out of a shell's way before it hit the ground. The answer was that you couldn't see a round coming, and even if you could, you wouldn't have time to dodge it. This unsettling intelligence was followed by a more encouraging realization: the shelling was over. Dave, a step ahead of me from the moment the shells struck, suggested that we help carry buckets of water to the fire. Moments after we began, the top American official in the province ran up to us, his eyes wild with excitement. Maybe the shelling had unnerved him, or maybe he was just trying to ingratiate himself with a journalist. Either way, he claimed to see heroism in our joining the bucket brigade. "I saw what you did!" he shouted. "I'm going to give you a commendation for bravery for this!" He did, too: it came in the mail a few days after we returned to Saigon.

Sprague's secretary was the only serious casualty of the shelling: she lost a piece of skin below her nose. One building burned down. The attack was so insignificant that it wasn't mentioned at the daily military briefing in Saigon the next day, and I wrote nothing about it. When I told McArthur about it, he said, "Now you've been shot at."

Shells weren't the only unexpected thing that Cheo Reo delivered up, for Sprague took us to see the King of Fire, a spiritual leader of the Central Highlands people known as Montagnards. Like American Indians, the Montagnards were tribal people exploited by an invading race. Physically, they were more appealing than the slight and angular Vietnamese: they were dark, robust, round-faced. And during the war they were a lot friendlier: they lived in huge communal houses, to

which Americans were readily invited. Their weakness, probably fatal, extended from their strength: they lacked guile. I'd
already visited Montagnard resettlement camps, into which they
were herded after free-fire bombing turned their traditional
lands into moonscapes; they looked demoralized, as if they figured they might as well die.

Sprague was an ardent Montagnard lover; in my opin-
ion he was a soldier gone good. He'd been a lifer, the recipient of
five Purple Hearts, and for a time Gen. William Westmoreland's
sergeant major, but after living and fighting with the
Montagnards for a few years, he threw his military career over,
essentially for them. He went back to the U.S., quit the army, and
joined the Agency for International Development, all so that he
could return to Vietnam as a Montagnard economic adviser.
Some of his colleagues thought he'd gone overboard, that he
cared too much about the Montagnards; the American who provided the commendation for heroism, for example, compared
Montagnards to ornate Victorian buildings that ought to be
demolished and replaced by modern high-rises. Sprague
despised such Philistine notions — he was indirectly responding
to them when he said, "The only Montagnards who know how
to lie are the ones who have been exposed to American or
Vietnamese society" — but he knew he was an isolated voice,
and feared his superiors would transfer him out of Montagnard
country if he drew too much attention.

Sui Anhot, the King of Fire, reflected the Montagnards'
predicament: his beloved traditional home was on a river bank,
but the South Vietnamese government deemed the area vulnerable to Viet Cong infiltration and forced him to move. Not that the
Vietnamese cared about Sui Anhot's well-being: they were worried that the government's prestige would be damaged if he
lived in a Viet Cong zone. The drive to the king's new house was
shorter and less dangerous than it would have been before he
moved; it was, however, still bumpy, a sensation intensified by
the speed at which Sprague drove. The king's visitors were
expected to give him an animal for sacrifice, so we stopped at a

marketplace to buy a live chicken; back in Saigon I took pleasure in filling in $1.25 on my expense account for a "sacrificial chicken."

The king's modest house was announced by an official-looking sign that made him seem an adjunct of the South Vietnamese government: I suspect the government intended the misleading effect. A Montagnard man arrived just before we did; in an effort to cure his sister of craziness, he had brought an earthen jug of homemade wine which he presented to the king. Her misfortune became an occasion for festivity: we'd all take part in the chief Montagnard social activity, wine-drinking. The jug, filled with wine and leaves, was tied to a pole in the center of the house's main room, and we sat on the floor around it, taking sips through a long reed passed from person to person. Sprague said some men could lower the jug's contents by a foot in a single intake through the reed, but an inch was all I could manage and, considering the taste, more than I desired.

The king looked anything but regal. An old man, he wore only a loin cloth, and a stroke had left him half-paralyzed. His face was alert, though, and his spirits were high: when Sprague showed him a pocket lighter, presumably an interesting object to a King of Fire, Sui Anhot giggled and asked where he could get one. I liked his tiny, darting eyes and leathery skin, his obvious enjoyment of simple pleasures and vain hope for a life free from interference by the Vietnamese. "To sit in a house, drink wine, hunt animals, and catch fish — that is the good life," he said to Sprague. "But now I have no place to fish."

From one rafter hung an old photograph of the king dressed in a French uniform bedecked with medals. He laughed when we pointed to the picture, and said it had been many years since he wore the uniform. Now he lived more simply, surviving on the donations and sacrifices of his tribesmen. Though frustrated by his relocation, he was confident that Montagnard traditions wouldn't die. "Tradition is not this floor or this roof," he said. "It is this wine jug, and that will never change."

I liked the King of Fire; I didn't know why. Was it his simplicity, his directness, his connection to feeling, or was it simply that he was victimized, as I believed I was? The condition we shared felt as if it had been a part of me since childhood, for even then, I knew, I harbored sympathies for voiceless sufferers. Once, when I was eight years old, a man came to our house to deliver rented tables and chairs for a party. He unloaded his goods, and since my mother was still in bed, asked me to sign for them in her place. It was then that he noticed the name written on the invoice: "Mrs. J. Leslie." Joan Leslie was a faded movie star, and since we lived in Beverly Hills, the home of movie stars, the man assumed my mother was Joan Leslie. He got excited, and asked if I would awaken her so that he could get her autograph for his son. I didn't know who Joan Leslie was, and I had no idea why he wanted my mother's autograph, but he was an adult, and I carried out his request.

Once awakened, my mother required only a few seconds to grasp the man's error, and then she was furious. She yelled down at him from the balcony overlooking our living room, "How dare you wake me up!" and didn't even bother to explain that she wasn't Joan Leslie. The man seemed to crumple, to implode. In the meekest of voices he apologized, and, looking smaller than when he arrived, shambled off. All my compassion went out to him. I imagined him slinking home and informing his son that he'd failed to get a movie star's autograph for him. I knew the man was wrong to awaken my mother, but that didn't matter: I wanted to complete the communication, to let my mother know that he had been sincere and that she had trampled on something genuine. I couldn't get the man out of my head, and I brought him up at the dinner table again and again over the next few months. Nobody understood. In time my preoccupation with him was regarded as a quirk, and the tale was treated as a family joke.

In my mind, however, the story lived; at eight years old I had a component of the mark. To me the man from the rental company, the King of Fire, and I were linked. My mission now was to defend other sufferers, and in so doing, defend myself.

It was obvious that there were all kinds of marks. David Elliott had the scholar's version: he even looked like the professor he later became, with bushy eyebrows, the beginnings of a paunch, and a stiff, slumped bearing that suggested an indifference to the physical world. Particularly when the subject was Vietnam, he conversed in long, erudite paragraphs that threatened to overwhelm the listener with information. Sometimes, as he responded to a question of mine with an explanation that began with Ho Chi Minh in 1945, or referred to a recent article of significance in *Nhan Dan*, the Hanoi newspaper, my mind wandered, and I had to struggle to pick up the thread of his reasoning. Dave was slightly more convinced of the justice of the North Vietnamese cause than I was, but he never twisted fact to fit his ideology: I liked him because he respected truth, and he thought elegantly besides. He was my resource, my best and sometimes only source. He suggested story ideas and then came along as my interpreter, all the while feeding me enough background information to make me feel like an expert, like him; my only recompense was to put his travel costs on my expense account. I was impressed by Dave's willingness to take risks, particularly considering that, unlike me, he would receive no payoff in front page stories. He wanted the historical perspective, he said: he looked forward not just to the end of the war, but to a time when the war was a dwindling memory in the American consciousness. He predicted, in fact, that one day the Vietnam War would be as obscure to Americans as the Spanish-American War already was: it was as if only then would Vietnam be truly his. Here was an American with more patience than a North Vietnamese general.

Ron Moreau's mark was more immediate. Like me, he was in his mid-twenties and a journalistic novice, having just made the unlikely transition from being a volunteer agricultural adviser in the Mekong Delta to being a reporter for *Newsweek's* Saigon bureau. Ron, too, spoke fluent Vietnamese, but unlike Dave, who had learned a proper Hanoi accent, Ron spoke the earthy Vietnamese of the Delta, the equivalent of a Texas drawl. Indeed, Ron had learned his Vietnamese talking with Delta peasants, and he understood the dynamics of village life. I loved listening to him analyze how peasants would respond to some government initiative; his predictions, usually correct, were never what the government intended. He represented the other end of my political spectrum: he hated the Thieu regime as much as Dave, but unlike Dave, he was equally suspicious of the Communists. He was a skeptic, an ironist; he seemed most pleased when he brilliantly, precisely debunked.

In some respects Ron's mark and mine were similar. Like me, he'd grown up in Southern California, he felt to some extent estranged from his parents, and he loved the abandon that Vietnam embodied. Gangly and rough-complexioned, hiding behind silver-tinted sunglasses, he must have had an awkward time with girls. In Saigon, he said, he often sat home at night, gravely determined to read a book; then a voice within him would scream until, his concentration broken, he'd put the book down and go looking for women. I went with Ron to a brothel once — I knew I'd never go alone. What I remember about the prostitute I ended up with is that she had a scar extending from her navel to her pubic bone, and grandiosely feigned enthusiasm for me. I could not reciprocate. Ron and I had planned to spend the night there, but I fled just before the curfew and took a taxi home. When I saw Ron the next day, he said he'd enjoyed himself.

Alex Shimkin had the deepest mark of us all. He was less a friend than Dave or Ron, but that was because he was incapable of friendship: he wouldn't let anyone get that close to him. As usual, Vietnam was what we shared: Alex knew more about combat than any other non-military man I ever met. He could recite the history of every unit in Vietnam, and kept track of their movements in notebooks filled with his tiny notations.

He didn't look the slightest bit soldierly: he wore glasses with lenses as thick as soda bottles and was comically gawky — I swear I once saw him walk into a pole. He was extremely shy, a condition he dealt with by pretending that the people around him weren't there, or by mumbling.

Though he was a *Newsweek* stringer, I doubt he considered himself a journalist: he was a military freak, a frustrated combat soldier who couldn't join the army, presumably because of his poor vision. Confrontation fascinated him. Years before he had participated in civil rights struggles in the American South; then he went to Vietnam as a member of International Volunteer Services, the same organization Ron had worked for. IVS was ostensibly non-military, but Alex wasn't; Ron said Alex once participated in an operation to force Vietnamese civilians to walk through mine fields at gunpoint. But Alex was more complicated than that suggests: I could never get a fix on his views on the war. After joining *Newsweek,* he discovered a statistical discrepancy that led to the uncovering of widespread civilian killings by American troops in the Mekong Delta; sadly, *Newsweek* was not enthusiastic about the story, and ran it in truncated form many months later.

The first time I went out in the field with Alex, I was surprised to find him jittery. He spoke of settling down with a Vietnamese girlfriend and of ending all his perilous adventures. Once he became infuriated with me for driving too fast on a deserted country road. He said I didn't know what I was doing, a point I was prepared to concede, but clearly more was going on: I think he hated his fear, and veiled it by denouncing as stupid the acts that made him fearful.

In mid-February I arranged to spend two days aboard the U.S.S. Constellation, an aircraft carrier plying the South China Sea. I flew to the carrier on a tiny Navy plane whose passengers all faced backwards, and which landed by trailing a hook designed to catch any of three wires stretched across the

width of the carrier deck. Looking backwards, I was still
dwelling on where I'd been — Vietnam, the supple jungle, the
land of mystery and the confused longings of the human heart
— and now, suddenly, I was engulfed in technology, released to
a vast metallic universe where nothing grew, where doubt had
no place. I was on a floating American outpost, population 5,000,
but I felt more like an outsider than I did in Saigon. The press
officers who took turns accompanying me could tell me all about
the astonishing mechanics of jet take-offs and landings, of how
the pilots got graded on their bombing accuracy, but they
couldn't say if the pilots thought of people below as they
dropped their bombs or ever felt regret. Most of the pilots could-
n't tell me either, preferring to dwell on the marvels of their flying machines. They got catapulted off the ship like pellets from
slingshots, and bragged of the "G-forces" they had to endure
those first few seconds. Landings were scary: if they came in too
high, they missed the wires and had to try again; if they came in
too low, they crashed. Some of them liked the danger: they had
an antiseptic version of the mark. Pointing to a distant jet banking for its landing, one pilot told me how a few days earlier
another plane had reached the same position in relation to the
carrier when it suddenly quivered and spun crazily into the sea.
Wasted. The pilot smiled slightly as he explained that nobody
knew why the crash occurred.

    I was in the company of little boys in love with their
toys. When the pilots returned after their bombing runs, they
buzzed the carrier upside-down or dipped their planes' wings a
few times before settling down to land: never mind the mission
(or taxpayer expense), flying was fun. Larger-than-lifesize
blowups of Playboy centerspreads adorned the walls of the officers' mess hall; torpedo-sized breasts hovered over the food. If
that didn't hamper digestion, the food itself did. It featured cor-
nucopian servings of hamburgers, soft drinks, cake, and ice
cream: it was amusement park food, and the Conny was the ultimate amusement park.

    One night a bomber pilot named Pete ushered me into

his room, a cramped cubicle with psychedelic posters on the wall. The girls in my high school would have called Pete cute: he had blond hair, a neat Navy mustache and beard, and an accommodating smile. Most of the pilots treated me as an unfathomable alien, a man with suspect motives, but Pete wanted to befriend me. He brought out liquor from a secret cache, put a Rod McKuen record on his stereo, doused the lights, and turned on a home movie projector. I found myself staring at film he'd shot while bombing the Ho Chi Minh trail. It wasn't great footage, but then, Cartier-Bresson never performed his craft while trying to demolish a bridge. Finally, Pete confessed that he was convinced the Communists would win the war, and thought that might be best for the Vietnamese "at this stage of development." That startled me: a pilot who bombed North Vietnam was cautiously advocating the Communist line. Yet Pete's politics hadn't kept him from bombing, hadn't ever led him to miss a target on purpose. And though he spoke of quitting the Navy, he was vague about a date.

I couldn't decide whether Pete and a few other pilots like him were heroic for admitting their doubts about the war, or, considering their lack of action to back their convictions, were just feeding me a line. (But with what motive?) At least I had a story, and after I returned to Saigon, I filed it:

ABOARD THE U.S.S. CONSTELLA-TION, Tonkin Gulf— Though pilots on this aircraft carrier are flying their missions with as much efficiency as ever, many of them openly admit doubts about the role they are playing in the Vietnam war.

"We're doing it because we enjoy flying, not because it's a great cause," one says. Nevertheless, he bombs the Indochinese peninsula once or twice a day seven days a week.

While many pilots still are enthusiastic about their mission, the change in American

public opinion about the war and the ongoing
military withdrawal seem to have affected most
of them. "We fly a little more carefully because
we know our efforts aren't going to the win the
war," says one pilot who generally favors the
war effort.

It is also obvious that more than a few
dissident pilots doubt the wisdom of their continuing to bomb Indochina. But they are by no
means firmly committed to an anti-war stance,
or even greatly troubled by their continued par-
ticipation in bombing....

A cable came from L.A. the next day. Addressed to
McArthur, it said, "GEORGE JACQUES STORY SLUGGED
PILOTS FAILS MEET STANDARDS AIRMAILING LETTER
EXPLAINING WHY BEST GIBSON." I was shaken. McArthur,
who had approved the story after hearing only its lead over the
phone, now read all of it and was mystified. Nick said it was just
the kind of piece *Newsweek* liked. McArthur told me not to write
anything else until we got the letter, so I just worried. What sin
was I accused of committing? While in L.A. I'd heard of another
reporter, a dovish one at that, whom Gibson had sent to Saigon.
After a year he returned to the States for a home leave, at which
point Gibson told him he wouldn't be going back. Would my
stay be even shorter?

Gibson's letter was a puzzlement. He said the story
lacked focus, and I could see his point, but the offense didn't
warrant the ferocity of his tone — why, I'd read dozens of L.A.
Times stories which committed that offense. I cringed when I
read such lines as "Why the hell should [the pilots] be 'troubled,'
as you put it, if they are not anti-war dissidents?" It seemed to
me that the issue at stake involved politics and morality, yet
Gibson couched his disapproval solely in journalistic terms, by
charging that I hadn't been "objective." He was so certain of his
point that he said he assumed McArthur must not have read the

piece before I filed it, for surely McArthur would have turned it down.

I thought the only thing I cared for in the world, my job, was on the brink of being taken away, and I reacted impetuously. I decided that if the *Times* wouldn't run my stories, I'd work for the Washington *Post*, which I admired more anyway. I was already a foreign correspondent; perhaps the *Post* would keep me in Saigon. I had a meal with a *Post* editor who was passing through Saigon and intended to ask him for a job, but I lost my nerve at the last minute. That was fortunate: as I learned later, the *Post* wasn't in the habit of hiring reporters with two months' experience and making them foreign correspondents.

It wasn't until many years later, when I was close to dismantling my mark, that I understood just how potent journalism's claim on me had been. Neither of my parents was a journalist, and I felt remote from both, but their professions pointed the way. My father was a prominent Beverly Hills lawyer, whose client list was studded with celebrities' names. He wanted me to attend law school and join him in his practice, but the cold logic of jurisprudence repelled me, and, anyway, I knew I couldn't bear his harsh tutelage. Boss was the role he played best, the only role he relished. I contracted polio when I was four, and for years afterwards he yelled at me almost daily for failing to do my leg exercises to his satisfaction; as a teenager I'd hear him yelling at his clients over the phone, and I'd cringe. After he died some of them told me they hadn't minded his tirades, that they understood the outbursts as his way of expressing care, but I was too stung by his fury to see beyond it. What impressed me instead were the liberties he took with his authority. It rankled me when, stopped by a policeman for speeding, he'd hand the officer his "honorary county sheriff"'s card, which he'd received in return for a political contribution, or when, after a stint as an interim municipal court judge, he insisted on retaining the title of "Judge" because he thought it enhanced his prestige.

By most's people's standards, my mother was as successful as my father: her writing credits included fourteen films, a long-running comedy radio program, two novels, and several plays. Yet her work never seemed to gratify her: the director ruined this show, she said, or the publisher made writing that book a burden. When she gave up writing, around age 60, she said she felt only relief. I thought she was right to feel dissatisfied with her work, for I, with adolescent extravagance, held it in contempt. My objection, that it lacked substance, was accurate enough; what I failed to perceive was that her work was her escape, her attempt to create the unfailingly benign and innocuous family environment she longed for. The main character in her radio show was a teenaged girl whose parents were at times befuddled but never malevolent, and whose biggest dilemmas, week after week, revolved around such issues as what clothes to wear on a date with her boyfriend. When my mother's first novel was published, while I was in high school, I registered my disdain by refusing to read it, until one day my father announced that I was not allowed to leave the house before I'd digested it. I could have left anyway, but I was too cowed to provoke a crisis. Instead, I read the book in silent fury, then informed my mother that it was shallow.

I wasn't soured on writing, however; on the contrary, my relationship to my parents underlined its value. At home I was usually too intimidated to speak out against the injustices I believed my parents perpetrated. It was only at a desk, alone, that I could find my voice; writing seemed my only hope of expression. At Yale, which I liked partially because a continent separated it from my parents, I began writing for the *Daily News*, and quickly realized I'd found my life's work. With its blend of writing and public affairs, journalism felt uniquely satisfying. It held the promise not just of uniting my mother the writer and my father the lawyer within me, in a way that they themselves were never joined, but of surpassing them, by writing more deeply than my mother and by serving justice more devotedly than my father. Journalism reinforced the treacherous link I felt to my parents, and then it offered hope of soaring beyond them.

For a few days after the Constellation story, I stewed; then I wrote Gibson, promising to "do better as time goes on and I get more experience." This act of fealty had its effect: Gibson's next letter was full of praise and my transgression was forgiven. And then, a week after that, I was even more firmly ensconced in Gibson's good graces, for reasons as nonsensical to me as his earlier wrath.

When an ad in the Saigon *Post* for a local cosmetic surgery clinic caught my eye, I saw a way to satisfy my sexual curiosity even as I dutifully performed my reporting chores: I called up the owner, Madame Ngo Van Hieu, and arranged an interview. The ad listed the sort of operations that appealed to Vietnamese who thought they'd be better off looking like Westerners, a category that apparently included Madame Hieu. She looked pretty in the way that mannikins are: she had long false eyelashes and big breasts that looked, if not inhuman, then certainly un-Vietnamese. Considering the hardness of her looks, I thought she was surprisingly congenial, even candid. She said that at her clinic a woman could have the bridge of her nose raised to look like a Westerner's, her eyelids could be given a fold and "rounded," her breasts could be enlarged, and after a pregnancy her vagina could be "tightened" to provide greater sexual satisfaction for her mate. A man's chest could be firmed up; both sexes could have underarm odor permanently eliminated. Mrs. Hieu's manner was matter-of-fact, as if these operations were humdrum. I sensed she'd failed to mention the *unusual* operations, and asked, "Is that all?" It is extraordinary what things some people will tell a reporter with pen and notebook in hand. Mrs. Hieu made a show of looking embarrassed; then she said a man could have his penis lengthened.

The more Madame Hieu explained, the more sordid her clinic seemed. She said, with characteristic candor, that 40 percent of her patients were prostitutes, most of whom catered to the tastes of GIs. One operation was strictly for the trade: to pass

themselves off as virgins, whom Saigon's rich Chinese business-
men considered the most desirable of sexual partners, the prostitutes could have their hymens reassembled. The operation was
expensive, but the sex afterwards cost more.

Madame Hieu disclosed all this without the slightest
acknowledgment that what she did smacked of impropriety. On
the contrary, she portrayed herself as a brave pioneer. Her husband, a politician as well as a doctor, started the clinic, and was
killed when somebody threw a grenade into it. "My work now is
full of tears and blood," she said. "But I believe it is my duty to
continue my husband's career, to make his name shine and
become more and more famous." Who wrote her lines? Because
of the fighting spirit she displayed after being widowed, she
said, she was known as "the Jackie Kennedy of Can Tho," her
home town. She was reticent only about revealing the identities
of the clinic's surgeons, for, as she confessed, they were South
Vietnamese military doctors doing illicit moonlighting; if the
army learned who they were, they might be transferred to hospitals far from Saigon.

I wasn't sure how to write the piece; I didn't even know
if the *Times* printed words like "penis" and "hymen." What I
came up with was this:

> SAIGON— The unspoken word at
> Mrs. Ngo Van Hieu's cosmetic surgery clinic is
> sex. Women who go there can have their breasts
> enlarged, the effects of childbirth repaired, and
> even their "virginity restored." Men can have
> their chests firmed up and enlarged, and, Mrs.
> Hieu claims, their penises lengthened.
>
> But Mrs. Hieu does not mention sex
> when she talks about the rationale for these
> operations. It is more cosmic than that. "My
> guiding principle is that we can take a person
> who has failed in life, and we can change him
> into a success," she says. "When a person

becomes beautiful, he becomes more self-confi-
dent, his prestige is increased, and he feels personal satisfaction."

For patients who are willing to
become only slightly successful, the clinic offers
less dramatic operations. The three surgeons
can put Western-style folds in eyelids, give eyes
a rounded shape, uplift enlarged noses, put
dimples in cheeks or chins, and even eliminate
underarm odor.

Mrs. Hieu operates one of the best-
known of about 20 Saigon clinics specializing in
such cosmetic surgery. Wealthy Vietnamese
considering such operations have been encour-
aged by the example of President Nguyen Van
Thieu's and former President Nguyen Cao Ky's
wives, both of whom have undergone "eye-
beautifying" operations....

The story ran a week later on the front page, of all
places, in the column that ran down the left-hand side of the
paper. Stories in that slot were called "non-dupes" because they
were meant to be "non-duplicative," or exclusive, features;
Gibson considered them so important that every six months he
mailed out box scores to all correspondents containing the numbers of non-dupes each had written. At first I was pleased: I had
my first non-dupe. Then I read the story. Under the headline,
"Playboy-Style Looks Catch on in Vietnam," it said:

SAIGON— The long American pres-
ence in South Vietnam has changed not only the
face of the nation, but the faces and even the
bodies of a growing number of South
Vietnamese people as well.

A score or more cosmetic surgery
clinics have prospered in Saigon alone in the

last few years, and others in the provincial capitals [sic].

Women who go to them can have
their breasts enlarged, and even, so it is
claimed, their "virginity restored." Men can
have their chests firmed up and enlarged and,
as it also is claimed, other physical attributes
enhanced.

A single busy clinic here boasts of up
to 1,000 operations a month, and it all has an
aura of respectability. The wives of President
Nguyen Van Thieu and former Vice President
Nguyen Cao Ky both underwent "eye-beautify-
ing" operations a year ago....

The foreign desk editors had transformed my dispatch
on hypocrisy into a titillating nudge in the ribs. Gibson even
wrote me a letter of congratulations on the non-dupe, advising
me in the manner of a teacher to "please note how the article was
recast." I was amazed at his presumption: he thought I'd like the
editing. I took out my frustrations in a letter home:

*Half the reporters here say they can't bear to see how
their stories come out in the paper. So they feel compromised and end up as wrecks. That's why so many
people quit newspapers in their early 30s. That's
why the main character in Graham Greene's The
Quiet American is a broken-down old journalist....*

With no conscious awareness that I was alluding to myself, I'd
accurately predicted when I'd resign from the *Times*.

Oh God, the things the paper did to my stories. All
things considered, it was surprising they appeared intact as
often as they did. I was in Vietnam, gorged with the richness of

life, embroiled in a million disputes that weren't just intellectual
arguments but questions with direct bearing on the lives of
everyone around me — were the Viet Cong malign or patriotic,
was "Vietnamization" a plausible goal, could the Americans win
the war by bombing North Vietnam's dikes, would the American
"pacification" program work?— while my copy editors sat in a
nearly windowless newsroom, waiting for the end of their shifts,
the end of their lives. Everyone of them was on the downside of
journalism: they were former foreign correspondents who'd succumbed along the way to alcohol or women or inertia, and sat at
their desks as if propped up there to personify the profession's
pitfalls. (The one who intrigued me most was a Catholic with
close to a dozen kids, who evaluated world events strictly in
terms of their impact on his tax bill. Thus the Vietnam War was
bad for the same reason welfare was — they both cost him tax
money — while the Sino-Soviet split, say, was of no consequence.) I didn't think any place was as vibrant, significant, por-
tentous as Vietnam; they considered Vietnam about on a par
with Anaheim. I carried around a list in my head of the outrages
they perpetrated on my stories, such as inserting into them inaccurate information gleaned from the wire services, or cutting
vital information so that Dear Abby could run in its entirety.
They had only a nodding acquaintance with grammar, hilarious
examples of which crept into my pieces. I reserved special contempt for the *Times'* chief copy editor, who decreed that the word
"a" be deleted from stories because it wasted space. Yet one of
the paper's saving graces was the laissez-faire spirit that deflated its line of command: McArthur, for example, steadfastly
referred to the Vietnamese Communists as the "Viet Cong,"
while I, after a few months in Vietnam, used the term they preferred, the "National Liberation Front," and, in case readers did-
n't know what that was, put "Viet Cong" in parentheses. The
editors never asked McArthur or me to agree on one usage; perhaps they didn't notice we used different ones.

I wasn't even sure McArthur noticed, for he gave my stories a cursory reading at best. I usually finished writing at night, when he was already settled in at the home of his girlfriend, who happened to be Ellsworth Bunker's secretary. At first I read my stories to him over the phone; then he settled for hearing just the leads. For a time after the Constellation imbroglio he resumed reading my pieces before they were filed, but he did it without enthusiasm: we both knew that beneath every objection he had to my stories simmered our differences over the war. Looking back, I give him credit for trying sincerely to separate his journalistic concerns from his political ones, but the distinction wasn't easy for me to perceive then, particularly as our concepts of journalism clashed almost as much as our views on the war. To me he was one more impediment in the way of my reporting the truth. I considered him guilty of all kinds of transgressions, from displaying artless figurines of copulating couples on his mantelpiece and serving canned peaches for lunch (in a country blessed with magnificent fresh fruit) to prohibiting a bureau subscription to the New York *Times* on the grounds that it was too dovish; I imagine he disapproved of me on a similar variety of counts.

My resentment of him boiled over only once, when I reached the low point of my professional behavior in Indochina. It's indicative of the insignificance of the story provoking my ire that I can't remember what it was about — all I recall is that McArthur refused to let me file it. At first I threatened to file it without his approval, and didn't back off until he said that in that case he'd have to write Gibson a letter. I thought I knew how to gain the upper hand: I wrote my father, who had doggedly cultivated a friendship with Gibson, and asked him to intervene on my behalf. I'd been in Vietnam for two months, and thought, astonishingly, that I'd already proven myself as a reporter, so I asked my father to feel out Gibson to see whether I could file my stories free of McArthur's supervision. I must have been so inflated with Vietnam's importance, or my own, that I thought Gibson would agree, but nothing came of my request: either my father failed to pass it on, or he did it so tactfully that Gibson wasn't offended. For months afterwards I continued to believe that McArthur kept me under wraps, but somehow I absorbed the lesson that my best chance lay in treating him diplomatically.

McArthur wasn't entirely rigid, either. For example, he'd naturally set up the bureau to meet his requirements, which, judging by appearances, consisted chiefly of a desire for feminine diversion, as both the bureau's Vietnamese employees were women. This made sense in the case of our secretary, who performed such chores as buying our airplane tickets and arranging for our visas, but it was harder to see the logic of a female reporter-interpreter, particularly since she refused to venture outside Saigon. Her unwillingness to travel didn't bother McArthur, as he rarely left Saigon himself, but it left me stranded. When I proposed that she be replaced, McArthur was fortunately agreeable.

In her stead I found Phan Phi Long, a man of enormous dexterity. Long was one of the huge cadre of Northerners who settled in the South after the partition of Vietnam in 1954 and then rose to a position of prominence. In his early 40's, he'd studied engineering in the United States and been a top instructor in the South Vietnamese navy; he was discharged only after being wounded three times. More recently he'd worked for an American research organization in Saigon. Now, asked to consider yet another unfamiliar profession, journalism, he was enthusiastic and obviously competent. I tried him out as an interpreter in interviews with a group of Vietnamese widows. I liked the way he drew the women out, even thought of questions I hadn't. He understood that interpreting meant more than manipulating words: he knew how to present my questions in a way that made sense to the women, and how to present their answers in a way that made sense to me. Interpreting is a hard job, requiring a command of two languages and a vigorous intuition, and Long was a find.

As time went on, I developed as much respect for Long as for any other non-Communist Vietnamese I knew. If that sounds like damning with faint praise, I don't intend the effect, at least not wholeheartedly. It's just that Long's extraordinary adaptability made me wonder where his core lay. He was decent and honest and remarkably capable, yet to me he wasn't a true Vietnamese: he was too Westernized for that. He was divorced, which few Vietnamese were, he drank beer, and he laughed easily at dirty jokes — in some ways he was more American than I was.

I found a noble plastic surgery clinic, the moral antithesis of Madame Hieu's establishment. There was nothing else like the Barsky Unit in Vietnam: it was a plastic surgery ward for children burned in combat or ravaged by disease. More than a third of the patients were war casualties, while many others were victims of noma, a disease induced by malnutrition. Noma could be arrested with penicillin, but so little medicine was available in South Vietnam that these children had gone without until it was too late; now they lacked noses or lips or cheeks. Each time I saw the back of a small head, I hoped not to see its front: I didn't want to know what was missing.

The Barsky Unit was an anomaly, a place devoted to good deeds in a country engulfed in bad ones. It even looked alien: it was too shiny, too antiseptic, as if it had been constructed in America and shipped in one piece; indeed it was supported by American donations. But what chiefly distinguished it was its spirit, so different from everything else I saw in Vietnam. I watched a nurse feed a baby whose lip had disappeared — there was no skin between the baby's nose and mouth. As the nurse poured food through that hole, she looked not repelled but serene. She obviously took pride in her work, she liked what she was doing. I thought all the nurses there were that way: it occurred to me that they were the first beautiful Vietnamese women I'd seen.

The paradox was that I never wrote a word about the Barsky Unit. I started a story several times, but it never felt right;

I didn't know how to write it without sounding maudlin. In its tenderness, the Barsky Unit felt saccharine to me; it was so straightforwardly virtuous that it lacked an element of the drama I sought to portray. Suffering, not healing, was my obsession; once victims were acknowledged and cared for, they no longer held my interest.

Even so, something in me was giving way. I couldn't put words on the change: I could only notice its effect, bracing and unsettling all at once. One facet was reflected in a conversation I had with Nick about what journalists' objectives ought to be. Nick said the key was making impact with a story, getting the White House or Congress to take notice. I was offended. I said concern with impact was unclean, subversive to journalism. I said a journalist's satisfaction ought to come from writing a good story, describing precisely, communicating truth. I believed what I was saying, but even as I argued I felt something yielding. Soon after that I started keeping a chart like McArthur's; the only difference was that I hid mine in a drawer.

At the same time, I was becoming seasoned. I went on a dozen trips my first three months in Vietnam and got used to the discomfort of provincial hotels that ranged from tolerable to scrofulous, seemingly infectious. Foreboding characters dwelled in those dark corridors: they included blind masseurs who advertised their services by ringing a bell as they walked down the hall and haggard prostitutes who advertised theirs by knocking loudly on my door. At a hotel in Can Tho, a prostitute with a tubercular-sounding cough greeted Dave Elliott and me as we entered our room; though we turned her down, she knocked on our door later that night, and got refused again. We heard her make her way down the hall until she found a customer at last.

I took my first helicopter rides, saw my first bomb craters from the sky, flew on commercial planes with Vietnamese who could endure everything but air travel: once a man sitting next to me held a vomit bag at his chin for an entire flight as we both waited in vain for something to come out of his mouth. I drove down country roads that were safe only in daytime, and put aside worries about the consequences of a flat tire or an engine breakdown. I liked my flexibility, my new-found courage. I could take care of myself in a war zone.

TAKING OFF
Chapter

2

By late March the Saigon air was growing heavy with the humidity of the approaching monsoon. At the northern tip of the country, it was already raining explosives: the North Vietnamese were firing thousands of artillery rounds each day at ARVN firebases in Quang Tri province, just south of the Demilitarized Zone. We weren't sure what to make of it until the fourth day, by which time the North Vietnamese had sent 15,000 troops across the DMZ and toppled twelve firebases. By then we understood: the Offensive was underway.

Nick was elated. Nineteen-seventy-two had been transformed from just another year in the war to a watershed, as significant as 1963, when Diem was assassinated, or 1968, the year of the Tet Offensive. Nick envisioned cover stories week after week, but I was worried — I hadn't contracted for a convulsion. All I'd hoped for was to survive a quiet year in the war, then make my escape. Now I was in for it.

It was Sunday. McArthur was in Hong Kong on R & R. Nick was planning to leave the next day for Quang Tri City, the province capital. Should I go with him, or should I stay in Saigon until McArthur returned? Gibson had instructed me to go nowhere without authorization, but this situation seemed to call for an exception: I'd be useless in Saigon, where I'd be lucky to gather half as much information as the wire services, but in

Quang Tri I could provide a first-hand account. After much ago-
nizing I decided to go, and sent a cable to Los Angeles saying so.

On Monday, Nick, Dave Elliott, and I took an Air
Vietnam flight to Hue, an hour's drive south of Quang Tri City.
Until a few days earlier we could have flown to Quang Tri, but
now those flights were cancelled, and for all we knew the Quang
Tri airstrip was in North Vietnamese control. Hue was as taut as
a trip-wire; already thousands of refugees from Quang Tri were
seeking shelter there. The streets were gorged with people,
buses, cars, trucks, bicycles, everything loaded down with
household possessions from electric fans to live chickens. We
hired a stately old Citroën and its owner to take us to Quang Tri
City. As we made our way north, along the two-lane highway
lined with sand dunes that the French during their war called
the "Street Without Joy," I slid down in my seat. Compelled forward by military trucks, troops, and armored personnel carriers,
we were bucking the tide of refugees. Some were in buses
packed to standing room capacity; others rode bicycles or
walked, carrying toddlers on their backs. Why was I advancing
towards what they were so swiftly fleeing?

We reached Quang Tri City ahead of the North
Vietnamese, but we weren't sure how much ahead. Inhabited a
few days earlier by 40,000 people, it was on its way to becoming
a ghost town: most houses were shuttered or boarded up. We
went to the civilian American compound to get a briefing, but
the advisers had disappeared, their desk calendars still set on the
day the shelling began. We scurried around town, stopping first
at a high school where a thousand refugees had taken shelter,
then at an ARVN division headquarters where we were turned
away, and at the end of the day we still knew nothing.

Abandoned by our Citroën driver, who'd loaded his car
with passengers and hurried back to Hue, we spent the night at
a U.S. military compound in the town. I was jittery. The
American soldiers there weren't excited about helping us cover
a military debacle, and threatened to throw us out. More worrisome, the North Vietnamese presumably were advancing

towards the city and might cut off our escape route by morning.
Even if they didn't reach us, we were within range of their 130-
mm. artillery pieces, whose destructive prowess Nick eloquent-
ly described to me. His words had more impact than he intended: I spent the evening considering how to prepare for a 130-mm.
shell coming through the roof. "If you're hit by a one-thirty,"
Nick said, amused, "it won't matter where you are."

I refused to believe that. While Nick and Dave spread
out their sleeping bags on the floor of a large room that seemed
to me an inviting target, I spotted a tiny elevated bunker just outside, and climbed in. Unfortunately, so did David Burnett, an
American news photographer. Burnett had seen plenty of combat, but something had gotten to him: he was even jumpier than
I was. When I reached down to take my boots off, he warned me
not to: if the North Vietnamese attacked the base, he said, I
wouldn't want to waste time putting them back on. That sounded logical, so I retied my shoelaces and for the next hour lay in
the bunker, sweaty, feet aching, Burnett's elbow in my ribs. At
last I gave up: I was frightened but I wasn't crazy. I returned to
the large room, took my boots off, and slept. The next morning I
told Nick about Burnett and the boots. Nick said some people
were fine until they'd seen too much fighting; then everything
scared them.

Tuesday morning we set out to find the front line. By
now I felt captive to my fear. I was afraid of going to the front
and afraid of not going: the compromise I made with myself was
to go, expressing my fear all the while. We'd heard that the
North Vietnamese advance had been halted at Dong Ha, a town
ten miles northwest of us, so we decided to hitch a ride there. A
jeep was our first conveyance; words among the solemn South
Vietnamese soldiers who shared it with us were as sparse as the
vegetation over the expanse it negotiated. We were deposited at
an ARVN intelligence center, which we weren't allowed to enter:
unlike American officers, who felt some obligation to speak to
us, the ARVN command had no use for reporters. Considering
that the ground was shaking because of nearby 130-mm. shell

explosions, I thought the ARVN officers were unreasonable; I
would have promised to filch no information if the occupants
had admitted me inside. Instead, we headed towards the front.
We got another ride on a half-track, then discovered that it was
loaded with ammunition. One bullet could kill us all, I thought.
The low-hanging clouds had robbed the surrounding terrain of
color; the world in front of us varied only in its shades of gray.
We were within mortar range of the North Vietnamese now; they
could even be hiding in the bushes a few hundred yards away.
Maybe they would intersect the road after we entered Dong Ha,
and then we'd never get out. I felt strapped into a roller-coaster
car climbing slowly before the headlong plunge.

On the outskirts of Dong Ha we joined a column of
South Vietnamese marines marching single file into the town.
We passed a shot-up jeep; the mangled corpse of a water buffalo, apparently run over by a tank; and some peasants working
their rice paddies. War reversed things: the jeep and the water
buffalo were understandable, while the peasants were shocking.
A terrible rumbled emanated from the northern side of Dong Ha,
followed by a rising cloud of white smoke: the low clouds prevented strafing, but nothing held back the B-52s. Further on was
the ruin of a bridge, blown up by two American advisers to halt
the North Vietnamese advance. As we walked by, I saw my first
corpses, of four North Vietnamese soldiers who had apparently
charged across and then were gunned down. Bloated and fly-rid-
den, with indistinct features and blotchy skin, they were frozen
into awkward poses that distinguished them from anything
alive. Some of the South Vietnamese soldiers in our column
pointed at the bodies in derision, but I was filled with wonder,
even awe: what made those men charge across the bridge when
they must have known they faced death at the other side? Were
they so certain of their cause that they were prepared to die? I
doubted the mocking ARVN soldiers around me were capable of
such unambiguous action; I doubted I was, too.

Entering Dong Ha calmed me a bit, just as a boxer might
feel more relaxed after entering the ring. I had an idea of the dan-

ger now, and it wasn't as severe as I'd expected. Fighting was confined to the river bank in the center of town, at least half a mile from where we stood; aside from that the chief danger was mortars, which had blown the rooftops off a few houses around us. For now, though, it was quiet: the inhabitants had fled, leaving behind boarded-up houses which the marines were breaking into, looking for lucre. Some found beer or soft drinks, which they drank with their rations. A few played harmonicas or guitars. Down the street a looted alarm clock went off.

Nick, Dave, and I walked closer to the river bank, ignoring soldiers who whispered urgently to us, "VC!" I was ready to turn around, but Nick wouldn't stop. He said he wanted to see combat; I couldn't understand how we could see it without becoming a part of it. Noticing that one of the tallest houses in Dong Ha, all of three stories, had already been broken into, we entered and climbed to the top to see where the North Vietnamese positions were. The house was like a museum display; we even found a child's opened schoolbooks on the dining room table. From the top floor we watched South Vietnamese jets making strafing runs, and then we heard the chilling rumble of another B-52 strike across the river. A voice from a propaganda plane advised the Communists, "No place is secure." Did they need to be told?

We waited within a few hundred yards of the river bank for perhaps an hour, while Nick hoped for something dramatic to occur and I hoped for continued calm. I was becoming obsessed with the notion that the North Vietnamese would cut the road back to Quang Tri City and we'd be trapped. Nick considered my anxiety entertaining, and professed to find something ominous in the fact that among some playing cards strewn on the ground where we stood, an ace of spades pointed at me. I wasn't amused. I was angry with Nick for wanting to stay and angry with myself for wanting to leave. Finally Nick gave in— he'd seen no gore, but he had enough color for his piece. The trip back to Quang Tri City did not go quickly enough for me. We hitched a ride out of Dong Ha, then walked for a long stretch along the crater-pocked road. Dave and I practically trotted, but Nick trudged behind, laughing at our haste and yelling, "Half step, you guys! Half step!"

I spent another fretful night wondering if we'd be able to get out of Quang Tri before the North Vietnamese blocked the road to Hue. The next morning the road was still open: as we drove south, we passed a row of corpses of North Vietnamese soldiers neatly lined up in plastic bags, all that remained of a surprisingly feeble attempt to cut the road. The Hue-Saigon flight on Air Vietnam was by now booked weeks in advance, but we were able to catch a military flight and were in Saigon by late afternoon. I had caught a glimpse of the elusive enemy, the juggernaut, and I'd survived.

A few days after returning to Saigon, Nick got a phone call from Ennio Iaccobucci, a photographer he'd hired to take pictures for the magazine. Iaccobucci was in Quang Tri, hysterical. The predicament that had animated my fears there had become his reality: the North Vietnamese had cut the road to Hue, and he was trapped. He was certain he'd be killed, and spoke as if his executioner impatiently awaited transmission of his last words. He asked Nick to tell his wife, mother-in-law, and friends goodbye. Nick hated all the treacly sentiment, but he obliged.

The North Vietnamese success, however, was temporary. The ARVN reopened the road to Hue, and Iaccobucci returned to Saigon unscathed. Only his stature was diminished: we couldn't forgive him for not dying. Sorry, one death to a customer. He'd used up his quota.

I loved stories that exposed my colleagues' pretensions. One of my favorites was about a network television correspondent who was covering the Quang Tri fighting. He wanted to depict himself in combat, though he was miles from it, and had his cameraman film him as he dove into a ditch as if taking cover; then he began his monologue from a kneeling position. The cameraman, however, said he missed the entire sequence, and asked for a second take. Again the correspondent jumped into the ditch and delivered his report. When the network's Hong Kong bureau chief reviewed the film, he saw both dives, and realized the footage was staged. The correspondent got a reprimand, just as the cameraman intended.

I returned to Hue after a four-day respite. This time I played it safe: I stayed there. I thought I was onto a story as good as any further north, where the North Vietnamese advance had stalled, for the area around the city was crammed with 75,000 refugees. At one makeshift refugee site, 2,500 people resided in twelve tents; at another, nearly 300 people lived in a single school room. I discovered that even though the South Vietnamese government had a large emergency stockpile of food in warehouses, it refused for more than a week to give it to the refugees. I wrote a piece 3,000 words long.

The *Times* cut the story in half and ran it on page 20. I was appalled. Cut the astrology column, cut some cartoon, I thought — there's got to be room for a full report on a cataclysm as wrenching as this one. For once Nick agreed with my editors: he said refugees weren't interesting. He pronounced the first syllable to rhyme with "be" and the second syllable to rhyme with "mug," explaining: "re-fug-ees — they've been fugged once and fugged again." Journalists have no heart, I thought.

Of the three fronts the Communists opened during the Offensive, the An Loc region was easiest to reach. An Loc was a province capital unremarkable in every way save that during the Offensive the North Vietnamese committed several thousand soldiers to seizing it; now the town's ARVN defenders were besieged and in constant danger of capture by the Communists.

We could leave Saigon at eight or nine in the morning, drive north to within ten miles or so of An Loc, spend an hour or two hovering near the rim of the big battle, and be back at the Continental in time for a mid-afternoon *citron pressé*. It was war without discomfort, or at least it seemed that way at first; we didn't have to take a poncho or a change of clothes, we didn't even have to buy plane tickets.

The Communists started the fighting around An Loc a week after the Quang Tri assault began. They quickly captured a district town, Loc Ninh, and began their siege of An Loc. Route 13 once connected An Loc to Saigon, but now the Communists used a detachment of troops to keep the road cut south of An Loc. The result was that even when we drove up Route 13 as far as we could, An Loc remained a mystery; we were dependent on officials in Saigon for information about the fighting there. We could retrace our path a few miles back to the base at Lai Khe, the ARVN mounting area for reinforcing An Loc by helicopter, but the South Vietnamese officers in command there customarily declined to speak to Western journalists, and we usually learned nothing. All Route 13 typically offered was color, a chance to watch ARVN troops in action, making one of their ineffectual attempts to open the road.

Once on Route 13 I hopped aboard the first truck in a long ARVN convoy intended to resupply troops near An Loc. The convoy began moving, and then, a few minutes later, it momentarily halted. By then I'd noticed that I was sitting on top of munitions crates, so I took advantage of the pause to switch to another truck further back. The convey started up again, and kept going until it ran into a North Vietnamese ambush. From my new perch I couldn't see the fighting; I gathered, however, that its focus was the truck I'd so recently debarked. It occurred to me to wonder whether I would have survived had I failed to move, but something had already changed in me: the thought of this close call, if that is what it was, hardly fazed me. I'd learned to shelter my fear behind a fortress of insouciance.

On another day I went up Route 13 with Shimkin and

Moreau. We followed behind an ARVN battalion trying to clear a North Vietnamese bunker a couple of hundred yards from the road. Visibility was blocked by bushes, and officers' estimates of the North Vietnamese force there ranged all the way from a platoon to a battalion — I knew the difference now. The most advanced South Vietnamese position was about 25 yards in front of us. Sometimes kneeling, sometimes lying in the dirt, I watched as the South Vietnamese commander yelled to his troops, "The VC are running!" He pointed to thick bushes in front of him and exhorted his troops, "Over there! Over there!" A soldier jumped up, fired an M-16 at point-blank range, tossed a hand grenade, shrieked to a companion to take cover, and dove back to the ground. The explosion moments later seemed only a few yards away from him. Did the grenade hit the North Vietnamese? Were the North Vietnamese running away? For half a minute I couldn't tell. Then, tentatively, the South Vietnamese soldiers got up and fired again into the bushes. The North Vietnamese responded with a rocket; apparently they were still there. It went on like that for several hours.

I couldn't believe it was real; the soldiers looked like my childhood friends playing war. I saw how tempting it was not to take the risks seriously. Before I went to Vietnam I told myself that I'd take any precaution, no matter how minor, to protect myself, but now I realized I was reluctant to lie prone on the ground because I didn't want to get dirty, and I left my flak jacket unbuttoned because the day was so hot. Made jumpy by the mere sound of distant gunfire a few weeks earlier, I was already blasé. I wondered how many men died because of such nonchalance.

That kind of carelessness enraged Alex. As we watched the fighting, he began swearing at a European television crew between us and the front line. The crew members didn't crawl from place to place; they stood up and ran hunched over. Alex said they were stupid to expose themselves to fire like that, that they obviously knew nothing about war, that they didn't deserve to live. I think Alex was angry because they were taking more risks than he was. In his mind they were braver.

The war turned bravery into a kind of measure, a standard by which we judged ourselves. At the top of my hierarchy of heroism, at an elevation far above my own aspirations, were the pilots of two-seater Light Observation Helicopters, or LOHs, which everyone called Loaches. Loaches were small and quick; flying "contour," as Loach pilots liked to do — skimming the earth's surface so rapidly that only split-second reactions to looming trees and telephone lines prevented crashes — was more riveting than a roller coaster. In search-and-destroy missions Loach pilots flew low over terrain where Viet Cong soldiers might be hiding, actually hoping to draw fire, so that the Communists would give away their positions; then the Cobra and Huey helicopters, far better armed than the Loaches, would swoop down for the kill from higher altitudes where they'd been lurking. "Loach pilots," a Huey pilot said to me, "have balls this big," and he held his hands a yard apart.

The boldest Loach pilot I ever met, John Whitehead, was also the surliest; he reflected the malignant tenor of the war. He wasn't imposing, just mean: he was short, with narrow shoulders and a reedy gray mustache that made me distrust him as soon as I saw him, and his face had a permanently pinched look, as if Vietnam had drained him of all possibilities of pleasure except what could be derived from killing. He'd won a Silver Star, which was my reason for interviewing him; the manner in which he earned the medal cast a shadow across my idea of heroes.

Ron Moreau heard first about the incident which yielded Whitehead his medal, but *Newsweek* wasn't interested in the story, so Ron passed it on to me. It turned out that the action had been preposterously conceived; indeed, to come across a plan like this one was to be reminded, in case one was in need of it, that military tacticians weren't necessarily rational. The idea was that Whitehead and another Loach pilot, David Ripley, would rescue three Americans who, along with 15 ARVN soldiers, were surrounded by a Communist battalion north of An Loc. To do so, other helicopters would first spread tear gas on the ground, so that everyone — Communists, ARVNs, and Americans — would be rendered unconscious; the two Loaches would land; Whitehead's door gunner, Ray Waite, would lift the three incapacitated Americans into the helicopters; then all would fly to safety. The plan didn't call for rescuing any of the ARVN soldiers because the additional Americans alone would strain the Loaches' capacity, but the omission also reflected the Americans' contempt for the ARVN.

Of course, the plan didn't come close to working. The tear gas blew away and had no effect except to irritate the eyes of the pilots in support helicopters 2000 feet above the ground. As Whitehead and Ripley reached the landing area, they came under intense fire from the North Vietnamese, and the ARVN soldiers, desperate to escape with the Americans, rushed the helicopters. North Vietnamese fire killed one ARVN soldier as he dove into Ripley's chopper. "His eyes went wide and he fell off," Ripley said. "That scared me, because if he hadn't been there, I would have been shot through the head." Ripley left the landing area with five ARVN soldiers hanging on his skids: three survived, and two fell off in flight.

Whitehead faced even more pressure. Six ARVN soldiers and the three Americans instantaneously leaped inside or onto the skids. Afraid that the helicopter wouldn't be able to fly, Waite, the door gunner, tried to scare the ARVNs away by pointing his machine gun at them, but he didn't shoot out of fear they'd return the fire. Whitehead slung two ARVN soldiers off by spinning the helicopter in the air. He left with Waite holding onto the pistol holster of one American to keep him from falling out, while two ARVNs dangled from the helicopter, clinging to the American's legs. The Loach was too heavily burdened to gain much altitude, but Whitehead managed to return to safety with all three Americans and four ARVNs.

As for the South Vietnamese left behind, Whitehead

said, "There was no way for them to live, no way." The thought didn't seem to upset him. He called the Vietnamese "gooks" and said, "You just don't put half the ARVN army on your skids and try to get them out."

I was repelled. It seemed to me that the American concept of heroism had become dangerously narrow, as if we no longer had allies on the battlefield, only enemies, and the best we could imagine was to extricate ourselves from the conflict we'd once come to settle. This conclusion struck me as so obvious that I figured my readers would understand it, too. Nevertheless, when a *Times* editor complimented me on the story a couple of days later — "Nice tale," he said over the phone — I assumed just the opposite. The editor wasn't prone to compliments, so I wondered why, out of all my stories, this one caught his eye. After a moment's reflection I thought I understood: he must have meant that it was good shoot-'em-up, as entertaining as TV. I felt angry, as if the story's moral had somehow been lost during cable transmission. Now, however, I realize I still don't know what provoked the editor's compliment; all I know is that I was disposed to believe that he couldn't have absorbed my meaning. I was so certain of the impossibility of conveying my version of truth that when a man praised me, I felt failure.

It was ironic: my job was to report on the war, to communicate, yet the longer I was in Vietnam the more I felt the futility of reporting, the impossibility of communication. My mother read my stories intently, yet she still wrote me about her fear when she discovered I'd gone "so near North Vietnam," as if the danger chiefly lurked there. It didn't matter how laden my dispatches were with facts; readers had been inundated with facts about Vietnam for years, and now their minds were as cluttered with them as attics with useless furniture. I thought I had secret knowledge, for I had seen the war, and facts couldn't touch the experience. The war Vietnam the war Vietnam the war

— my beloved, resplendent Vietnam War. I ceased caring about anyplace else. Anyone aspiring to be my friend was required to have spent time in Vietnam and share my rhapsodically jaundiced perspective about it. Nick and Dave qualified, and so did Ron, though Ron now had a girlfriend who took up much of his attention. A fragile Francophile, she did not qualify: though she was Vietnamese, her chief interest in the country was how to get out of it, and I therefore held her in contempt. My letters to the States concerned only Vietnam, regardless of recipient. My sister wrote me describing life with her new child and asked me to describe my living conditions, and I wrote back chastising her for the narrowness of her interests: I thought that compared to my activities, those of the people I wrote to didn't seem significant enough to comment on. I was full of theories about the Offensive, denunciations of other journalists, and accounts of my adventures. I made carbon copies of my letters, for at some level I knew I was talking to myself.

One reward for the helicopter rescue story was a chance to fly with the squadron. Ron and I joined the unit at Bien Hoa one morning and flew towards An Loc for search-and-destroy operations there. Helicopters fascinated and scared me. I loved staring down from them, for Vietnam looked best from the sky, where its beauty was far more visible than its despoliation, where the farmland looked ordered and the jungle lush, but I never quite gave up my fear of crashing: the aircraft banked too dangerously and changed directions too abruptly for that.

Ron and I took turns flying on one of the gunships that hovered at 2,000 feet while Whitehead and the other Loach pilots tried to draw fire near the ground. During one of my stints in the air somebody spotted something that looked a Communist truck convoy, but we had no time to attack, as we'd run out of fuel. I was more relieved than anything else. After refueling it was Ron's turn. An hour later he returned, shaken. The squadron had gone back to the area of the suspected convoy. As the helicopters prepared to attack, a door gunner handed Ron an M-16 and assured him he'd want to defend himself. When they descended, however, all they found were piles of rocks, each pile about the size of a truck. Somebody guessed that long ago the U.S. Army had started a road but never got around to finishing it. Ron said he didn't know what he would have done if he'd had to use the rifle. I was relieved that he didn't have to find out, more relieved that I didn't either. I didn't think I was a killer, and didn't want a chance to prove myself wrong.

Even from 5,000 feet up, I found evidence of American arrogance. The U.S. Army's First Division, the famous Big Red One, had been stationed at Lai Khe, the base near An Loc, until shortly before my arrival in Saigon. From my vantage point inside the helicopter, I looked down and discovered, carved out of the thick forest, a huge "1" surrounded by the outline of a shoulder patch; it was the Big Red One's insignia, cast on a Brobdingnagian scale. The Army apparently used bulldozers to cut a swath many yards wide; the insignia must have covered several square miles. It infuriated me, more than most killing did. It was simple defacement, the ultimate in graffiti, made by a division of Kilroys.

In mid-April, Dave Elliott and I went south to see what impact the Offensive was making in the Mekong Delta, the most populous of South Vietnam's four military regions and the only one where no major battle was being fought or imminently expected. Dave's theory was that despite the relative calm there the Delta was the key to the Offensive; he believed that the Communists' strategy was to divert ARVN troops there to the big battles while they gradually rebuilt military and politically in the Delta, where they had been weak for several years. I am sure that the theory had much truth in it, though it probably was not as vital an aspect of the Offensive as I believed. I embraced it because it was subtle and elegant and disproved McArthur and all the American officials who saw the war as a straightforward clash of armies. The theory explained how the Offensive might work to the Communists' advantage even if they became mired on the major fronts, as now seemed conceivable. It allowed me to maintain my faith in the Communists' military wisdom: it all but implied they intended to be bogged down in the big battles.

Dave, a driver, and I went through eight provinces in four days, staying in the usual scabrous hotels, passing through or near locales with such evocative names as the Plain of Reeds and the U Minh Forest. It was useless trying to get information from South Vietnamese officials — they considered journalists only slightly more trustworthy than Viet Cong — and after a few fruitless attempts to interview them, we found ourselves forced to rely on American advisers. At the entrance to the American compound in each province, we usually were stopped by an ARVN guard. Using a mirror attached to a long pole — the device looked like a giant dental tool — he checked the underbelly of our car for plastique, then waved us inside.

Most of the civilians among the advisers looked as if something they valued in life had passed them by and now they were trying desperately to catch up. The top advisers in each province, known as Province Senior Advisers, or PSAs, spoke of their jobs as great "management opportunities," as if they were running a J.C. Penney's or a Woolworth's, but instead some unfortunate perversion of their ambition had led them to dreary backwater towns with names like Rach Gia (mistakenly pronounced "Rock Jaw" by most Americans) and Long Xuyen, so far from the consumer society they seemed to have in mind that there Formica was a luxury. Some PSAs showed us statistics on military casualties, while others said the statistics were secret; some said the situation was "pretty good," while others said it was awful; some refused to talk to us, or were at lunch, or were out fighting the war. I noticed a correlation between an adviser's degree of candor and the extent of his pessimism: thus, the more unfavorably his comments reflected on the South Vietnamese cause, the more likely it seemed that he was telling the truth.

The most open official we found was a debonair colonel whose reward for candor appeared to be his tour in the remote province of Chuong Thien. His comments happened to coincide exactly with Dave's theory. An ARVN division had been relocated from Chuong Thien to reinforce An Loc, and in the resulting upsurge of Communist-initiated combat, the remaining ARVN forces in Chuong Thien had been "set back considerably." My story, which illustrated Dave's theory with the example of Chuong Thien, was cut in half and run on an inside page, while McArthur's more prosaic analyses ran day after day on the front page.

The fighting at Quang Tri and An Loc had come as a surprise, but at Kontum and Pleiku, the Highlands province capitals which for months American officials had predicted would be the focus of the Offensive, the Communists had caused the air to be filled with nothing more lethal than ominous expectations. I felt an attachment to the Highlands — it was, after all, where I'd spend my first night on a firebase, Ben Het, back in January— and I thought I knew my way around a little. I returned to the Highlands in late April, viewing the prospect of an assault with my usual combination of eagerness and dread. The battle might start any day: Communist troops had surrounded Kontum for a week, and they'd overrun eight nearby ARVN firebases. In normal times a pretty town of tiled roofs and bougainvillea, Kontum was now overcome by panic. Its shops were boarded up and most of its 30,000 residents wanted out. The wealthiest ones paid bribes of up to $250 for a helicopter ride to Pleiku, 20 miles away and somewhat safer. ARVN pilots took the money and left wounded soldiers behind.

I stayed in Pleiku and commuted daily on U.S. Army helicopters to Kontum. At night in Pleiku I'd watch illumination flares floating slowly to earth, as American and South Vietnamese troops searched the terrain to protect against a surprise attack. Some nights "Spooky" gunships — World War II-vintage C-47s outfitted with machine guns — circled overhead and fired streams of bullets, the tracers among them forming golden dotted lines in the sky. I was staying on a base just outside the town, and felt relatively secure. I was beginning to understand that for every ten predictions of an attack, perhaps one was accurate. That made me sleep better, as did the fact that the base put up journalists in bunk beds and even provided sheets. Once during the night sirens went off, and several of us in various stages of undress jovially convened in an underground bunker to wait out what proved to be an uneventful alert. Another time I was dictating a story by phone to Saigon when a shell struck somewhere on the base; I crawled under my desk and kept on dictating, immensely enjoying my fortitude.

The North Vietnamese captured Quang Tri City without resistance on the first day of May. The ARVN simply bolted and ran, and didn't slow down until they got to Hue, where they went on a day-long rampage of rioting and looting. A few thousand South Vietnamese marines stood between North Vietnamese troops and Hue — the Communists could practically claim the city at their leisure. That would be a blow few thought the ARVN could recover from. The resulting gloom enfolded government-held territory throughout the country. From Kontum I heard a story about an evacuating American military adviser who left a sign on the door of the U.S. compound there that said, "Will the last one to leave please turn out the light at the end of the tunnel?" In Saigon, for the first time since the Offensive began, citizens were taking seriously the idea that the regime might fall. Everyone's mood turned a shade darker: one day a beggar, angered when I turned down his request for alms, kicked me, and I surprised myself by kicking him back. I was horrified to realize how intensely I didn't want the war to end, ever — I was attached to just those attributes of Vietnam I professed to hate. I was afraid I'd be transferred to some sedate

foreign capital, or worse, L.A. I was an intensity freak; my mark
was already deep. I walked around with a checklist in my head:
Had I seen corpses? Had I seen men die? Had I seen hand-to-
hand combat? Had I been wounded? Somehow the list never got
any shorter; instead, each new experience opened possibilities
for previously unimagined ones. The trick, I thought, was to
move down the list, gathering as many checkmarks as possible
without reaching the bottom, death itself.

Of course, some people were impervious to shifts of
mood. I thought McArthur was one of them: whenever we discussed the war, no matter what aspect I mentioned, he claimed
that the Americans and South Vietnamese were making
progress. Once, in frustration, I cited a notoriously disastrous
American-backed program.

"Sometimes you can advance only an inch instead of a
mile," McArthur said.

"But the program's going backwards, not forwards," I
said.

"Well, that's negative progress," McArthur said.

A phrase to sum up the war.

McArthur only reflected the American credo, the
American religion. The assumption was that if the war effort
made sense, then it had to make uninterrupted progress, like,
say, the GNP. When the war was going badly, which was most of
the time, believing in it thus required finding evidence of
progress in unlikely places, much as certain religionists find
proof of God's existence in odd-shaped gourds and smiling
slum-dwellers. The most commonly cited proof of progress was
the Honda statistic: an American official in Province X would
profess to see overwhelming evidence of gains for the Thieu
regime in the fact that Honda motorcycle sales had increased
there by ten or twenty or forty percent in the previous six

months or year. The Vietnamese were embracing our way of life!
(Supporters of the Communists presumably eschewed Hondas.)
My favorite progress statistic was uttered to me by a fat, cigar-
chewing USAID official who'd lived in Vietnam for five years.
He was sure the war was going well, since, he said, "When I
came here, almost all Vietnamese were barefoot. And now one
out of three wears socks!"

The Communists clearly weren't making that kind of
progress, so why did anyone support them? My friend Dave
would have started his answer with Ho Chi Minh in 1945, stressing their greater claim to Vietnamese legitimacy, but his theories
only confirmed what I already felt. The Communists fought like
heroes. They left the North knowing they were unlikely to
return, and marched down the Ho Chi Minh trail wearing crude
thongs made out of tires, enduring malaria and B-52 strikes, carrying on their backs (on their backs!) pieces of tanks to be
reassembled later. The Americans claimed they found
Communist soldiers chained to their tanks, as if without the precaution they would have fled, but I couldn't believe it. Coercion
didn't explain why the Communists fought when they had only
a tiny chance of survival and when even that tiny chance didn't
exist. They displayed more courage than I imagined within me
to summon — I was awed. They opposed the entire American
arsenal and somehow they held their own. They represented an
enclave of human possibility that machines hadn't yet overrun;
they stood up to the William C. Westmorelands and Lyndon
Johnsons and Gibsons and McArthurs of the world. They spoke
for me.

Yet I didn't want the Communists to win. They were
attractive as underdogs, not obnoxious victors. Communism
itself held no appeal — I didn't want to live in a collective. I
wanted to feel adrenalin pulse through me as I watched the war,
I wanted to come back to my villa at night and smoke a joint, I
wanted my name on the front page day after day. I wanted the
world to stay exactly as it was. I would oppose the war forever
into the brilliant, bloody future.

Back in the Central Highlands, I found myself in the company of Véronique Decoudu, a French reporter for Agence France Presse. We'd already teamed up on several stories, and found that our skills were complementary: I spoke to the Americans, she spoke to the French-speaking Vietnamese, and together we emerged with more elements of an story than either of us could have gathered singly. A woman in a man's profession, Véronique was compelled to put her masculine attributes constantly on display, and was appropriately tough: she chain-smoked Gitanes and talked a Marxist line, which I considered at least preferable to McArthur's hawkishness. I liked her for the hint of vulnerability she exuded despite her efforts, for her elfin appearance and magnificently frizzy hair, a white woman's whimsical sandy-colored Afro.

One morning in mid-May Véronique and I walked into the regional military headquarters in Pleiku hoping to get information. Previous efforts there had been fruitless, but we figured we had to keep trying. This time it was different, as if we'd said a magic word. No less a personage than John Paul Vann, the top American military adviser in the region and the closest thing to an American legend the war produced, appeared and asked us if we'd like to join him for a helicopter ride. Nobody's mark was deeper than John Paul Vann's: he'd been obsessed with Vietnam since 1962, when he arrived as a lieutenant colonel and developed a reputation for being wily and fearless. He fell out of favor for criticizing American strategy, and then he fell back in, and now, defending American policy at his press conferences in Pleiku, he sounded as gung-ho and blustery as Lyndon Johnson himself.

Now Vann had what he considered excellent news, and we happened to be the beneficiaries of his desire to spread it. During the night the North Vietnamese had launched an attack on Kontum, and, surprisingly, were repulsed. Exhilarated, Vann wanted to show us the battlefield from the air. He ushered us into the two rear seats of his four-seat helicopter and gave us head sets so that we could listen to the radio interplay. As we flew towards Kontum, he informed us that we'd soon be witnessing a B-52 strike. Here was another item for my checklist: I'd never seen a B-52 strike from the air. The prospect filled me with anticipation: it was like looking the devil in the eye. On our earphones we heard voices warning planes in the area to stay away so that they wouldn't be struck by the descending bombs. Suddenly gray clouds took shape on the ground in front of us and billowed to a height of a thousand feet or more. Insulated from the explosions by earphones and helicopter vibrations, I was surprised to feel so little: no horror, no pain, just marvel at the dubious wonders of technology. Had men been killed beneath the smoke? Did they mean anything to me? I knew I should be appalled, but I felt only numbness: it was like watching people die on television.

As soon as the clouds began to disperse, we swooped down for a closer look. I saw charred tree trunks shrouded in smoke oozing from the ground; the only visible colors were black and gray. Vann yelled "I see some bodies!" as if he were announcing wonderful news, and counted out nine of them. I looked and looked but I couldn't see any. Vann offered reassurance: "You have to be very experienced to see them." He was yelling over the din of the helicopter engine. "They're almost invariably on the edge of bunkers, running lengthwise from the center of the hole. You don't mistake trees for bodies after you've seen them for a long period of time." I looked harder, and thought I saw inert human masses, arranged as neatly as logs in a bonfire. Vann boasted: "We could go down into those holes because anything still living in there is in such a state of shock that he couldn't pull the trigger for thirty minutes." Not even Vann's pilot believed that, I noticed, for he made frequent sharp turns, as if evading someone drawing a bead on us.

Vann wouldn't leave the battlefield until he'd pointed out three destroyed North Vietnamese tanks. Then he took us for lunch at division headquarters in Kontum. Despite the rockets that exploded nearby and the flies that buzzed over their food, the officers there were exultant. When Major General Nguyen Van Toan, the commander of the division spearheading Kontum's defense, told Vann that the soldiers who had knocked out the tanks would receive cash awards and home leaves, Vann answered, "This should motivate them — you may have hundreds of cowardly soldiers trying to knock out a tank just to get leave!" The two men laughed heartily, as if they were sharing a dirty joke.

It hadn't yet occurred to me that the wellsprings of all our marks weren't necessarily identical; all I could see then was that the focus of Vann's obsession wasn't mine. I needed proximity to violence, but only, I thought, in the service of quelling it. Vann, on the other hand, celebrated it. It seemed to me that he was crazed.

Surprisingly, the North Vietnamese failed to parlay their advantage in Quang Tri, and by the end of May, all three fronts were stalemated. Gibson therefore authorized my first R & R. Before going to Vietnam, I thought I'd treat each R & R as an adventure, going to places I'd never visited, but when the time came, all I wanted was something comfortable. I chose Hong Kong.

I'd run the gauntlet of South Vietnamese customs procedures once before, when I left the country for a short reporting stint in Cambodia. Back then I was handed a declaration asking how much South Vietnamese currency I was carrying. I knew regulations prohibited leaving the country with more than 500 piasters, barely more than a dollar, so I wrote in that amount even though I was carrying ten times as much, enough for a taxi ride home plus change when I returned to Saigon. The customs inspector glanced at my form, then asked to see my wallet. Bracing for a reprimand or worse, I slowly handed it over to him, but when he saw my 5000 piasters, all he did was add a zero to the "500" I'd written on the form and wave me on.

Now, headed for Hong Kong, I intended to follow the procedure correctly. I again had 5000 piasters in my wallet, so I wrote that amount on the form. The inspector looked at it, crossed out the last zero on my "5000," and allowed me to pass. Were the customs inspectors closet anarchists of the (Harpo) Marxist persuasion? I laughed all the way to the plane.

I stayed at the Mandarin, a swank hotel on the plush side of the Hong Kong harbor. For a day or two I luxuriated in the soft bed and had room service bring me breakfast and tried out living the way I imagined a foreign correspondent on vacation should. It was no good. I felt contempt for the tourists, with their Bermuda shorts and tinted hair, who seemed not to notice that Asians scorned them as much as they scorned Asians. I searched the papers for news about Vietnam and was frightened at how much I missed the place. A day after I got back, I felt like I had never left.

On the last day of my R & R, Huynh Cong Ut, a Vietnamese photographer for the A.P., shot what became one of the most famous images of the war. The photograph depicted three children running down a road after being accidentally hit by napalm dropped from a South Vietnamese plane; in the foreground a girl held her arms outstretched in pain.

Nick filled me in on what had happened, for, as it turned out, Alex was there. He'd been watching a skirmish, and the incident happened right in front of him. He saw the napalm cannisters explode, saw the girl tear off her burning clothes, saw the children scream as they ran down the road. The only problem was that the scene didn't interest him. When he got back to the *Newsweek* office that afternoon, he told Nick all about the fighting, as usual emphasizing its tactical dimension, and mentioned the napalm only in passing. Nick, on the other hand, wasn't interested until he heard about the children; then he urged Alex to write an account for the magazine. Alex wrote the story as he had told it, full of references to battalions and flanking movements and only a fleeting description of the napalm. Nick told Alex to do the story over, but Alex never came close to getting it right. Nick didn't even bother to send the piece to New York.

I could imagine Alex's frustration as he sat at his typewriter, yearning to think like a general while being asked to write about children. Alex wanted to breathe the rarified air of military abstraction, for it was safe from children, safe from emotion, nearly safe from life itself.

Vann was killed on the night I returned to Saigon. His helicopter crashed while he was flying between Pleiku and Kontum. The obituaries emphasized his heroism and his obsession with Vietnam. Arthur Higby, U.P.I.'s Saigon bureau chief, wrote that he was once in Vann's helicopter as Vann fired his rifle through the window at North Vietnamese troops. Apparently he *was* crazed those last few months, acting as if he could win the war single-handedly. I didn't fail to notice that I was one of the last civilians to fly in Vann's doomed helicopter.

I was edging closer and closer to death. By mid-June the ARVN had succeeded in relieving An Loc by helicopter, breaking a two-month siege. Véronique and I drove up Route 13 to Lai Khe to ask if we could board a flight in. An Loc was still being heavily shelled, and I wasn't enthusiastic about going there; the ARVN obliged by refusing our request. Instead, we continued driving up Route 13, stopping a few hundred yards south of a row of ARVN tanks. We pointed our car back down the road, in case we got shelled and needed to leave rapidly, and walked toward two American officers standing just behind the tanks. On the way we passed two colleagues, photographer Horst Faas of the A.P. and reporter Charlie Mohr of the New York *Times*. Experienced in war coverage, they were crouched in the dirt just off the road, wary of shells. I hoped our bravado would impress

them, and confidently walked by. We at least impressed the
American officers: one of them, a full colonel, greeted us by saying, "You're the first journalists with enough courage to come up
here." For a moment I basked in this achievement, or whatever
it was. I noticed that the ARVN tanks were starting a sweep; it
was apparently designed to clear the area of North Vietnamese
troops blocking the road. Then the first shell landed a few yards
from us. A shock wave sent us to the ground. I felt something
warm embedded in me, followed by a tiny ecstatic moment of
recognition: *I'm wounded!* Several more shells came in, each one
landing a little further away than the one before it. Lying prone,
I looked around. Véronique and I exchanged assurances that we
were okay, but she added that she'd been hit, too, in her crotch.
She didn't appear to be in pain; I assumed her wound was no
more serious than mine. The second officer, a lieutenant colonel,
took cover on the ground next to us, but his superior only knelt:
he looked reassuringly calm, a trace of a smile on his face. I
thought how military of him not to stay down, how self-consciously brave. The worst casualty was the lieutenant colonel's
shaggy dog, which ran around in circles, yelping pitifully.

My wound was a tickle, a tease. I wondered, *is this all?* I
reached behind me and pulled a piece of shrapnel out of the seat
of my jeans. I cupped the metal in my hand and examined it. It
was ragged, hot. A war souvenir. I put it in my pocket. I was puzzled: how could this be enough to kill anyone, when it was barely able to penetrate my jeans? Or had it? Maybe I wasn't even
wounded. I reached behind again and stuck my finger through
the hole, then brought my hand back to eye level. My finger was
red. From time to time I'd half-seriously contemplated the ideal
wound, grave enough to draw attention without leaving a visible scar. Now I realized my good fortune: I had the perfect
wound.

Véronique and I waited until the shelling paused, then
trotted back towards our car, past Faas and Mohr, who stared
blankly at us. To my surprise, Véronique began blubbering. As
soon as we were out of shelling range, she sat down at the side

of the road, unzipped her jeans, and looked inside her panties to see how badly she'd been hurt. I started to look, too, then thought better of it and drew back. Véronique recognized a French colleague nearby, and yelled to him that she'd been wounded. Anxious to share the spotlight, I added that I was wounded, too. He drove us back down the road to a dispensary.

My wound was mended with three stitches, while Véronique was bandaged and sent to a Saigon hospital where she underwent an operation to remove the shrapnel. Her wound was nearly major, as a fragment had lodged dangerously close to a vein. We found out later that an ARVN soldier was killed by the round that wounded us, and that the dog died. And a few minutes after we left the area, more shells came in, killing the lieutenant colonel who'd joined us on the ground. His death was full of pathos of a kind that was by then commonplace in Vietnam: that day in 1972 was to have been his last on duty before a five-day leave. His wife had planned to meet him in Hawaii, and was en route when he died.

As minor as it was, my wound received news coverage. The *Times* ran a story headlined, "Writer Wounded in An Loc Attack," and later the paper's editor-in-chief emeritus wrote a column ascribing heroic qualities to me. Two wire services distributed stories on the event; one said I'd been wounded in the "upper thigh," while the other specified my "lower back." Pleased by my notoriety, my mother informed me that I'd become "a legend."

I didn't know what to make of the wound. Nick, once more in his rationalist pose, said it was odd that those who suffered war wounds were regarded as heroes, while, say, people injured in car accidents were considered only victims. Which was I? I liked all the attention, but I didn't think I merited it. I'd taken a conceivably foolish risk, and for my trouble got a warning: wars are dangerous, the hot metal said. On the other hand, I'd been close to death, closer than many people get in a lifetime of avoiding the prospect. I directed my confusion at the nearest targets of opportunity, the newspaper stories about the incident:

in letters home I mocked the wire services' euphemisms for "buttock" and called the editor's column about me "garbage.... I see that column as a kind of symbol of how people misinterpret things, how truth becomes lost." Gibson, meanwhile, sent a jovial cable:

> JACQUES YOU WILL BE GRATIFIED TO KNOW THAT TIMES SOCIAL BEHAVIOR COMMITTEE COCHAIRMANNED BY HAVEN AND MYSELF HAVE STUDIED POSITIONS OF WOUNDS INFLICTED UPON YOURSELF AND FRENCH FEMININE COMPANION AND COME TO TENTATIVE CONCLUSION THERE WAS NOTHING OCCURRING AT THE TIME TO REFLECT ANYTHING EXCEPT CREDIT ON CITY OF LOS ANGELES...

I'd been wounded in a war, so I was glorious, and I'd been hit in the ass, so I was not. The cleverer of my colleagues warned me afterwards to "Keep your ass down!" and I did my best to laugh. Yet something in me grieved: for four days afterwards I couldn't get out of bed. I thought I'd reacted adversely to a tetanus shot, but I don't think so now. Something inside me was singing out, in fear and primordial awe, "I've been wounded!" Unlike the American officer and the ARVN soldier, I hadn't been killed; I'd merely been given a glimpse of death from another angle.

As far as I could tell, the wound delighted my mother: she seemed to regard it as a windfall, an opportunity for both of us to bask in the spotlight of my unexpected acclaim. Concern about the danger did not seem to occur to her, and, indeed, I was so used to her numbness in the face of my imperilment that I hardly noticed it. It wasn't until years later that I found her coolness noteworthy, and then I remembered how I'd gotten sick. I was four. On vacation at a San Diego resort with my mother, father, and sister, I became feverish, and the next day I noticeably limped. First the hotel doctor and then another doctor examined me; both passed their findings on to my parents out of my hearing. I remember no discomfort; all I recall is that I enjoyed the strange solicitude everyone displayed towards me. My parents had learned that I was a victim of the polio epidemic then engulfing the country; their manner of coping was to keep the information from me, thereby staving off the pain my response would cause us all. Instead, after a day or two in San Diego, they announced that we were cutting the vacation short and going home, back to Beverly Hills, and we packed up and climbed in our car. We didn't go home, however; my parents took me to a hospital in Los Angeles. I didn't understand where I was until I was separated from them, whisked through swinging metal doors, surrounded by stern-faced doctors wearing white masks and white coats. I realized then that my parents intended to leave me there. I cried out for them, but they were on the other side of the doors, where I couldn't reach them. Instead, I was consigned to a wheelchair and sent rolling past my fellow patients, who lay deflated and inert in beds clogging the wards and hallways. I was a hostage in an embattled country of disease.

I was well into my 30s before my mother told me that I'd nearly died in the hospital. Though I have no memory of being close to death, the information didn't surprise me exactly, but rather registered as a vital piece of evidence, the proof of a hypothesis I hadn't yet formed but which lurked, simmering, just outside the range of my awareness. Somehow my struggle with death had impinged upon my fate, but I couldn't say how. I stirred through my recollections of the hospital, searching for harrowing events, but I'd expunged them from my memory and installed more mundane ones in their place. I remember, for instance, that on her visits to the hospital my mother invariably struck a light-hearted pose. Once she gave me a book in which she'd pasted a picture of me, smiling, on the back page; the center of the other pages had holes in them, through which my face appeared. The book was about careers, of all things: on one page my face was framed with a fireman's uniform; on another page, I was a policeman; and so on — we talked about what I would do when I grew up. The book embodied what she wanted from me, which was to focus cheerfully on the future, as if my polio did not exist. Desperate for her company, conceivably anxious to join her in conjuring up a future for myself, I was happy to oblige.

All I can remember about my stricken right leg is that I could neither move it nor feel it. I walked with a limp through my childhood, enduring first a brace and then a succession of plaster-of-Paris casts designed to straighten out my inwardly curled foot. Eventually I could run, but so slowly that I was self-conscious about it, and I fell down often. Despite all this, I loved sports, particularly baseball. On afternoons I could find no one else to play with, I created games by fielding balls I threw into the air, and announced the results to an imaginary radio audience. In real games I played catcher, the only position that didn't require mobility, and became a solid hitter. My happiest childhood memory is of being carried off the field by Little League teammates after hitting a game-winning triple. It's clear to me why I loved baseball: it offered my only chance for something like communion.

The first story I did after recovering from my wound was about a cemetery. I was already back in my reporting mode, telling myself that I was just gathering information for a story, but timing like that is seldom accidental. The terrain I chose was the national military cemetery outside Saigon, the likely gravesite of the South Vietnamese soldier killed when I was wounded. The drive there was aptly cheerless. Long and I passed first through the slum-ridden outskirts of Saigon, where ramshackle houses on stilts loomed above the muddy banks of a putrid, garbage-infested river. Then we took the American-built

Bien Hoa Highway, a modern thoroughfare complete with fuming diesel trucks and buses. At the cemetery turnoff was a garish statue depicting a soldier staring dejectedly into space. The statue's absence earlier in the year, when a temporary cast was removed before installation of a permanent one, frightened local residents, who claimed to see the soldier walking near the highway at night, begging for food and water. For weeks Saigon newspapers carried accounts of the soldier's reputed activities.

I was reluctant to intrude on the mourners at the cemetery, so Long and I talked to a gravedigger. In South Vietnam the gravediggers were women: men just fought. The digger we approached looked haggard. She sat on the brick-lined edge of a tomb and provided as trenchant an assessment of the impact of the Offensive as any military analyst could. "Last year we dug 200 holes, then stopped for many months," she said. "But since April we have been digging and digging without any rest. People keep dying."

In an enclosure abutting the gravesites, flag-draped caskets bearing bodies were stored until families could arrive for last rites. One old woman moaned, "Oh my God, my God." To no one in particular she said, "He was a soldier for eight years and now he's gone. We were refugees from North Vietnam in 1954. If I had known this was going to happen, I would have stayed in the North, so that my son wouldn't be killed by the Viet Cong."

A distraught young widow walked around the enclosure carrying a small child on her hip. She wore traditional mourning clothes, consisting of a blouse and pants made of frayed white cloth. The clothes were meant to look tattered, for the woman symbolically was wearing them inside out, revealing the emotions inside her. For the same reason, her hair was uncombed and she wore no makeup. She faced a long mourning period: some widows never remarried, while less tradition-bound ones regarded three years before remarriage as the minimum.

Another sobbing woman and her family gathered

around the gravesite of a soldier killed a week earlier. On the burial mound they put flowers and four burning candles to alert Buddhist spirits to the soldier's new dwelling place. The family also left behind items of symbolic usefulness to the soldier in afterlife: two bowls of rice, a wad of play money, and a tiny ladder made of sugarcane to help him into his grave.

In the fresh row of graves where the soldier was buried, at least half the dead were South Vietnamese marines, who had taken heavy casualties on the Quang Tri front 400 miles away; it was likely that the corpses of some of the marines I walked with in Dong Ha three months earlier were here. Frugal in every other respect, the South Vietnamese government took good care of its war dead: the regime transported bodies, hundreds of miles if necessary, to gravesites chosen by the dead soldiers' families, and it paid all burial expenses. The gesture seemed appropriate in a country where war was the dominant industry and death the leading product.

I felt comfortable at the cemetery. I took down all the information in my notebook, pleased to see a story taking shape from all the details, unmindful that I, too, grieved.

Alex died next. I walked into the *Newsweek* bureau and Nick gave me the news. Alex had been at the Quang Tri front, and wandered across a de facto boundary into Communist territory. His companion at the time, another frustrated soldier-cum-journalist named Chad Hundley, said he started to run as soon as they were confronted by Communist soldiers. Alex, though, chose to yell, "*Bao chi! Bao chi!*" — Journalist! — instead of running. Hundley said he looked back and saw a grenade explode at Alex's feet, and then Alex "crumpled." It was odd that Alex had made a dumb mistake like entering Communist territory in a combat situation, odder still that he of all people threw himself on the Communists' mercy instead of running — Alex, who trusted no one, was the most innocent of us all.

Officially, Alex remained "missing" for the duration of

the war. A few weeks after his "disappearance," an officer at the
U.S. Army morgue asked Nick to try to identify Alex's body, as
the morgue had obtained part of a finger suspected of being his.
Nick understandably wanted company, and Ron and I were curious, so the three of went together to the morgue. We entered
warily, afraid of confronting cadavers, but all we saw were large,
empty, ominous vats. A captain greeted us warmly, a bit too
warmly for the job at hand, I thought. He looked like the mad
scientist in a horror movie, smiling when he referred to the
"remains" and giving every indication of immensely enjoying
his work. He was in his forties, old for a captain: clearly he
stayed in the Army because he'd found his niche. Our discussion
established that the bits of corpse the morgue had recovered
couldn't be Alex's, and we left without viewing them. Alex's
body was never found.

By early summer the Offensive had begun to wane. The
Communists never took Kontum or An Loc, and far from having
the strength for an attack on Hue, without warning withdrew
deep into Quang Tri province, leaving the surprised ARVN to
organize a counter-offensive to retake Quang Tri City. Press
attention focused on ARVN efforts to regain the walled citadel in
the center of town; U.P.I. reported the citadel's recapture three
times before it actually happened, and McArthur, a dreary sentimentalist underneath his hard crust, served notice that he might
rouse himself to cover this grand event personally. McArthur's
threat turned out to be empty, and so, for a while, was the
ARVN's: the South Vietnamese didn't retake the citadel for
almost three months after their counter-offensive began. In mid-
July Long and I flew to Hue to cover the fighting's progress.
    I didn't like the Quang Tri front. The central Vietnamese,
who inhabited the area, were notoriously haughty, and the war
was particularly bitter there. Even the climate was contrary—
through a quirk of geography it was rainy there when other
regions of Vietnam were dry, and dry when other regions were

wet. While in Hue I stayed in the Huong Giang Hotel, a notch above other provincial hotels in that it provided shower thongs so patrons wouldn't have to place their feet on the grimy floor. One hotel employee made me shudder: he looked like a weasel, with a volcano-shaped growth topped by a black mole extending improbably from a point directly between his eyes. Corpses didn't hold as much morbid fascination for me as did that man and his growth; in my mind he cast a pall over the entire hotel, over all of Hue. All the hotel guests were journalists — the Vietnamese who could afford to were going in the other direction, south, to Danang or Saigon. We displayed none of the jovial behavior that characterized life among journalists in Saigon. I reported my stories during the day, wrote at night, and went to bed early, yearning — was it possible? — for Saigon.

So deep was our aversion to the hotel that Mark Meredith, a Canadian who worked for the Reuters news service, and I spent a night aboard a sampan in the Perfume River, which runs through Hue. The sampans were an institution, serving as floating hotel rooms, frequently floating brothels. We bargained with some sampan owners early in the evening and settled on one at $3.50 for the night — the same rate as the Huong Giang's. We were propelled by pole from the shore to the center of the river, where we anchored. Other boat dwellers, surprised to see Westerners in their midst, yelled "Americans! Americans!" and prostitutes offered their services, which we declined. The owner and his family, all permanent boat residents, retired to the aft, leaving the rest of the sampan to us. The interior was decorated with pictures of pretty women and a calendar featuring a photograph of a South Vietnamese Navy destroyer. Was the latter the owner's fantasy of a proper kind of boat?

In the middle of the river I could momentarily convince myself that the war was someplace else. Dinner was delivered by female vendors in tiny vessels constructed in typically ingenious Vietnamese fashion out of gasoline containers cut in half. With easy smiles showing beneath conical hats, the women paddled up to the edge of our sampan to sell us soup, noodles, and fruit.

After our meal, the owner's wife served tea. Kerosene lamps in nearby boats illuminated the warm wood colors and threw long shadows across the water. Bits of conversation and radio music wafted within hearing distance as our sampan pitched gently in the current.

Then, as we lay on reed mats, we saw distant mountains light up with a row of golden explosions. In the clouds, we saw what looked like purple lightning, the reflections of the blasts. We knew what it was long before the deep rumbling noise rolled through Hue half a minute later. Arclights. The B-52s.

A day's exploration on the edges of the Quang Tri front convinced me that until the ARVN recaptured the town, covering the fighting wasn't worth the risk. Instead, what caught my attention were the Quang Tri civilians. Trapped in their homes by the Offensive's sudden onset, they'd lived underground for months, while the province was flattened. Americans had been bombing it for months with B-52s and tactical air strikes and had shelled it from ships offshore, the South Vietnamese had added their own air strikes, and the two sides had exchanged heavy artillery fire. Now that the ARVN had regained part of the province, the surviving residents were surfacing and at last fleeing to refugee camps in Hue.

For two days Long and I went from one refugee camp to another, interviewing people who had lived under the shelling. All the camps were muddy and squalid, exuding demoralization. The refugees were country folk with missing teeth and wizened expressions, used to scrabbling their existences out of the earth, but abruptly they had no land, no home, no possessions of their own, and might not ever again. It is testimony to the astonishing Vietnamese capacity to survive that few refugees exhibited self-pity or even regret. With typical toughness they haggled over the meager portions of food and supplies meted out to them and cast steely eyes on the camp administrators and American officials who now wielded such power over their lives.

About 100,000 Quang Tri residents had lived in under-ground bunkers for months, while the ordnance fell around them. In some areas the shelling was so frequent, they said, that people never left the bunkers, not even to bury their dead. They had months to watch the corpses of family members and friends decompose or be eaten by animals. An old woman said, "We didn't talk, we didn't do anything while we were in the bunkers. We just lay down and feared dying."

The best thing the refugees could say about the naval shelling was that it was regular; people exposed to it said that after a while they knew at what time of day to expect the bom-bardments, and went for walks during the intervals. The most feared weapons were the B-52s. A man said he saw children killed by a B-52 strike even though no bombs struck them: the shock waves, which caused blood to gush from their ears, were enough.

I found an American official, a "war victims adviser," who came close to apologizing for the B-52 strikes. He blamed them on the American military bureaucracy, which took a week to stop bombing an area after being notified that civilians were living in bunkers there. Five thousand civilian deaths had been tabulated, he said, and the final figure would be much higher. Ten thousand deaths, maybe 15,000 or 20,000 quiet deaths, with instant burials.

Because refugees were such an unglamorous subject, my story was an exclusive. The *Times* ran it on the front page. A friend who worked for a Congressman saw it and had it insert-ed into the *Congressional Record*. From there it went into oblivion.

Oblivion was what I expected, always. By now I thought I understood my mission, and I also knew I couldn't possibly fulfill it. With the inflated gravity of a 25-year-old, I considered myself the sole journalist who told the truth. I was to look hard, to see freshly, until every clichéd way of describing disintegrat-ed before my gaze. Nearly every other correspondent was compromised, I thought, by his indifference or his embrace of false ideology or the requirements of his publication. I looked through the roster of journalists and dismissed them one by one: this one worshipped his C.I.A. sources, that one was undermined by his haste, this one loved only his byline, that one never wrote stories longer than five hundred words. McArthur, for instance, bought the American line as neatly as if he'd conceived it, and even Nick's work was trivialized by that myth factory he worked for, *Newsweek*. I felt alone, stooped under my self-bequeathed burden of bearing witness. I described my frustration in a letter home:

> I'm filled with Vietnam and everything I do in my spare moments is an effort to get away somehow, and there's no way to get away. I'm not particularly disturbed by anything as cosmic as the amount of suffering here or the course of the war. It's the job, it's working for the L.A. *Times* and McArthur, it's having no real way to enjoy myself here, it's all the frustrations.... McArthur has written a couple of stories recently that drive me crazy. One, incredibly, was the lead story in the L.A. *Times*. It said that ARVN troop strength was now greater than it had been before the offensive. Big fucking deal. That's not the point — George seems to be the U.S. government's biggest flack. The question is whether as fighting units, ARVN units are as good as before. Obviously with the casualties that officers and men of experience have taken, there's no way the answer to that question could be yes.... I wonder if the attentive reader of the L.A. *Times* can detect the dialogue that now takes place in its pages between George and me. I have to stick my jibes in subtly. I'm proudest of the story I

did on refugees, wherein I managed to drop the
fact that American bombing had killed "at least
5000" civilians, and probably more than twice
that number, in Quang Tri alone. I can't put this
sort of thing in the lead, though, I don't think.
Or my story on minibase operations in the
delta, showing that things had deteriorated
there as a result of the offensive. Meanwhile
George has chalked up an ARVN   victory....

   For some reason I seem to care how
this war is reported. I don't know why that hap-
pens to be true. I'm fascinated by the waltz of
American leftists and rightists around Vietnam.
None of them approaches the truth. They all
seem to be engaged in propagandizing.... Being
here is making me much less sure of long-range
ideals. What's desirable, what's not? Who is a
villain? Who is not? I'm becoming much less
interested in attaching blame and more and
more interested in simply trying to describe
what is happening. Certainly it is easier to con-
demn policies than people. What accident of
birth makes one fellow a VC and another an
ARVN? We're dealing with fundamental questions of being, of guilt and innocence, and I'm
growing tired of people with glib answers to
these questions. I think of Lyndon Johnson as
probably being guilty, but guilty in the way
Oedipus was, not because he was innately evil
but because somehow that was his fate, and the
recognition of his guilt would genuinely benefit
and enrich humanity. In other words, my vision
of his guilt is not the same as "LBJ, LBJ, how
many kids did you kill today?"

   I find myself constantly trying to
gauge suffering. I talked to refugees who had

been in bunkers three months trying to survive
B-52 strikes, tactical air strikes, naval shelling,
and artillery. Undoubtedly, what they went
through was terrible. But they do not seem to
feel sorry for themselves. Some of them seem
almost satisfied with their new, lousy lot living
in a refugee camp. One day I went to the
refugee camps with a reporter who'd covered
the India-Pakistan war. Indian refugees, he
said, were far less stoical than Vietnamese: they
would scream at the mere sound of outgoing
artillery fire. Well, how does one gauge suffering? Are the Vietnamese worse off because they
went through something more terrible than
what the Bengalis went through, or are the
Bengalis worse because they *thought* they were
going through something terrible? You wonder
about these things, and then it doesn't help to
hear someone in the U.S. saying that the war is
the world's greatest atrocity. And at the same
time, one thinks, yes, maybe it is that bad. But
it's much more subtle than anyone in the U.S.
imagines....

It seems like about ten years ago, it
was possible to have discussions about Vietnam
in which people would actually wonder, admit
there were things they didn't know, try to find
out things. But now there are two camps trying
to score propaganda points for an audience out
there (the American public) which is basically
unconcerned but at best has what can be called
a shallow interest (my son is fighting in
Vietnam, is Vietnam causing inflation?) in the
whole thing. Almost on whim, readers decide
one day one thing, another day another. At
times I become impressed with the futility of it

all — I can't even get my own editor to see
what's involved in the war — how in hell can I
get all these readers who don't recognize
bylines and of course don't know when I'm trying to tell them something and anyway see
George's stories on page one rather than mine
on page 28. And besides, I only write two or
three stories a week, and some of them aren't
even very good....

One Sunday in Hue five of us declared a unilateral
moratorium on the war so that we could spend the afternoon at
the beach. Ten miles away was an accessible island; a U.S. military installation covered part of it, but the rest was deserted. We
reached the island by car and motorboat, found a stretch of
white sand that sloped grandly into the South China Sea, and
took off our clothes. Meredith, the fastidious Canadian, was so
foresighted he'd brought swimming trunks to Hue, and was
modest enough to wear them; the rest of us went naked. Pale and
unshapely, we were no advertisement for nudism: I felt our vulnerability, our incongruity in a war zone. We sat at the water's
edge, and, in the wry manner of reporters, began discussing
whether we'd want to cover the war if the Communists were as
well-armed as the Americans and ARVNs. Just as I was about to
answer "no," rifle fire rang out and bullets zoomed over our
heads. Because of the steepness of the beach we couldn't see who
was shooting. I thought I heard two different kinds of rifle fire,
which suggested that a skirmish was taking place; perhaps the
Communists were attacking the nearby base. I half-expected
North Vietnamese troops to stumble upon us as they retreated
across the sand; then we'd be killed. Nobody said a word. Two
of us began swimming parallel to the beach, hoping eventually
to reach our motorboat on the other side of the island. Somebody
else swam straight out to sea. One guy lay prone in the sand and
began digging with hands at his side, turtle-like; another never

moved. After a minute or two we realized simultaneously that our separate actions were futile. We hurried back to our initial spot, threw on our clothes, and, keeping low, ran along the shore to the motorboat. By the time we got there, we could see what was going on: three GIs were holding target practice on a dune behind our beach spot. We yelled at them for being so careless. They answered our indignation with contempt.

On the way back to Hue, we made up headlines summarizing the tragedy that hadn't quite occurred. My favorite was "Five Correspondents Killed While Swimming Nude on Hue Beach."

When I got back to Saigon, I found that Gibson had given me a raise. I read his letter over and over again, trying to feel good about it. Nick had warned me that editors' praise was always insufficient; now I saw that he was right. Gibson wrote, "You have worked very hard, been conscientious, and produced some high-grade copy." I hated that word "some."

Like everybody else in Saigon, I was horny most of the time. Sexuality was what kept the city in motion between crises: it was as if the war inspired more frenzy than the citizenry could absorb, so the excess was played out in lubricity. Sexuality was as palpable in Saigon as the late-evening artillery serenades audible from my window; it was the city's fuel, as much a propellant as the diesel oil whose fumes settled over the capital, mingling grittily with our sweat. American GIs were justly held responsible for turning the country into a brothel, but Vietnamese men, too, were swept into the sexual vortex: according to Long, this was not obvious only because the Vietnamese kept the locations of their own preferred bordellos secret, as they considered the flesh of prostitutes who'd been touched by Americans contaminated. For Americans, Vietnam was a sexual testing ground, a place for acting out fantasies far less easily realized at home. Would you like two girls at a time? A virgin? A 14-year-old? McArthur himself was reputed to have been a connoisseur of barely post-pubescent girls, back in the days before he settled in with Bunker's secretary. Dave Elliott theorized that if Vietnamese women hadn't been so attractive — if they had worn, instead of the graceful and seductive national costumes known as *ao dais*, say, rings in their noses — the Americans would have quit the war years earlier.

The only difference between me and everybody else was that I was ashamed of my obsession: I didn't like the idea of being seen with a whore. I eventually figured out a solution. That flimsy four-page English-language rag, the Saigon *Post*, carried ads for a female escort service, which I knew was no escort service at all. I imagined calling the number, describing the woman of my fantasies, and having her arrive at my villa as straightforwardly as if I'd ordered a pizza. One night I waited until Sinh had gone home, smoked a joint, and called the number in the ad. The woman who answered the phone spoke a kind of pidgin-English that reminded me of butchers' knives being sharpened, and she thought my idea was crazy: why didn't I just come into her office and pick out a girl? She didn't understand. I declined her invitation, but her next question set me back further: she wanted to know what kind of girl I wanted. How could I sum up my desire in a few words, when I didn't begin to know what I longed for? Should I say I wanted someone pretty? Kind? Thoughtful? — it was absurd. The knife voice grew impatient, and narrowed the question down to a choice between fat and thin girls. In despair I opted for "medium." She took my address and said the girl would come right over.

I started worrying. What if my landlady saw the prostitute arrive? What if I didn't like her looks? Why had I made the phone call at all? Half an hour passed, and the girl still didn't appear. My chance for pleasure was dwindling with each minute, for now the grass was wearing off.

I knew as soon as I answered the doorbell that my fantasies would not be fulfilled. The prostitute was not the slightest bit provocative: she was plain-looking and had fear in her eyes. The first thing she did was ask me to pay her. Only then did I see the man outside, sitting on his motorcycle, waiting for the money. I wished desperately for him to leave, and got out the money as quickly as I could. I paid her, she paid him, and then she and I went upstairs and took off our clothes. Her belly was all rubbery: I was so unworldly that I didn't recognize stretch marks. The sex was over in a few minutes. She didn't pretend to have an orgasm, and I noted her guilelessness with relief.

I still wasn't done with her: I wanted something close to absolution, but not exactly that. As we lay naked on McArthur's old rattan bed, I asked her to tell me about her life. She was surprised: that wasn't what her customers usually wanted. In broken English, she let me know that she was 21, only four years younger than I was, and had given birth to a boy fathered by an American soldier. Now the soldier was gone, and the child was treated with contempt by most Vietnamese, including her parents. The only work she could find was prostitution. I looked for signs of bitterness, but I couldn't find any. I lit up another joint, and she implored me not to smoke it: marijuana, she said, was bad for me. I was touched by her concern for my well-being. I hadn't been satisfied, at least not in the sexual sense, but what I truly sought had only a little to do with sex. To my amazement, we'd made a connection. People like us saw the world without being seen; we were invisible, except to one another.

I was a loner who hated to be alone. I think I cared so much about journalism in order to fill the void. The feeling was worst on nights when I had no story to write, when I sat in my villa trying to read a book until I noticed I'd turned several pages without absorbing a word. My shelves became filled with Vietnam books I'd started and abandoned. I told myself that at least I owned books on Vietnam, at least I knew what they were about — most other journalists didn't know that much. When reading was futile I took out my stash, which a departing colleague had bequeathed to me, and lit a joint. I believed the marijuana relaxed me, but I don't think so now; that couldn't have been relaxation, whatever it was. All I'm certain of is that it intensified my feelings: in the most intense place in the world I took drugs to feel more intensely. My idea was to pile sensation on top of sensation, hoping that the next one — the orgasm on top of the marijuana on top of the B-52 strike I'd seen that day— would end my longing, but in the end a voice always whispered, "You're still not satisfied." Sometimes the grass provoked my fear, taking me to the edge of the abyss, close enough to look down and for a moment believe I was falling. Other times it made me feel brave, untamed, brilliant, worthy. I was the Los Angeles *Times'* man in Saigon, I was Clark Kent undisguised. I liked to think up story ideas stoned and fall asleep before the grass wore off. The next morning I'd sift through the debris of my ideas, occasionally finding something useful.

This is how much the Offensive changed me.

Long after the Offensive peaked, I returned to the Central Highlands. At an officers' club in Pleiku, I ran into the captain with the scar I'd met at Ben Het; he told me that while the Communists had overrun most of the firebases in the vicinity, Ben Het still stood. The Communists had attacked with tanks and hundreds of infantrymen, and the battle had been touch-and-go. Now the ARVN troops lived underground, as the North Vietnamese kept rocketing the base. The dead North Vietnamese were as much a problem as the live ones: Ben Het was suffused with the smell of half a battalion of rotting corpses, draped on the barbed wire and lying on the ground surrounding the base.

The captain gave me enough information for a story, but I thought I should get a Ben Het dateline: it didn't matter how much time I spent on the base as long as I was actually there. The captain said I could fly in that afternoon on a helicopter evacuating wounded soldiers, but the trip would be risky, as the Communists had the landing pad bracketed; the helicopter was going to stay on the ground for as short a time as possible. That was fine with me: as long as the helicopter touched the ground, I figured I could claim the dateline — I wouldn't even have to debark.

I didn't get nervous until the helicopter began its descent. From the air Ben Het looked deserted, but as soon as we touched down, soldiers suddenly appeared and loaded the chopper with stretcher-borne wounded, then ran back to their bunkers. The rotors churned up so much dust I barely noticed a rocket explosion twenty or thirty yards away — the door gunner pointed to the smoke as we pulled away. It wasn't until we'd regained altitude that I breathed out. I had risked my life for two words.

One reason I loved Vietnam is that in every respect it was as far from Beverly Hills as I could imagine traveling; it persuaded me that I'd escaped the shackles of an arid and joyless childhood. My parents, my sister, and I were solitary beings who happened to inhabit the same house. We ate dinner together, and that was all: by the time I was a teenager, my parents occupied separate bedrooms, to which they withdrew when the meal was over. We were Jewish, but we observed no Jewish holidays; on the other hand, one of the few holidays we did celebrate was Christmas. My parents kept their distance from our relatives; even of my grandparents, I have only fleeting memories.

An insomniac, my mother stayed in bed until noon, and my mornings were punctuated with admonitions to be quiet so as not to awaken her. In the afternoons she worked; child-rearing chores were left to servants. The arrangement reflected more than simple convenience, for apart from sewing, my mother possessed no domestic skills. I never once knew her to clean the house or cook a meal, and her fear of fleshly matter was so pronounced that I can't imagine her changing diapers, though she must have, from time to time. In her place, a battalion of nurses, maids, and cooks trooped through our house over the years. Most of them stayed a few weeks or months and then quit or were fired. I surmised that only unstable people took such jobs, for many of them displayed symptoms of mental disorder, which my parents enjoyed ridiculing.

When I was 14 we moved from one part of Beverly Hills to another; the new house was built in 1927 by William Randolph Hearst. It wasn't San Simeon-sized, but it was large, very large. My parents considered it elegant, their just due, but I hated it for the very features that caused them to love it. With its steeply inclined driveway and pink swimming pool, its bas-relief ceiling in one room and checkered marble floor in another, the house seemed to them the validation of their importance, but all it made me feel was my insignificance: I felt imprisoned inside a museum display. Nothing in the house was to be moved from its designated position; every flower pot, every ash tray, even the daily newspaper had its exact spot. Even in my own room, my mother dictated the decor: I couldn't put pennants or posters on the walls because my mother insisted on a butterfly collection instead, and I wasn't supposed to sit on the bed until I'd folded and removed her hand-sewn quilt. From that vast white room I looked down on the palm tree-lined street and felt not my wealth but my poverty, my insulation. I kept the door locked, and pretended not to hear when my mother called.

At dinner we sat at a pink marble table, while my mother conducted monologues as long as the meal, smothering the silence with false cheerfulness. Often my father didn't acknowledge my mother's discourses. He began his salad as soon as he sat down, and then he consumed his main course and dessert, and sometimes said nothing besides asking my mother to ring the bell that summoned the maid with second helpings and dessert. The silence only lent urgency to my mother's task of talking: she would do anything to avoid acknowledging the disinterest around her. I raged at my mother, my father, the bell, at the numbing superficiality of our domestic scene, but only inwardly: the avoidance of havoc seemed to require that I remain invisible, so I willed myself into acquiescence, and said even less than my father.

Politics was the exception to the rule I've described, the one subject which aroused my parents to something like genuine conversation. Politics was what my parents believed in instead of religion. My mother was so fearful of turmoil that she continually convinced herself that she was not, indeed could not possibly be, unhappy; only other people were, and politics was the potential antidote to their unhappiness. My parents hung upon politicians' pronouncements as if salvation were at stake, as if even their own unacknowledged sadness could be healed with legislation. Their vehicle for change was the Democratic Party, to which my father gave much money. While a child I met Averill Harriman and G. Mennon ("Soapy") Williams at fundraising parties held at our house, and my father's study was adorned with photographs of him standing with Lyndon Johnson, Ted Kennedy, and Hubert Humphrey. I caught my parents' political bug osmotically: in 1960, at the age of 13, I stood with my mother in the gallery of the Democratic convention in Los Angeles, cheering in vain for the nomination of Adlai Stevenson. I liked the political arena: it was where truth conceivably had power, where injustice could be redressed, where underdogs (such as I considered myself) might rise up and vanquish their enemies.

The six thousand miles from our dinner table to Indochina felt more like a light year to me, and still it was not enough. It wasn't until I understood my mark that I realized the different realms were related, that in fact they were two sides of the same coin. In the rawness of the experience Indochina offered, in its triumphant outpouring not just of blood but honest-to-God tragedy, it represented what my parents declined to acknowledge. I felt comfortable in Indochina: it spoke for me.

And it didn't just speak, it fulminated. My agreement with Gibson was that I'd work in Vietnam throughout 1972; at the end of the year either of us could decide it was time for me to go home. That had suited me: I figured a year in Vietnam would be like ten anywhere else. Once the Offensive began, I knew my year was a big one—the only story conceivably bigger was peace itself, and by October it appeared that 1972 might deliver that up, too. Superstitious Vietnamese, i.e., most of them, were saying that since their history reached a crescendo every nine years — the repatriation of the Japanese and establishment of a Communist government in Hanoi occurred in 1945, the Geneva Accords were signed in 1954, and Premier Ngo Dinh Diem was assassinated in 1963 — something momentous, such as a ceasefire, was inevitable in 1972. All I knew was that I was on a jag: by then I didn't want to leave Vietnam at the end of the year or maybe ever.

In August I tripped over evidence of ceasefire preparations without grasping its significance. An American major in the Mekong Delta province of Dinh Tuong told me that villagers under Viet Cong control there were being assigned tasks to perform in case of a ceasefire, including flying Viet Cong flags. I considered this an interesting tidbit, nothing more — I couldn't see why the Communists would be interested in a ceasefire — and put the item in the fourteenth paragraph of a seventeen-paragraph story. Gibson, however, evinced rare evidence of reading my stories in their entirety: he cabled back asking me to expand the ceasefire paragraph into a separate piece. I arranged interviews with three American officials in Saigon, and to my surprise all of them corroborated the major's statement. "There's a tremendous amount of talk of ceasefire at a low level from the other side," said Charles Whitehouse, the deputy U.S. ambassador, but even he thought the purpose was only to demoralize ARVN troops by dangling the possibility of peace in front of them.

The story was the first one anywhere giving solid evidence of an impending ceasefire, a subject that in another month or two would be the only one worth talking about in Saigon, but I had no more inkling of this than anyone else. On the contrary, when I learned that the piece ran on the front page, I thought that proved only that stories requested by editors got good play. Now I'd say that if it proved anything, it was that even editors sometimes use good judgment.

As the ceasefire story supplanted news of the waning Offensive, I had less and less reason to travel, but if I was going to stay in Saigon for long stretches, I needed sources to justify my existence. I would have liked to have been the sort of journalist who could check out any rumor with a phone call or two, but of course I would have distrusted the answers: I presumed that officials who dealt in that kind of information lied, or were ignorant, or manipulated journalists for their own purposes. Anyway, it didn't really matter that I lacked good sources inside the American bureaucracy, for McArthur had plenty of them. He and his sources got along too well, in fact; McArthur trusted them more than he did most of his journalistic colleagues, while the sources were relieved to be talking to one of the last hawks in the press corps.

At the same time, McArthur ignored the Vietnamese as if they were unfortunate tenants on Big Power turf; what I could do, therefore, was to reflect the Vietnamese side of the equation. Unfortunately, it was impossible to get close to the men who held power in South Vietnam. Thieu rarely gave interviews, and then only to journalistic luminaries. Hoang Duc Nha, Thieu's assistant whom I'd met at Con Son Island, did not return journalists' phone calls. I tried to alert Prime Minister Tran Thien Khiem to my existence, even sending him flowers when his grandson was born, but he never responded. The regime's generals stayed similarly aloof. The only accessible Vietnamese officials were the men on the periphery of power, the front men who played to a foreign audience. I interviewed Foreign Minister Tran Van Lam, a delicate, round man whose chief qualification for his job appeared to be his acquaintance with the English language, and learned nothing more earthshaking than that he supported President Nixon's reelection. I occasionally saw

Economics Minister Ngoc, who seemed rather candid in describing the regime's economic woes, but of course he had a reason: he was pleading for more American aid.

That left the legal opposition, commonly referred to as the "Third Force." Third Force politicians portrayed themselves as democratic alternatives to Thieu and the Communists, a fact which made them seem attractive to many American liberals, but I was never sure how much of their democratic rhetoric was simply convenient, to be abandoned if they ever attained power. Many journalists understandably saw no reason to get to know the Third Forcers, but I wanted to — I was hungry for an opposition, any opposition.

The best known of the Third Forcers was Duong Van Minh, who a decade earlier had been South Vietnam's chief of state. Now "Big Minh" — physically imposing by Vietnamese but not Western standards — kept to his Saigon villa, tending his orchids, clinging to the faint hope that Thieu would falter. The Third Force politicians I interviewed all had less stature than Minh, which usually meant very little stature at all. They included Senator Vu Van Mau, the pear-shaped leader of a faction of Buddhists, whose giggly manner mitigated against my taking his frequent denunciations of the Thieu regime too seriously; lower house deputy Tran Van Tuyen, a lawyer whose typically earnest but downcast demeanor and musty office evoked for me the grand futility of his station; and Senator Nguyen Van Huyen, a gaunt Catholic, the father of a priest and a nun, whose extreme caution in interviews suggested his discomfort with power. One of the best known in the United States of the Third Force politicians, Truong Dinh Dzu, was among the least respected in South Vietnam; universally considered corrupt, Dzu made the mistake of running second to Thieu as a "peace" candidate in the 1967 presidential election and ended up in prison as a result. I interviewed Dzu's wife, who complained that because of his imprisonment, the family had been forced to give up both its chauffeurs. The Third Forcers were at once laughable and brave; I was unsure only of the proportion of the ingredients.

The first ceasefire rumors began after Henry Kissinger and Nguyen Van Thieu conferred in Saigon in mid-August. The rumors built all through September, and in early October a negotiations breakthrough occurred, so that suddenly a ceasefire, if not peace itself, was considered likely. The tension in Saigon grew as oppressive as the monsoon air. For many Vietnamese the war had the advantage of being familiar; a ceasefire, on the other hand, was mysterious and therefore frightening. Why would the Communists agree to a ceasefire if they didn't have some strategy for usurping the government? Was the ceasefire a pretext to allow the United States to leave Vietnam without the ignominy of a military defeat but with the same result? Even during lulls Vietnam produced as many rumors as combat casualties; now it led the world in rumors. According to them, Thieu was going to resign — the alleged proof was that his wife had left for Paris with 27 pieces of baggage — and the C.I.A. was leading commando attacks against the ARVN to force the South Vietnamese to give in at the bargaining table. Bunker began visiting Thieu almost daily, until Thieu, apparently displeased with the deal being offered him, refused for a time to receive Bunker. Then Kissinger came for a visit of his own, and stayed for five days of talks. We became accustomed to being held up in traffic for five or ten minutes until a limousine bearing one of the dignitaries whisked by, flanked by motorcycle policemen and jeeploads of security men. Those caravans so bristled with stern-faced authority that it became impossible to believe that anything salubrious would emerge from the negotiations.

Indeed, the limousines were about all anybody had to go on. Saigon became inflated with reporters from around the world, including the sort of journalistic celebrities who fly from capital to capital being rewarded for their ignorance of local conditions with interviews of heads of state, but even those knights-errant couldn't come up with much more than the one fact which the U.S. Embassy was willing to divulge: the number of minutes that Thieu and American officials conferred each day. The Communists added to the drama by launching skirmishes on every road extending from the capital, thus precipitating some precautionary hoarding by Saigon residents. I suspected— wrongly — that the negotiations constituted the penultimate phase of the Offensive, that if Thieu and the U.S. didn't come to terms with the Communists, the Communists would launch a devastating final assault on Saigon. "I am observing what must be called a brilliant military campaign," I wrote, fortunately only in a letter.

The truth is that I missed the drama of combat. I wasn't the sort of journalist who pursued fighting wherever he could find it, but I'd been altered by exposure to it. Risk was a part of the mark, I figured: to cover a Vietnam story without risk was to be cheated, to pretend, to be on a trapeze with a safety net; you might as well be in Washington wearing a tie. I could at least console myself with the thought that thanks to the negotiations, Vietnam dominated headlines around the world. For a week or so dramatic developments broke several times a day; they emanated not just from Saigon but also Washington, Paris, and Hanoi, and made me feel I lived in the world's cockpit. I felt superior to reporters in the other capitals who dared to write about Vietnam without being there; their stories amounted to interpretations of interpretations, as close to reality as an art critic's description of a painted tree is to the tree itself. Yet at least they had stories to write: I didn't. Relying on his coterie of insiders, McArthur wrote all the significant negotiations stories, while I, frustrated, nibbled at the edges. I ran about with a thousand anxieties rattling around in my head: *Write a story. Call up Nguyen Van Huyen or Ton That Niem, call up anyone, get a comment. I've gone three days without a story: am I any good? McArthur's holding me back, Gibson doesn't understand, nobody in L.A. understands. Don't let anybody beat me to a story! Should I talk to more people, should I ask more questions, should I check my facts? Gibson doesn't care, the copy editors don't care, if I died would they care?*

Even though the military story was relatively inconse-

quential now, in my frenzy I returned to the battlefield, up Route
13 with Véronique. We walked up to a command post where an
American adviser and his Vietnamese counterpart were watching South Vietnamese planes drop napalm on a hamlet a hundred yards away. We saw the planes make several passes, and
then we left. A few minutes later Communist troops fired a few
mortars at the command post, lightly wounding Ennio
Iaccobucci, the photographer who'd been trapped in Quang Tri
at the beginning of the Offensive, and the ARVN officer. When I
heard about the incident back in Saigon, my first reaction was to
regret that I hadn't stayed. I thought, "How much glory two
wounds must be worth!"

Most maddening of all, I thought I understood the negotiations better than McArthur. Nick had an inside source, whom
he called "Supersource," and he told me what the source said.
At first Nick wouldn't reveal the source's identity — he was just
a Vietnamese who for unknown reasons was leaking the secret
contents of the ceasefire agreement to an American news magazine. Nick's editors sent him congratulatory cables, and for a few
days afterwards, while he awaited the magazine's publication,
he soared: alone among journalists in Saigon, he thought he
knew the whole story. And since Nick couldn't keep a secret —
it is, after all, the nature of journalists to be unable to abide even
self-imposed confidentiality — he passed it on to me. His information — that the United States had agreed to the formation of
a coalition government including the Communists — evoked my
envy: I felt inconsequential, reduced to watching the heavy hit-
ters practice journalism. Before Nick's story reached print, I told
it to McArthur. To my amazement, he dismissed it out of hand:
the United States, he said, would never agree to a coalition government. Part of me looked forward to seeing McArthur's naive
trust in the U.S. punctured at last; another part rooted for the
negotiations to break down so that the Communists could finally erase any doubts about their military superiority. In my ver-

·sion of the war, Communism wasn't pitted against capitalism, nor Nixon and Thieu against the legacy of Ho Chi Minh; it was just me against McArthur and Gibson, me against the *Times*, me against the world.

The negotiations drama reached a climax on October 26, when Radio Hanoi, reflecting North Vietnamese frustration with delays in signing the accord, revealed its main provisions. Then, late that night, when I was stoned and practically asleep, Veronique called to say that the American armed forces radio station was about to carry a live press conference given by Henry Kissinger in Washington. I turned on my radio and heard Kissinger proclaim, "Peace is at hand." He sounded so wise, so astute, so fatherly that it was hard to hate him. He was our expedition leader, describing for us the dark side of the moon that only he and a few others had seen; a ceasefire was an unknown to us, but to him it seemed comprehensible and thrillingly concrete. Remaining differences, he said, could be settled "in one more negotiating session... lasting... no more than three or four days."

And McArthur was right about the contents of the agreement: it didn't call for a coalition government. Nick's source, Tran Van Don, a South Vietnamese lower house deputy and former general who claimed to be close to Thieu, had, for reasons of his own, duped Nick. The odd thing was that in the excitement of the crisis, nobody noticed the error. If anything, Nick's reputation was enhanced, for his editors remembered he'd reported an exclusive long after they'd forgotten it was wrong.

The morning after Kissinger's press conference I did a quick story on the reaction of South Vietnam's opposition politicians: they were frightened, for they assumed that the Communists would usurp power during a ceasefire, and were, of all things, rallying around Thieu. Thieu entertained similar fears, as I found out later that day. I was walking on Tu Do Street when I noticed a demonstration. I'd already seen a few Saigon protests, led by ragtag anti-Thieu students who were usually dispersed with teargas, but this clearly was different: it was pro-Thieu, concocted expressly for the foreign press. The marchers, all dressed in white shirts and ties, were South Vietnamese legislators and provincial officials who'd been ordered to come to Saigon to protest the ceasefire agreement which the Americans were pressuring Thieu to accept. Some of them were considerate enough to carry placards in English for the benefit of American journalists; a typical one read, "Coalition with the Communists Means Suicide." I followed along, scribbling every detail into my notebook, thinking that at least I was covering the story while McArthur basked lazily in his house, until the procession reached Thieu's palace. I assumed it would break up there, but to my amazement guards removed the barricades and the gates swung open. At the top of the steps stood Thieu himself, looking tense and fragile in a white safari suit, like the host of a party he wished he didn't have to give. Thieu was no populist: this gesture of openness was so uncharacteristic of him I looked for the catch, hesitating before joining in the ensuing scramble up the stairs. I'd never seen Thieu up close before, as he usually surrounded himself with layers of security men. Now I was able to walk up to him and introduce myself before his bodyguards shoved me aside.

Thieu led us into a hot and surprisingly drab reception room where he delivered a long harangue in Vietnamese on the evils of the ceasefire. The Vietnamese around me said he was denouncing the agreement because it made dangerous concessions to the Communists. I rushed over to McArthur's house to tell him what had happened. He listened impassively; then he told me to go through the details slowly while he took notes. I realized then that McArthur was going to incorporate the material into a piece of his own. I was still a second-stringer.

For a few days we held our breaths, and then gradually we let go: the ceasefire was not imminent, or if it was, peace wasn't. What prevented the negotiations from reaching success was Thieu's conviction that the Americans had sold him out, particularly by accepting the post-ceasefire presence of North Vietnamese troops in South Vietnam. Thieu knew they wouldn't stay in place just to enjoy the scenery: they were in the South to fight, and most likely would remain until they won. Thieu therefore refused to sign until the Americans wrung more concessions out of the North Vietnamese. In late November Kissinger and Le Duc Tho, the North Vietnamese negotiator, held four days of talks, which failed. They met over a ten-day period in December and failed again. Then the Americans tried another gambit: in return for Thieu's signature on the ceasefire pact, they pounded North Vietnam. They unloosed the biggest bombing campaign in the history of warfare, striking canals, highways, factories, air and sea ports, and three days before Christmas they leveled a Hanoi hospital; in case the bombing was perceived as unbecoming, they imposed a blackout on all news related to it. For the first time in my Vietnam tour, the daily news briefings, labeled "the four o'clock follies," got interesting, though certainly no more informative. One reporter asked an Air Force briefer if he was "ashamed" of hiding the truth from the American people; it was a bold question even though its premise was dubious, since it implied that the Air Force normally conveyed truth. One thing in particular may have embarrassed the Americans: newly armed with advanced versions of Soviet surface-to-air missiles, the North Vietnamese for the first time were succeeding in shooting down American bombers. Altogether, 15 B-52s went down; the North Vietnamese captured 82 airmen. Nixon had been saying for months that the American military withdrawal envisioned by the ceasefire would be justified by the release of American POWs, yet in a few weeks his bombing campaign increased the number of POWs by 20 percent. South Vietnamese government officials, many of whom were born in the North and still had relatives there, nevertheless were delighted with the bombing. One of them called up Agence France Presse to pass on a news tip. "Here is a Christmas present," the official told Félix Bolo, the A.F.P. bureau chief. "Giap [North Vietnam's famed military leader Vo Nguyen Giap] is dead." In fact Giap was in good health, but it took a day or two to confirm that, and in the meantime some wire services carried the official's fabrication.

Of course, we were all captives of our sources. They were our lifelines; without them we might as well have been essayists or editorialists. If you knew who a reporter's sources were, you knew a lot about him, including where he placed his trust. Reporters were passionate about guarding their sources' identity not just to protect the sources but to protect themselves: to know a reporter's sources was to strip away his facade, to find out where he was exposed. And yet, after a while every journalist knew who his colleagues' sources were, if not by name then at least by institution: once you knew who the candidates were, it was just a matter of deduction. Whenever I read a colleague's story, I tried to figure out the source, to determine, in effect, the story of the story: I believed I knew about 90 percent of the time. The effort was essential, for if I could identify the source, I knew how much stock I could put in the story. Most readers, of course, had no way of knowing this story of the story; that was why I knew Americans would never understand anything as complicated as Vietnam by reading newspapers. On one level we tried to communicate to the American public, but on another we wrote only for each other. We were a closed circle, talking among ourselves.

McArthur made a point in conversation of stressing his differences with American policy, but that just showed me his insecurity about being labeled an Embassy stooge: the fact that virtually all his sources were American officials alone refuted his bluster. He was Mr. Inside, subject to the misjudgments to which insiders are prone. All that was left for me was to write from the outside, which was where I was anyway, where I wanted to be.

Then, abruptly, my list of sources grew much more unconventional than even I had imagined possible. In mid-November, when the ceasefire was beginning to seem like one more broken promise in a war littered with them, I thought of the ceasefire story Gibson had set in motion three months earlier, and wondered whether the Viet Cong were still telling Mekong Delta villagers how to prepare for the end of combat: if they were, prospects for a ceasefire presumably were still high. To find out, Véronique and I decided to ask the villagers themselves: we were tired of relying on the third-hand reports of American advisers. We knew our plan was foolhardy, since Vietnamese peasants considered contact with foreign journalists only slightly less dangerous than B-52 strikes, but all we risked was wasting a day. Indeed, having hired a car and driver and driven to the Delta with Long, I was ready to call off the project after just a morning, during which we interviewed peasants who for our edification couldn't quite recall who the Viet Cong were, never mind receiving instructions from them about a ceasefire.

Véronique and I were discussing giving up when Long had a brainstorm. He said he had a hunch that two men he knew in Long An, the Delta province closest to Saigon, could help us; he'd met them years earlier while working in an unsuccessful political campaign for a local candidate opposed to Thieu. What had Long, a Northerner, a sophisticated city dweller, been doing in a backwater like Tan An, Long An's capital? What was he doing in politics, anti-Thieu politics at that? I'd heard him deplore Thieu before, but that wasn't unusual, as nobody had kind words for Thieu. And Long was assuredly anti-Communist: after all, he'd been wounded three times while fighting the Communists as an officer in the South Vietnamese Navy. Yet now he was confessing that he'd publicly opposed Thieu, as if doing so was a lark, like working for Gene McCarthy in New Hampshire: it was yet another facet of a man who seemed to have an endless supply of them.

Long's two friends lived within sight of an ARVN outpost no more than a hundred yards from the main highway through the Delta. We parked our car in front of their house, which, considering the customary absence of both cars and foreigners in the village, was tantamount to announcing over a loudspeaker that the residents were unusual. This bothered the two men not at all: they greeted Long buoyantly, and when he explained that Véronique and I were journalists and he was our interpreter, they invited us to sit around their table and served us tea. The men looked like bumpkins: one had a smile full of gold teeth, and both wore dirty peasant clothes. Yet, unlike the other Vietnamese we spoke to that day, they didn't retreat behind generalities when we asked about their contacts with the "other side." Instead, over the next two hours they recited a list of 21 points of ceasefire-related instructions Viet Cong officials recently had given villagers; my hand got tired writing down what they said. Once the ceasefire began, they told us, villagers were supposed to display Viet Cong flags, hold anti-Thieu demonstrations, even plant flowers around the tombs of dead Communist soldiers.

Of course, no one except Viet Cong cadres themselves would bother to memorize such instructions: the men confessed that their information came from Viet Cong district headquarters, and left us to speculate on why they'd have access to it. I felt as if I'd stumbled through a warp in Vietnam's logic. American journalists couldn't have Viet Cong agents for sources: the idea was laughable, preposterous, like being handed the answers to a test my colleagues were cramming for. The two men seemed to understand the joke: I never saw two Vietnamese who enjoyed themselves as much as they did. Even as they led us behind their house to whisper some tidbit they considered especially provocative, they giggled, yet what they said behind the house was no more or less revealing than anything else they disclosed.

They were thumbing their noses at someone, but whom? The obvious candidate was the Thieu regime, for if they could operate so openly while living in the shadow of an ARVN outpost, then support for the Communists was more widespread than I'd imagined. The men didn't even bother to lower their voices when neighbors dropped by; their roles seemed to be common knowledge in the village. Even so, nothing explained their candor. Did Communist officials really want their plans revealed to the first couple of Western journalists who asked for them? Alternatively, if the men were practitioners of disinformation, hired, say, by the CIA, then why weren't their disclosures more obviously slanted? And what would be gained from deceiving two journalists with as little influence as Véronique and me? Of course, Long would have had to be in on the conspiracy, too, and until the previous day he didn't even know what story Véronique and I planned to work on. I'd stepped into a puzzle so vast I thought I might not escape it: the best explanation I could think of was that even among the Viet Cong, perhaps solely at this low level, friendship sometimes was a stronger bond than politics. The men were daredevils, and they apparently trusted Long.

One of the men said he'd take us to talk to Viet Cong supporters in the province if we returned the next day, and we agreed to meet him at a rendezvous point on the highway. When we got there, something disturbing occurred: after Long got out of the car to greet him, our driver, the same man who'd been with us the previous day, picked up a camera and pointed it at them. It was widely assumed that drivers employed by Saigon's big hotels, as this one was, collected extra money by telling the police about their passengers' activities: the photograph the driver nearly took looked to be a supplement to his oral report. Before he snapped it, Véronique and I told him to put his camera down. He obliged. Then Véronique, Long, and I returned to Saigon, dismissed the driver, rented our own car, and drove back to Long An.

Unperturbed by the incident, our man led us far from the main road. In other circumstances I wouldn't have strayed from the highway — even the most gung-ho of American officials conceded that the Communists were strong in Long An — but our guide's presence reassured me. I was reconnoitering terrain that until then had been no more real to me than a movie backdrop; at last the Delta took on three dimensions. The rice in the fields looked golden, and the water in the paddies shimmered.

The house Long's friend led us to had an austere, jungly grace that was underscored for me by the glimpse I caught of a beautiful Vietnamese woman combing her long, black hair. It was as if the Viet Cong occupied a different aesthetic realm, where Coca-Colas and painted faces had no place. Véronique was transported — I could see the elation in her eyes — but I recoiled, afraid of being smothered in all the rapture. My doubts became more urgent: What if our source was misleading us? What if the Viet Cong were truly evil? For an hour or so we talked with the house's owner, an old man of dignified mien who did not quite state outright his support for the Viet Cong. Did his willingness to belittle the Saigon regime prove our source's veracity, or was his reluctance to praise the Viet Cong more telling?

I wrestled with the questions all the way back to Saigon. The two men's claims were so unlikely, yet an instinctive voice told me to trust them. I finished my story at three in the morning. It began:

> TAN AN, South Vietnam — While negotiations in foreign capitals suggest problems in reaching an accord, Communist cadres a few miles from Saigon are continuing to hold nighttime meetings telling villagers to prepare for an imminent ceasefire....

I said my sources were village "residents," a true statement as far as it went. I didn't say they were Viet Cong cadres because doing so might have endangered the two men, and, anyway, I doubted Gibson would have believed it. The irony was that Gibson had set the search in motion back in August: the thread that connected his request for a story about Viet Cong ceasefire preparations to our story about of the men in Long An was tenuous, but it held.

The next day I told the tale of the two men to Nick. I waited for him to tell me that I'd located a gold mine, but instead he dismissed the story out of hand: the men were undoubtedly impostors, he said. He even had a phrase for their disclosures: "black information." Nick was so convincing that I assumed he was right, and   panicked. Should I have been more cautious? Could I ever fathom Vietnam's layers? Was I too naive to be a journalist?

I was so frightened I started to cover for myself. I had lunch with Lee Lescaze, a visiting Washington *Post* correspondent who had just been selected that paper's foreign editor. I was worried that he'd hear about my conceivably crazy story, so I thought I could at least impress him with my honesty: I told him I'd written a piece whose accuracy I now gravely doubted.

Later in the day I saw Véronique, who was still high from all the excitement. I felt like a wise elder indulging the charming innocence of youth, and mournfully told her Nick's reaction. To my surprise, she was not swayed. She believed in the story, she said, and having written it, so should I. Something clicked: I saw I'd never make up my mind by seeking a consensus of other journalists. I was stuck with my instincts. The two men probably were telling the truth; no other theory made half as much sense.

I had a chance to redeem myself. Lescaze called, saying his editors were intrigued by my story and wondered if they should run it. Before he advised them, he said, he wanted to know if I still had doubts. I was afraid another vacillation would cause Lescaze to conclude that my judgment was as variable as the tides, but I knew what I wanted to say: I told him I believed in the story. As it turned out, the *Post* ran it. So did the *Times*, on the front page.

As soon as we met the two men, Véronique and I had the same thought: could they take us into Viet Cong territory?

Such a journey would be one of the great journalistic coups of the war, for no non-Communist Western reporter had ever entered a Viet Cong zone and lived to write about it. Now the possibility of a ceasefire raised the prospect that the Communists would at last open their territory to us; in Saigon we'd already started speculating on which journalist was most likely to pull off a visit. That first afternoon we asked the two men whether they could take us. They said that as soon as the ceasefire began, they could.

We wouldn't let them forget us after that. Every week or two Véronique, Long, and I drove to Long An to see them. Once they told us they feared surveillance, and asked us to meet them later in a nearby town. Another time one of the men shaved his head to disguise himself as a Buddhist monk. With his abundant stubble he looked even seedier than usual, and we laughed when we saw him; he laughed, too. These rudimentary acts of deception confused us, for we couldn't understand whom they were designed to fool: didn't everyone in the village know the men's identity? The men didn't elaborate, and after a while we shrugged off what we couldn't explain. I wrote one more story based on their information, but stories weren't the main reason for our visits. Each time we asked the men if they could take us into Viet Cong territory, their answer was the same: once the ceasefire began, they would.

Working with Véronique was a little like having a girl-friend. Indeed, we'd done so many stories together that some colleagues suspected us of being lovers, a misconception I did not try to dispel. It made me seem cosmopolitan, and besides, I wasn't certain I disapproved of the idea. At the same time, her hardness frightened me, and I didn't feel sufficiently bold to try to change the terms of our relationship.

Once, as Véronique drove us back from a jaunt into the countryside, I asked her permission to lay down across the front seat and rest my head on her thigh. When she consented, I gently placed my head there and tried to convince myself that I didn't feel awkward. It reminded me of the time I'd had a date with the prettiest girl in my high school. We went to a movie, and after half an hour or so, I got up the courage to hold her hand. I gripped it very, very carefully, like a fragile trophy, and kept it pinned to the armrest between us. She understood not to pull her hand away immediately; she knew this was important to me. She waited a few minutes, and then, delicately, respectfully, she removed it in order to scratch her nose. I kept waiting for her to put her hand back, but I knew she wouldn't. In the same way I now wondered whether Véronique would ask me to sit up, but she didn't, until I made a realization: even if the prettiest girl in my high school had left her hand in my grasp throughout the movie, it wouldn't have made any difference. When the movie was over we would have returned to our separate houses, ruefully aware of the fine filament of intimacy that had briefly connected us, knowing that we never wanted to endure that tension again. That was as close as I ever came to crossing any boundaries of decorum with Véronique. We worked well together, I told myself, and I didn't want to jeopardize that.

Instead, I picked up prostitutes. It was as if I were trying to corner feeling, to pin it down, to bracket it the way artillery gunners found their target — from one direction I'd approach estimable women like Véronique, and from the other I'd hire whores — but the target was too elusive for me: I could never find the target, I could never feel. Whenever I picked up prostitutes I knew in advance that the sex would be dismal, but I couldn't stop. I clung to the notion that the woman of my fantasies was out there, around the next corner, somewhere, even after I got gonorrhea and crabs. The most appalling of the prostitutes were the streetwalkers, so haggard that not even the bars would employ them. I cannot forget one who lurked on Tu Do late at night, wearing a pink chiffon dress that only accentuated her death mask of a face, slightly obscured by cheap, thick make-up. I knew I'd never be desperate enough to pick her up, but once in a moment of inexplicable late-night recklessness I took on a streetwalker just like her, and I went with her to her house. She led me by several people eating dinner. I couldn't look at them. By the time we had entered her tiny bedroom and she had taken off her clothes and revealed her sad, sagging body, I knew I couldn't go through with sex. I paid her and left.

Journalism was all I had. Soon, in fact, I'd be without almost friends: Dave Elliott had left months ago, Nick would soon depart for Beirut, and Véronique was going back to Paris in February. I still had one American friend with whom I enjoyed talking about the war, but he'd fallen under the darkly sexual spell of his Vietnamese girlfriend. She hated for him to talk about the war: seduction was the only language she spoke. Sex was her only weapon and she wielded it with the same excess as Americans displayed in expending firepower on the battlefield. When conversations about the war broke out, she'd clear her voice, wiggle provocatively, interrupt, embrace her man if necessary, do whatever it took to keep his attention riveted on her. He was as weakly defended as a militia outpost, and he'd surrender his ground immediately. If she looked angry, he'd scurry to placate her; if she hinted at sex, he'd giggle — in either case our conversation was over. I'd feel superfluous, invisible. I'd resent her, and wonder why he couldn't see through her, and then I'd remember where I was. In Vietnam, I knew, you were supposed to dream, but you weren't ever meant to be satisfied.

Two days before Christmas, McArthur learned that his stepfather had died, and departed for an emergency visit home. Vietnam was all mine now: Gibson trusted me enough not to send in a replacement for McArthur. In his absence I wrote four stories in five days, and celebrated by holding a Christmas eve party at my villa. Véronique brought her French cronies, and my Vietnamese landlady brought her children. At last I used the living room. I moved the coffee table and straw mat aside and set up a borrowed record player. Then, under the spinning ceiling fan made in Hanoi, on the checkered marble floor, we danced. Despite everything, it was truly a party, I swear it was.

I'd passed my apprenticeship. When McArthur returned, he acknowledged the fact by ceasing even cursory inspections of my stories before I filed them, and Gibson informed me he wanted me to stay in Saigon a second year. That pleased me, though I didn't like Gibson's backhanded way of conveying the news: "As long as there is need for two correspondents based in Saigon, we would want you to be one of them." Oh. I imagined myself an old Vietnam hand, and, nearly a year after moving in, bought curtains for my office.

By now I had one other unusual source, though he was unable to help me cover the negotiations. He was Edwin Banks,* a low-level bureaucrat so erratic that I didn't trust his word on any subject. That was no problem, however, for the information he gave me was all in documents. I'd stumbled onto Banks months earlier, while trying to do a story on American civilian advisers in Vietnam, but the alley he led me down was so murky I abandoned the whole project. Still, I didn't forget him. He'd been referred to me by a government press officer, who must have assumed Banks would give me the standard vague answers that officials were expected to provide journalists, but nothing Banks did was standard. His appearance was deceiving: he looked as if he'd just emerged after twenty years in some Washington cubbyhole, with skin so pallid it appeared never to have been touched by sunlight, a stooped, paunchy bearing, and thinning hair combed straight back, like Lyndon Johnson's. When he said he'd cooperate with me, I thought surely that was his unctuous line, and didn't trust him: I'd never come across the species known as Disaffected Bureaucrat before.

Banks was the sort of man who'd come to Vietnam to

* A pseudonym

experience the good life, his version of which entailed orgies, enjoyment of a standard of living higher than he could afford in the States, and the occasional thumbing of his nose at his superiors, which he seemed to want to achieve by being my source. He wasn't a dove, exactly: living in the heart of Saigon, he didn't know much about the war, and hadn't heard of the leading antiwar books of the time. What outrage he possessed was focused on what he considered the American government's wastefulness, the perquisites he himself received being a notable example. Indeed, he was fond of rattling them off: a generous travel allowance, frequent home leaves and   vacations, free housing, use of a government car, and, my favorite, hardship pay. All this, he said, was provided for jobs which could be performed in an hour or two a day, by men making as much as $42,000 a year in base pay. Such was Banks' preoccupation with waste that the first documents he gave me all had to do with the size and performance of the American bureaucracy in Vietnam. My files bulged with such nuggets as a memo on the number of U.S. Agency for International Development automotive "sedans" (as opposed to station wagons and scouts) in Vietnam, broken down by year and military region; a "management fact sheet" claiming such accomplishments as creating "an effective radio-controlled taxi service which is making a significant contribution to vehicle fleet reduction program"; and pages of statistics concerning air conditioners, furniture (office and residential), vehicles (passenger and utility), generators, telecommunications equipment, and prefab buildings (including house trailers). Most of the stuff was bureaucratic gobbledygook.

I called Banks in November with some question about the American presence, and during a subsequent interview realized he might be a find: that was when he began plying me with documents. In the hope that something interesting would turn up, I took everything he had to offer, and tried cultivating him socially besides. Banks seemed titillated by having a journalist around, and in turn he titillated me. He was Henry Miller as a Republican, flamboyant and dull at the same time. On the one hand, he spoke not English but bureaucratese: he didn't know "people," he knew "individuals." On the other hand, he was a member of the "Saigon Social Society," an organization devoted to holding orgies. I knew Vietnam was a sexual playground, a magnet to thousands of men fleeing families and responsibilities in the States, but I'd assumed the female participants were Vietnamese prostitutes: Banks said no. At his orgies everyone was American: bureaucrats, construction workers, secretaries. They met for weekend-long trysts in villas with swimming pools, surrounded by high walls. I was ready to dismiss his tales as fantasies until he gave me an engraved invitation to a costume party billed as a "Hedonic Halloween Happening." The invitation listed eighteen hosts, with names like Troy, Ric, Floyd, and Mac, plus Banks himself. My curiosity wasn't as profound as my concern for my reputation, and I decided against going. From then on I tried to confine our conversations to politics.

The ceasefire rose phoenix-like from the ashes of the Christmas bombing. Nixon called off the attacks on New Year's Day, and Kissinger and Le Duc Tho resumed negotiations in Paris a week later. The North Vietnamese looked like paper tigers now; I couldn't understand why, after being being subjected to such belligerent acts, they so meekly rejoined the perpetrators at the negotiating table. A week after the renewal of the negotiations, Nixon said the talks were progressing and called off all hostile acts towards North Vietnam. In one more week Kissinger and Le Duc Tho initialed an agreement that the North Vietnamese clearly had been prepared to sign all along.

The ceasefire was coming at last, but this time no one was foolish enough to confuse it with peace. Combat might or might not stop, and if it did, the halt would last only as long as the two sides' purposes were served by subterfuges that did not quite amount to war; the struggle would endure. I was cynical about the ceasefire and I was exhilarated by it. I knew the agreement was hokum: it instructed the Vietnamese parties to negotiate a final settlement but offered no incentive to do so. Instead, the U.S. was already busy rearming the ARVN, while the North Vietnamese kept their troops in the south as part of the agreement. The accord's major achievement was in providing for the two sides to slug it out alone, while the United States, together with its POWs, finally went home. This was Nixon's "peace with honor."

At the same time, the ceasefire was history, the most significant development in Vietnam since the partition of the country in 1954. I reveled in my luck: my Vietnam years would be known as the years of the Offensive and the ceasefire. I wasn't sure, however, that we'd be able to cover the ceasefire: rumors were circulating that Hoang Duc Nha, newly appointed South Vietnam's "Commissioner-General of State for Information," or press czar, was planning on shackling the foreign press with roadblocks, a twenty-four-hour curfew, even censorship. I fretted that I'd never make it to Viet Cong territory, or that if I did, I'd be censored. I didn't even have Nick to offer me reassurance — he, his wife Marti, and their baby boy Paine (as in Tom), had left for their new home, Beirut. Ron was instructed to ship COSVN to Beirut after the Proffitts were settled there.

By now we'd all been reduced to putty. The ten months in which we'd endured an offensive, negotiations and hope of ceasefire, suspension of negotiations and no hope of ceasefire, the Christmas bombing, and the promise of a ceasefire at last had rendered most of us numb. And just when I thought I'd reached overload, just when I thought nothing more could touch me, I was awakened by a blast that sounded like an artillery explosion: I opened my eyes and dove under the bed. The blast was followed by a continuous firecracker-like sound, as if the Battle of Saigon were underway. I crawled to the phone and called MACV, and found out there was no battle, no artillery, no assault on Saigon; Communist saboteurs had merely set off the biggest ammo dump in South Vietnam, located six miles outside Saigon.

It was perhaps the first time in Saigon's history that all its residents awoke at the same moment, and it took a few hours for the
blast's explanation to circulate; in the meantime I heard muffled
sobs and shrieks whenever the rumbles got loud. Upon learning
the explosions' explanation, most people just shook their heads,
half-smiling: we'd been duped again. Vietnamese and
Americans alike, we were suckers, captives of our imagination.
We were the detritus of war, propelled from fear of battle to fear
of ceasefire back to fear of battle, until every crisis felt the same
and all we asked was to survive.

Once it became apparent that a ceasefire was in the
works, the paper prepared to publish a ceasefire supplement.
My assignment at once appalled and excited me, and made me
think Gibson understood me better than I thought: I was to
depict a Vietnamese family whose war-provoked tribulations
were so horrific, so enormous, that it could symbolize the entire
nation's suffering.

At first it was hard to find anyone who met the criteria,
as if Vietnam's suffering was a trick with mirrors, another ingenious deception. Everybody said families who'd experienced
unimaginable tragedies were plentiful in Vietnam, but nobody
knew any: they certainly didn't travel in the same circles journalists did. The first woman I interviewed said she'd lost her
husband and all her sons in combat; I was puzzled that she was-
n't more upset. She rambled on, about one inconsequential thing
after another, and skirted discussing her family history whenever Long brought up the subject. After an hour she confessed that
the dead men she'd referred to weren't her immediate relations,
but rather those of her sisters, none of whom wished to be interviewed. For the sake of politeness we talked a couple of minutes
longer. Then we left, annoyed.

Several more interviews were unsatisfactory. I felt like
the emcee on Queen for a Day, watching the swinging needle of
the applause meter in my mind as the interviewees spoke of

their misery. I couldn't tell them why I was asking them questions; I couldn't say, "I'm trying to determine if your suffering is sufficient to symbolize the suffering of all Vietnamese." And if their stories weren't tragic enough, I couldn't tell them that they failed to meet my requirements.

Long and I decided on another approach: we'd search for our family in a refugee camp, where at least everybody'd endured *one* tragedy. We told the director of a camp outside Saigon what we were looking for. He led us to a woman who told us she had lost a son in combat. We begged off: sorry, one dead son was not enough. The director thought harder and then hit the bulls-eye: I knew it as soon as I saw the next woman he introduced to us. Tears were flowing down her cheeks, in streams as fine as thread. This wasn't mere crying; the tears issued from somewhere deeper inside than her eyes. Yet even as she cried, she never stopped working. She was sitting barefoot on her wooden sleeping platform, making biscuits for sale in the camp. She had high, high cheekbones, from which her skin stretched taut, and wore her gray hair in a bun held in place by a brass pin, her only ornament. The holes in her earlobes were big enough to see through — she later explained that she left behind her only set of earrings when fighting forced her to flee her village in haste. What I liked about her was that she grieved openly, yet without apparent self-pity; she looked like the ultimate in self-pride. Long told the woman I might want to write about her, and she agreed to tell us her story on the condition that I not use her name. We learned that her husband and two of her six sons had died of illness, and that in the previous three months two more sons had disappeared in combat and were almost certainly dead. The two others remained in the army, and saw her only once a year. Roughly translated, this is what she said: "I know nothing of government or politics. All I know is that I think only of my sons. I remember their faces, their ways of walking. I still hope one is alive. I know that if he came into this room now, I would be happy to die.... I know how I suffer. I don't want other people to suffer like me. I want peace to come soon."

Like thousands of other Vietnamese families altered by the war, hers effectively consisted only of women. She lived in the camp, formerly a U.S. army base, with her two widowed daughters-in-law and eight grandchildren. Once inhabited by perhaps a dozen GIs, her barracks now was the home of eight families, including fifty-nine women and children and one old man. A month earlier she'd almost run out of money; now she and her family subsisted by selling the biscuits. On a good day she earned thirty-five cents. Though survival on such a sum was inconceivable to me, the experience hadn't made her acquisitive. The return of one of her sons, she said, "would be worth more than any fortune Buddha could give me."

I ended up devoting half my story to the woman, half to another family with different war-related problems. I sent off the piece to Los Angeles, and was pleased to get a return request for photographs: that meant the story would get good play. The other family I wrote about agreed to have a picture taken, but the refugee woman refused — she considered a photograph an invasion of her privacy in a way that words weren't. I thought that was reasonable, and cabled the news back to L.A. "Offer her $100" was Gibson's cold reply. I was appalled. Gibson's response assumed money bought everything, including principles; it was a metaphor for the American experience in Vietnam. I thought of ignoring the cable, but I lacked the resolve: in the end I sent Long and the photographer to the camp to make the offer without me. When they came back, however, they still had the money. Though a hundred dollars was more than the woman could hope to earn in a year, more than the value of all her possessions, she turned it down. When Long related her decision, I cheered. She remains my model of integrity.

The ceasefire was announced in late January, so long after Kissinger's promise of it that even the dimmest peasant residing at the remote southern tip of Vietnam should have known better than to confuse it with peace. Yet if the ceasefire didn't presage peace, the war was still irrevocably altered. Its rules were now dictated by the 70-page "Agreement on Ending the War and Restoring Peace in Vietnam" and three Protocols. What the hell was a protocol? We were handed the document two days before the ceasefire; a few hours later I was an expert, not just on that word's definition but on the entire agreement: its nine chapters and 82 articles comprised a condensed version of *War and Peace*. Some parts were signed by four parties, others by just two; each omission and commission reflected the shifting tides of a power struggle represented by years of negotiating. The agreement established a "Joint Military Commission," an "International Commission of Control and Supervision," and a "National Council of National Reconciliation and Concord": it was poetry, a minuet, if you could stand back far enough to see it that way, which nobody could.

I referred to the agreement constantly: it was my bible, I was its theologian. My favorite passage was Article 11, little-mentioned because it was so droll. It said the two sides would "immediately after the ceasefire...achieve national reconciliation and concord," as if everybody'd just shake hands and forget the war. More notably, the article commanded both sides to "ensure democratic liberties of the people," including "freedom of move-ment": the ARVN forcibly clung to their populace, as size was their biggest claim to power, so I knew they'd never obey that. Still, that was just a quibble, my pet article. The essence of the agreement was that the United States would take its prisoners and soldiers (but not its weapons, which it would bequeath to the ARVN) and go home; then the two sides would fight it out, politically and/or militarily, until the Communists won. Was that interpretation cynical? No other theory made sense: consid-ering that the ARVN and U.S. Army together hadn't been able to defeat the Communists, it was hard to see how the ARVN alone could do the job. The agreement simply codified Kissinger's "decent interval": enough time would elapse between the American withdrawal and the inevitable ARVN collapse for the

U.S. to deny responsibility.

Saigon again swelled with a thousand journalists, gorging on the agreement's complications and willing to pretend that the war was truly ending. *Newsweek* had jumped the gun, having run a "Goodbye Vietnam" cover along with Nick's specious coalition scoop two months earlier; now all the newspapers carried their special Vietnam supplements and war histories. It was ethnocentrism, no- thing more: Americans perceived the war as over because Americans would no longer fight it. Yet the ceasefire looked to be the most interesting period of the struggle so far. The stage was actually expanded, to include Canadians, Hungarians, Indonesians, and Poles, who were expected, improbably, to man a peace-supervisory force together. And the Americans weren't leaving, just not fighting: they sent in a legion of civilians to perform many of the same non-combatant functions the military had before. Could the two sides make any headway at all towards reconciliation? Would the Communists open up the areas they controlled? How would the two sides coexist where their territories met? What would released American prisoners of war say about their treatment in North Vietnam? How would Saigon's inhabitants react to the presence of North Vietnamese officers overseeing the ceasefire? Would combat pause, or continue unabated?

On the morning the ceasefire was to begin I drove north from Saigon on Route 13 as far as I could: it turned out that wasn't far at all. At 5 a.m. Communist troops had crept into a village straddling the highway 20 miles north of Saigon and blockaded the road. They apparently intended to dig in until the ceasefire took hold; they assumed they'd then have grounds for claiming all territory from the village north to their zone of control. This scheme may have adhered to the letter of the agreement, but it certainly violated its spirit. The ARVN understandably resisted, joining one of many battles that day actually provoked by the ceasefire. The villagers displayed typical Vietnamese sang-froid:

from a knoll where dozens of journalists watched, 200 yards outside the hamlet, I could see them cranking a water bucket up a well, tending animals, sweeping doorsteps, as if the fighting had nothing to do with them. At eight a.m., the designated ceasefire time, the fighting paused, and the sound of President Thieu instructing countrymen to be vigilant wafted over the village via radio. Then came more rifle fire and artillery: so much for the ceasefire. ARVN troops filed out of the village half an hour later, but not out of respect for the ceasefire; they figured their artillery would be sufficient to drive the Communists out of the village, and were withdrawing to prevent casualties. Minutes after that, two sobbing, profusely bleeding women, one carrying a small child on her back, came running out of the village towards us. A television cameraman and sound man followed closely behind them, recording their shocked screams, inadvertently tipping off journalism's priorities: news was more important than first aid. These two women, after all, were newsworthy: they were the first civilian casualties of the ceasefire.

I rushed back to Saigon, wrote a story, filed it, and went to the airport to cover the arrival of the peace-supervisory force. No bloodletting here, just slapstick comedy. When a Soviet propjet arrived with the first contingent of the Polish and Hungarian delegations, Deputy U.S. Ambassador Whitehouse and some thirty lesser officials stood waiting, practicing their synthetic smiles — but nothing happened. South Vietnamese authorities refused to roll out a staircase so the passengers could debark. Ten minutes later some American soldiers pushed a ramp to the plane, but it didn't reach as high as the door. By the time they got the right one in place, 15 minutes had elapsed. At last a hundred Hungarians and Poles emerged from the plane, blinking in the brightness, dazed and puffy-eyed after the 27-hour, five-stop flight from Budapest. With their heavy winter uniforms they looked ready for a siege of Moscow, but now, to their seeming surprise, they were in the tropics, already sweating. The soldiers were ushered to a waiting room where they stood uncomfortably under a photograph of a stern-looking Nguyen Van Thieu and faced an unfamiliar crush of Western journalists. I felt sorry for them: according to the agreement they were supposed to be in place throughout the country and prepared to begin work within a day, but they were ready only for a nap.

I was still laughing to myself when I checked in with McArthur by phone. By contrast, he was testy. Was I aware that elsewhere in the airport a plane full of arriving Viet Cong officials had been sitting on the tarmac for hours, its passengers barred from debarking because of a dispute with South Vietnamese authorities? I said I didn't know that. Watching the Eastern Europeans' arrival, I'd felt like a veteran correspondent; now, once more, I was a cub.

As soon as I got off the phone, I looked around the airport, and realized it was packed with South Vietnamese police whose task apparently included keeping journalists away from the Viet Cong plane. They were easy to elude: I hitched a ride on an airport service truck driven by an American GI, and he dropped me near the Viet Cong plane. I kept my distance and tried to look inconspicuous, particularly after I saw a colleague detained for approaching the aircraft. Viet Cong officers, distinguishable by their pith helmets, occasionally stuck their heads out the door of the plane as below them waited a crowd of South Vietnamese officials and government photographers, the latter almost certainly intelligence agents in disguise. By striking up a conversation with an American official, I learned that the source of contention was South Vietnam's customs forms: the Viet Cong delegates refused to sign them to avoid acknowledging the government's legitimacy. In response the South Vietnamese wouldn't let the Viet Cong off the plane. I stood around for three hours, and nothing changed: it seemed to me that unless the stalemate was settled, the ceasefire itself would be stillborn. When, calling in to McArthur, I expressed this thought, he again sounded exasperated; the ceasefire wouldn't flounder on a technicality, he said. He was right, too: 20 hours after the planes arrived, long after I left to write my story, the South Vietnamese government, under pressure from the U.S., relented, and the Viet Cong officials debarked without signing the forms.

The prospect that journalists might make contact with the Communist visitors in Saigon enraged South Vietnamese officials. Since the North Vietnamese and Viet Cong representatives were to be housed at a fenced-in outpost inside the airport, the officials proclaimed the entire airport off limits to journalists, and briefly detained 20 of us after we penetrated it the next day. The authorities confiscated our film and took away our useless press cards; thereafter, reporters at the airport pretended to be American officials, and photographers hid behind trees. All this was tame, I knew, but what I had in mind might evoke a more severe response. How would South Vietnamese authorities react to a visit to Communist territory such as the one Véronique and I planned? The two men in Long An had agreed to take us the next day, and showed so much confidence in the success of the trip that some of their conviction rubbed off. I thought we had a chance.

SOARING
Chapter

4

At dawn on the third day of the ceasefire, Véronique, Long, and I left for Long An in my rented car. Only McArthur and Félix Bolo, Véronique's bureau chief, knew of our plan; we told them that if we didn't return to Saigon that evening, they could assume we were on the other side. However, when we arrived in Long An, the two men were surprisingly subdued: they told us they couldn't take us. They'd been overwhelmed by the extent of South Vietnamese police vigilance since the ceasefire started, they said, and had to lie low. I saw our dreams of glory evanescing, but I didn't feel entirely deflated: it wasn't yet time to give up. We talked with the men for an hour, ostensibly gathering information for a story, but all we truly wanted was the answer to one question, which we asked repeatedly in different forms: if we walked into Viet Cong territory by ourselves, would we be welcomed? The men said yes.

I had begun to consider the possibility of crossing into Viet Cong territory without a guide a day earlier, when Ron told me he'd seen Viet Cong flags in the distance while driving down the main highway through Dinh Tuong, the Delta province immediately south of Long An. In the back of my mind it registered then that if for some reason the men couldn't take us into Viet Cong territory, the flags would show the way. As far as we knew, no colleagues had attempted such a journey, or even had contacts like our Long An friends, so the story would still be an exclusive: now we had to decide if we were ready to take the gamble. Of the three of us, the least committed to the journey should have been Long, who, unlike us, had little to gain in return for risking his life. Nevertheless, when Véronique and I spoke of going without the two men, Long didn't resist. Perhaps he felt he bore responsibility because he introduced us to the two men, or perhaps he just didn't feel comfortable turning us down. Conceivably, like us, he was intensely curious about the Viet Cong. In any case, when he said he'd go, we didn't argue — he was indispensable. We were so bound up in thoughts about the trip that I doubt we fully appreciated the magnanimity of his act.

We left the two men and drove down the main highway into Dinh Tuong. Sure enough, it wasn't long before we saw a Viet Cong flag — a gold star on a red and blue field — waving above trees a half-mile or more from the road: I felt like a New World explorer who'd found his Eldorado. Though I'd lived in Vietnam for thirteen months, until that moment the Viet Cong were abstract to me, like electrons, leaving traces but never visible; now at last they were revealing their positions. And doing so might have been a misjudgment on their part, for the flag we saw brought retribution to the hamlet displaying it: ARVN troops were attacking in an apparent effort to get it taken down. If the maneuver I'd witnessed two days earlier on Route 13 represented Communist chicanery, this was the ARVN equivalent: the Communists clearly controlled this territory, a fact the ARVN found too embarrassing to accept. As we drove on, we found that wherever Viet Cong flags appeared, the ARVN were attacking. Once we spotted a Washington *Post* reporter, my competitor, watching an assault. I was tempted to join him, for I didn't want him to have a story while I ended up empty-handed, but instead we drove on. We figured that there were more unfurled Viet Cong flags than ARVN troops to force their dislodgment, and hoped that eventually we'd come across one that hadn't provoked combat.

An hour later we found what we were looking for: a few flags were flying from above a row of trees half a mile from the road, and no troops were in sight. Only a rice field separated us from the trees: suddenly we felt very close to Viet Cong territory. We left the car on the shoulder of the highway, and walked on the mud walls between the paddies until we reached an old man. Long cagily told him we wanted to take pictures of the Viet Cong flags and asked how we could get to them. The man was wary of us, but said he'd take us there if we could wait an hour while he finished his work. Not wanting to waste time, we told him we'd go by ourselves. He pointed out a route and said he could "guarantee our legs"; only when I heard Long translate the phrase did it occur to me that the paddies might be mined.

To follow the old man's route we had to walk back to the highway and reenter the fields at a different point. By now the sun was overhead, and large ovals of sweat formed on our shirts. I carried a backpack, a notebook, and a new camera, all of which made balancing on the treacherous mud walls difficult, and Véronique had a bad cold. By the time we returned to the highway we were already tired.

As we resumed our walk towards the treeline, I looked back at an elevated ARVN outpost a few hundred yards down the highway. I could see soldiers there watching us through binoculars, and I wanted time to dive into a paddy if they were preparing to shoot. Our presence didn't seem to disturb them, however, so we kept going. We encountered a gap in the retaining wall, and had to wade through mud up to our knees while holding our cameras and packs high. Now we considered giving up. It wasn't the danger that was getting to us: I'd already learned that danger is easier to accept than discomfort. Véronique was feeling weak, and her face was flush red; all of us were muddy and exhausted. Véronique suggested turning back so that we could cover the combat down the road, but I said no. I had a feeling we could make it.

We walked as far as we could on the mud wall, until it gave out. Now a muddy lagoon blocked our way. Had we taken the wrong route? On the opposite bank was a rowboat, and beyond that was a house displaying a South Vietnamese government flag. Our only hope was to find someone who could fetch us in the boat. Instantly we spotted a farmer, and Long yelled our request to him. He obliged, and poled us across the pond; then he invited us into the house to rest and drink tea. Eight little children, some wearing only shirts, sat on the floor in front of us; they looked astonished to find such unusual visitors in their living room. Véronique collapsed onto a mat and tried to regain her strength. The farmer must have been ravished with curiosity about our mission, but he betrayed no particular interest. Long in turn didn't reveal more than was necessary — the government flag painted on the farmer's house was reason enough for caution. As he had done with the old man in the rice paddy, Long said only that we wished to take pictures of the Viet Cong flags. The man offered to show us the proper path. A few minutes later he took us behind his house, pointed where to go, and shook our hands. His solemnity surprised me, but later I understood it: his was the last house with a government flag we saw before reaching Viet Cong territory. We were about to cross sides.

As we walked on, a dozen gleeful children suddenly swarmed around us, as if we were Pied Pipers; in their presence it was impossible to feel fear. Then, as quickly as they appeared, they vanished, like characters in a dream. For a minute or two we were engulfed in a stilted, ominous silence that suggested we were being watched. We walked on until we reached the trees we'd seen from the highway, and noticed several houses without flags of any sort. Suddenly, as if on cue, more villagers surrounded us and greeted us with smiles. To protect myself in case the people were hostile towards Americans, I was prepared to say I was Canadian, and the three of us took the precaution of speaking French among ourselves, but now we decided there was no need. We said we were journalists, and asked to see the village leaders. The people pointed us further into the interior. Viet Cong flags waved from the trees we passed, and the villagers cheerfully posed for pictures in front of them. The people's daring surprised me; such pictures in government hands would have been grounds for arrest or worse. We'd penetrated the outermost circle of the secret realm.

There was nothing reticent about these people, nothing that remotely suggested danger. The three of us were on a stroll, a jaunt, as if we were the missing guests of honor in a celebration the villagers had long planned. The world in front of us continually seemed to expand, to burst, to somehow overtake mere 360-degree vision. I'd been in the Delta perhaps a dozen times, but only now could I see that it contained an intricate network of canals and streams and a variety of mechanisms for navigating them. I realized that my heavy army boots, which I'd bought in the Saigon black market and treasured for their manful aura, were a liability here, for several times we had to cross a stream by walking on bamboo planks, and I was in constant danger of falling; one of the villagers saw my difficulty and handed me a wooden staff to stick in the stream bed for support. In contrast to the hard-edged zone I came from, this one seemed supple, nurturing, feminine.

When we reached a canal, a familiar face was there, smiling: the farmer who'd "guaranteed our legs" had come back, and directed us into his sampan. Shorn of his wariness, he looked proud to be taking us to see the village leaders. I thought of all the interviews I'd had with Vietnamese peasants who behaved as the old man had an hour earlier, when he didn't know if he could trust us: they were vague, uncommunicative, monosyllabic. Did they all harbor the same secret the old man did — their support for the Viet Cong?

As we glided down the canal, word spread that we were journalists, and people greeted us by waving Viet Cong flags: I felt like a passenger on a Rose Bowl float. Once Véronique told me to look towards the canal bank, and I turned quickly, for I could hear excitement in her voice: two Viet Cong soldiers stood there, coolly regarding us. With their black pajamas and AK-47s, they looked like the Platonic ideal of VC soldiers. I took pictures. We had arrived.

A few minutes later other soldiers waved and called us ashore, and guided us along a path. All the friendliness was eerie, and it took me a while to see why: we never took anyone by surprise. Word of our presence always preceded us; in this zone without telephones, communication triumphed. More and more villagers followed us, looking pleased, like fishermen with an unexpected catch. At last we were delivered to the village chief, who stood on the trail, quietly watching us. In my mind the idea of a Communist village chief conjured up a steely build, chiseled cheekbones, and a hero's pose, and this man looked stamped out of the mold. Just one feature was discordant, and it only added to his mystique: he was missing a thumb. He was dressed just like the villagers: his flashlight and radio were what set him apart. He said his name was Le Hoang Oanh, and asked for our business cards, of all things. Perhaps he intended the gesture to convey formality, but it struck us as innocent — compared to the net of South Vietnamese visas and press cards in which we were constantly entangled, a request for a mere business card was practically amusing. My card all but announced that I was an American, but if Oanh understood that, it didn't show. All he did was pronounce, in an even, understated tone, "We are happy to welcome the foreign correspondents to visit our liberation area. This is the first time the press has come here." To him "here" perhaps meant the village, but to us it encompassed all Communist territory in South Vietnam. We felt flushed with triumph, one far more astounding to us than Oanh or the other villagers understood. The people around us cheered, and Oanh smiled. A woman handed glasses of iced tea to the three of us. It tasted like ambrosia.

We had reached the quiet center. The Viet Cong soldiers looked us over and didn't shoot; the village chief welcomed us. We were in the forbidden dark zone, and found that the sun indeed shone here, seemingly more brightly than in Saigon. The people around us didn't look murderous; on the contrary, they displayed more warmth than I'd seen in 13 months in government-controlled areas. My heart opened, swelled with the notion that Véronique and I were explorers, not just of Viet Cong terrain but of the humanly possible, and that what sustained our journey was not so much our courage as our trust.

"Be sure to provide double protection for our guests," Oanh told the village security cadre. He instructed three messengers to report on our presence to the Viet Cong district secretary, the chairman of the village revolutionary committee, and ordinary villagers respectively. The orders were carried out immediately, a fact which distinguished the messengers from their languid Saigon counterparts. Discipline in the village was impressive, perhaps overly so: when the village chief asked us to cease taking notes, as we'd been doing since we entered the village, we considered it prudent to accede.

Oanh proposed an afternoon tour beginning with an inspection of war damage he said was caused by ARVN ceasefire violations. As we walked to the first site, we were escorted by a barefoot soldier and a few children whom Oanh had instructed to carry Viet Cong flags on long bamboo poles. A festive mood pervaded our entourage, which constantly grew larger. Children giggled. I was handed a conical straw hat to shield my head from the sun; when I put it on, the people pointed and laughed good-naturedly. One boy pointed to a Viet Cong banner and said to us in awkward English, "My flag." I surmised that he'd spent time in ARVN territory, as probably most of the other villagers had; some of them may have crossed back and forth between the two zones daily.

As we walked, Oanh answered our questions about the village. We were in Binh Phu, a 100-percent Viet Cong-controlled village of seven square miles and 6,800 people. We were amazed that the Viet Cong occupied territory so close to the main road through the Delta — from where we stood at one point, we could see cars plying it. I'd driven that stretch many times without suspecting the Viet Cong were so close.

Considering that we could see battle smoke twisting

upwards in the distance, I thought Oanh's claims of ARVN ceasefire violations in the village were plausible, but the evidence he showed us undercut his assertion. We saw bomb craters, splintered rooftops, houses burnt to their foundations, but the damage almost certainly was done months or years earlier, not in the previous two and a half days. A bomb crater filled with murky water obviously had been there a long time. So Oanh was prepared to lie to us.

Continuing on our tour, we were confronted by surprising evidence of the thoroughness of the village's ceasefire preparations, as several peasants greeted us with harangues and angry gestures. Véronique and I were momentarily puzzled, but since we couldn't understand what they were saying, our attention was soon diverted. Later on, when Long told us what the villagers said, we realized they'd mistaken us for members of the peace-supervisory force, and were demanding payment for war damage. It was a planned performance, delivered before the wrong audience, which unexpectedly revealed that the Communists had high expectations for the ceasefire. The peace-supervisory force, for instance, never came close to playing a significant role, and combat hardly paused in some areas, yet all the ceasefire preparations in Binh Phu suggested that the Communists expected a peaceful struggle at least for a time after the ceasefire began. No wonder Binh Phu's residents greeted us so enthusiastically: taking their cues from Viet Cong preparations, they probably believed the ceasefire would hold. To them we were harbingers of peace.

Oanh led us inside a pagoda partially destroyed by explosives, another example of alleged American and ARVN-wrought damage. With 50 people gathered around us inside that shattered shell, the setting appeared sufficiently theatrical for a formal announcement, which was what Oanh had in mind. Implicitly acknowledging for the first time that he wasn't entirely sanguine about our presence, he announced, "The people are happy to receive all journalists, including those who work for the rebel government of Saigon, but on the sole condition that they do their job fairly." A man behind Oanh whispered in his ear, and then Oanh announced that we could take notes. Grateful to be relieved of the burden of trying to memorize everything we saw and heard, we took out our notebooks, and Oanh invited us to ask questions. We began gingerly, first asking what his job as village chief entailed. "My function is to command politically and militarily with the goal of conquering the American aggressors," he said. We asked how many villagers were members of the National Liberation Front, the umbrella Communist political apparatus. "Because this is a question of defense, I can't say how many people there are, but I can say that the Front represents the whole population of the village, all religions, and also men who work for the Saigon government."

It was another rhetorical reply, more evidence of Oanh's suspicions about us, but I wasn't bothered. It was enough for us to know that our lives weren't in danger, that we faced no threat of punishment, that we were free to leave the Viet Cong zone when we wished. Oanh's evasions were the least of what we had to fear, and were understandable considering that the United States had ceased being his archenemy only two days earlier. I was more struck by his decorousness and restraint than his unwillingness to give us accurate information. My job was to check his assertions against the physical evidence, to distinguish the truth from his rhetoric.

In the midst of our questioning a messenger handed Oanh a pink slip of paper. It had obviously come from his superiors. He read it, then announced, "The members of this village are very happy to invite you two journalists to spend the night here to celebrate together a ceremony of peace." Véronique and I exchanged glances, recognizing the elation in each other's eyes; the journey was surpassing our expectations. Our only worry was that some other journalist might have duplicated our feat in another Communist zone and would report on it that night, but we'd happily take the gamble. When we accepted, Oanh applauded, and the surrounding villagers joined in.

We had one problem: our car, parked on the highway

shoulder, gave our presence away, and the police might already be looking for us. Oanh ordered someone to find out if the car was still there, and assured us that the next day we would be taken back to the government side by a different route. We were relieved to have an alternative to facing down the police, but we knew, too, that in agreeing to abandon our car we entrusted ourselves entirely to Oanh.

Oanh gave another formal statement, in which we were told to write "what our consciences dictate" — he was again revealing his distrust. Then we were led out of the pagoda, and immediately more villagers hailed us. We were football heroes; they were cheerleaders. They shouted, "Welcome the correspondents! Welcome peace! We support peace! Welcome!" Long told us the next day that Oanh had instructed villagers to make the chants, but at the time we were more mindful of the villagers' apparent enthusiasm than their lack of spontaneity. Wherever we walked for the next hour, people hailed us on a cue from a cadre with "Welcome!" Youths appeared to carry our packs and help us across the gangplank-like bamboo crossings.

As we walked to a villager's house where we would have dinner, Oanh, more relaxed now, explained a bit of his background to Long. Forty-three years old, he had been an N.L.F. member for many years. He said he was arrested by government troops in 1969, then paid a bribe for the substantial sum of $125; as a result, he was released from prison three months later. He said villagers donated the money; I imagine that "villagers" was a euphemism for the N.L.F. Despite Oanh's revolutionary rhetoric, he didn't give the impression of being a one-dimensional zealot. He had his bourgeois habits, such as chain-smoking, and he wore, of all things, a Seiko watch, set on Hanoi time.

The conversation between Oanh and Long had an unquestioned potential for volatility. On the one hand, Oanh's flashlight, radio, and lighter had all been taken off the bodies of American soldiers, and he had lost his thumb fighting against the U.S. Ninth Infantry Division in 1969. For his part, Long never told me his feelings about interviewing Oanh, but he couldn't have been wholly enthusiastic about a representative of the army which had wounded him three times. Long sometimes revealed his bias by, for example, referring not to the "National Liberation Front" but to the "Viet Cong," a neutral term to most Americans but a pejorative to Oanh. It was to Oanh's credit that he did nothing more than correct Long each time a slip occurred, and never asked about Long's background. Oanh must have sensed that he wouldn't like the answers, and that any indication of his displeasure might jeopardize his chief objective, which was impressing Véronique and me.

The sun had set by the time we reached the house where we'd have dinner. At first Oanh, Véronique, Long, about fifteen villagers, and I crowded inside the tiny earthen-floored house, uniquely situated in the middle of a rice field. We were offered a sweet candy, our appetizer, and then the four of us had a chat. Still preoccupied with our trustworthiness, Oanh asked if we intended to write the truth. "You came here unexpectedly," he said. "We have nothing to hide. We hope that what you see is the truth." Then he asked if we believed what we had seen so far. Searching for the right word, I said I'd been impressed. Oanh asked Véronique what the flag of the French Communist Party looked like, and after hearing the answer, asked us what parties we belonged to. I said, "As a journalist I don't belong to any party." Véronique later told me she was appalled by this un-Marxist comment, while Gibson, when he found out about it, was so pleased he cited it in a *Times* newsletter as evidence of my objectivity. I disagreed with both of them: I meant the remark to reflect not objectivity, which I considered an illusory standard of journalism, but independence.

Véronique was exhausted by her cold and the long walk, and asked to rest for fifteen minutes before dinner. Oanh, Long, and I left her with the others inside the house, and ate at an outside table in the light of a kerosene lamp, underneath a

starry, moonless, royal blue sky. Even considering the distant
sound of artillery, the setting bespoke romance, and indeed a
kind of ideological flirtation took place, for Oanh was less dis-
trustful now. I asked him how he felt about eating with an
American after having fought against the United States for so
long. He sounded as if he'd been preparing his answer for years:
"We consider that there are two kinds of Americans. One we call
imperialists, who come with bombs and weapons to kill our people and destroy our land. They are our enemies. However, the
ceasefire is an agreement of reconciliation and we don't see anyone as our enemy any more.

"The second kind of American we call peaceful and pro-
gressive. They do not come here to destroy or kill — they are
people like Martin Luther King and the movie actress Jane
Fonda. We do not see them as our enemies but as helping us. We
really appreciate Americans such as those in the women's movement who prevent their sons from fighting in South Vietnam.
You can recognize friendship easily. If we were not friends we
would not sit down and eat at the same table. If we were not
friends, we would not talk about the things we are talking about
now."

I appreciated the precision and grace of Oanh's
response. A man who lived in a remote corner of Southeast Asia
had enough political sophistication to distinguish between "two
kinds" of Americans and even knew the names of an actress and
a civil rights leader from a distant continent. Even if he'd heard
it all on Radio Hanoi, he was a superior man. I liked the way he
accepted so readily what he was given, and responded with
appropriately measured action; his understanding seemed to go
beyond politics to something more profound, to the core of
Eastern tradition. After all, if the war had consumed four gener-
ations of Communist cadres in a decade, as Dave Elliott asserted, Oanh was extraordinary simply for having survived.

Our meal, consisting of overflowing servings of soup,
chicken, beef, and rice, was so bountiful I wondered who'd gone
hungry so that we might eat well. As soon as we finished, Oanh

told us we had to leave for the "peace ceremony" at a site two miles away. In the darkness, with the expanse in front of us illuminated only by flickering lights from a few houses, we reluctantly set out on this new trek. Already tired, we again had to walk on the mud walls of the rice paddies. Our guides carried flashlights and the kerosene lamp we'd used at dinner, but we still made many false steps. Véronique, Long, and I each were assigned two soldiers, one in front and the other behind us, to catch us when we fell. Usually stern-faced, my two teenaged barefoot escorts walked spryly while we frequently lost our balance trudging through the mud. Sometimes the guides couldn't contain laughs induced by our clumsiness, but they always caught us before we tumbled into a paddy. It was an odd sensation, feeling myself the butt of a joke on Westerners; the usual roles assumed by Americans and Vietnamese had been reversed.

Our party originally included a dozen people, but after an hour of steady marching at least a hundred others were following us in single file. Oanh said the ceremony had been decided upon three hours earlier in honor of our appearance, but if that was true, the news spread quickly. People waited on the trail until we passed by, then cheerfully joined the end of the column. No one looked surprised to see two Westerners. Sometimes we'd wait at a designated point until a cadre with a flashlight arrived; then he'd lead us along the portion of the trail he knew. I was amazed by the thoroughness of the Viet Cong's organization.

At one point we passed booby traps set just off the path, and I realized we were walking on Viet Cong military trails. Dead vines were draped in front of the traps to provide warning, and could be removed if ARVN troops attacked. Our guides warned us not to make a misstep, an instruction I scrupulously followed. A little further on we passed a graveyard for Viet Cong soldiers. A sign in front said, "Cemetery of Dead Heroes," and each gravestone was adorned with a red star. I was stunned: as unambiguously as I could imagine, this tidy cemetery almost within sight of the highway proclaimed the total absence of a government presence in the area. Perhaps I'd vastly overestimated the extent of ARVN territory; perhaps the ARVN controlled only roads.

The longer we walked, the more difficult the path became. Frequently we encountered breaches a yard or two wide, filled only by a board or bamboo poles; my escorts had to support me as I walked across. One gap was bridged by a piece of metal which bore U.S. military insignia on it; a soldier said it was part of a crashed U.S. Cobra helicopter. Knowing that, I felt ghoulish as I walked on it. The soldier added that his army had nothing like Cobras, those ferocious war machines. He said, "We have no airplanes. We have no tanks. All we have are men with legs of brass and shoulders of steel. Those are our tanks."

Did all Viet Cong soldiers speak poetry? I felt like the discoverer of an uncharted land of sentiment. I alone knew the secret that the Viet Cong sometimes smiled and acted nobly; it was hard for me to believe that in a day or two I might be able to share the information with a few million readers.

Thunderous explosions broke my reverie. It was artillery: judging by their force and loudness, I thought the rounds had struck no more than ten yards away, and people behind us shrieked. I dove head first into a ditch. A woman yelled miserably, "My God, what will we do now? Where will we run? Please help me." The Viet Cong also felt fear.

It was probably nothing more than good old ARVN Harassment and Interdiction fire, shot randomly into Viet Cong territory, but Véronique and I couldn't avoid thinking that the shells were meant for us, that somehow the ARVN had learned of our location and were gunning for the turncoat journalists. For the first time I wondered whether we'd survive the journey, and whether it had been worth the risk of death. Véronique began to cry. "I don't want to die here," she said. It was our guides who restored our confidence: they weren't the slightest bit worried. They said the shells struck 200 yards from us, not even close enough to merit taking shelter, and assured us we were safe. How could they be sure?

We needed a break. Our guides led us to a house to rest.

While we strove to regain our calm, the house's owner, an old
man with a wispy white beard, told us indignantly that ARVN
artillery was nothing new: it had struck his house five times in
eighteen years. He readily agreed when we asked him to pose
for a photograph in front of a Viet Cong flag displayed on his
wall. Some of what we saw that day was manufactured good
cheer, but I knew that the look of pride, nearly defiance, that
came over the man's face as he sat in front of the flag was genuine.

As we left the house to resume our trek, one of the soldiers smilingly asked, "Now have you seen an example of a
ceasefire violation?"

The trail grew progressively worse, then gave out
entirely, and we found ourselves wading through muddy water
up to our thighs. Sometimes I got stuck and the soldiers had to
haul me out. We became separated from most of the people
behind us, who, we were told, had taken an even more arduous
route. At last we stopped, at the bank of the Ba Rai River, where,
our guides informed us, the Viet Cong sank more than twenty
American vessels in a battle three years earlier. Now we waited
for a sampan to take us across. We had walked for more than two
hours, and the distance we covered was almost four miles, not
the two we'd expected. I thought of another theory Dave Elliott
espoused: he said the government survived by catering to the
passivity of the populace, whereas the Viet Cong required active
involvement of its supporters. Government troops rode to battle
in the backs of trucks on smoothly paved highways, while the
Viet Cong trekked through muddy trails like the ones we tra-
versed. I tried in vain to imagine the ARVN functioning here,
and felt I understood why almost all difficult terrain in South
Vietnam was controlled by the Viet Cong.

When Oanh first mentioned the peace ceremony, I imagined that perhaps 25 people would participate, but the size of
our traveling entourage alone indicated that at least a hundred

people would be there. Now, as we neared the site of the ceremony, we heard voices on loudspeakers, and my estimate leaped
again. Loudspeakers! So close to the highway, how could the
Viet Cong dare to proclaim their presence so boldly? More startling, the loudspeakers were announcing our arrival —
Véronique and I heard our names. As we got closer, we heard the
buzz that a crowd makes, and the buzz grew ever louder. We
reached a clearing and saw a large crowd, in front of a stage with
a Viet Cong flag for a backdrop, and flashbulbs went off in our
faces, the old kind that newsmen in '30s and '40s movies used,
and the crowd applauded, the crowd cheered, several thousand
people cheered. The reception both astonished and pleased me:
most people, after all, pass their lives without receiving an ovation from a crowd of strangers, much less from people of a different civilization and language. For a moment the notion
crossed my mind that Véronique and I would be asked to speak,
and I was horrified, but fortunately Oanh didn't intend that: he
led us to the front of the stage and sat with us on the ground. I
kept my head in my notebook, scribbling down everything I saw.
Who knew that the Communists held gatherings of this many
people in the middle of the Mekong Delta? Véronique and I possessed a secret that not only confirmed the Viet Cong's strength
but gave us validation. We weren't the dreamers; the hawks,
people like McArthur, who said the Communists were "bandits"
without popular support, were.

On the stage a man dressed in black pajamas and thongs
was giving a political speech, but instead of listening, most people talked jovially among themselves. I was surprised that none
of the officials present, including Oanh, minded the chatter. The
atmosphere contrasted dramatically with a village meeting of
Thieu's newly-formed Democracy Party I'd observed two weeks
earlier; there villagers looked bewildered and frightened, and
were compelled to chant mechanically "Anti-Communist!" and
"Constructive!" when a leader called out "Democratic Party!"
while here the villagers were required to do nothing, not even
pay attention. The speaker ended his speech with a call for "*hoa*

binh"— peace — and the people applauded.

Now the crowd rustled with excitement, for the enter-
tainment, the main attraction of the evening, was about to begin.
The stage was suddenly filled with performers of both sexes
wearing rouge on their cheeks; they appeared to have borrowed
their costumes from a revolutionary Chinese opera.
Accompanied by musicians playing a generator-powered electric guitar and mandolin, they sang such songs as "Liberation
Troops Going to War," "Enjoying Peace," "In Memory of
President Ho," "Spring in the Base Area," and "Salute to My
Liberated Country." In an apparent effort to counter the anti-
Montagnard prejudice common among Vietnamese, one song
made a point of praising Montagnards who supported the
Communists. Intriguingly, the performers playing Montagnards
executed the kind of kicks that are a staple of Russian folk dancing but bear no connection to the Central Highlands tribal people. Maybe the performers learned the dance from Soviet advisers.

A satirical play engaged the audience more. In it a buf-
foon of a government village chief tries to force a young pro-
Communist woman to pay him for painting a government flag
on her wall. Instead, the woman bites his arm and chases him
out of her house with a broom. "What kind of flag is this that
must be put everywhere — in front of the house, in back of the
house, in the bathroom, and even on the floor of the boat, so that
when you sit down you get paint on your pants?" the woman
says. The people in the audience roared.

I was amazed. In Saigon such a performance was blas-
phemous, yet here, in the middle of a rice field, the Viet Cong
showed no sign of fearing retaliation, not even when distant
artillery strikes were audible. Surely the gathering presented an
inviting target to ARVN gunners, yet when I asked a Viet Cong
soldier about the possibility of shelling, he just said, "If it comes,
it comes." The only security precaution I saw taken was to cover
lights when a South Vietnamese Air Force plane flew overhead.
It seemed inconceivable to me that of the several thousand

people in the rice field, not one informed the ARVN of the meeting. Maybe the Viet Cong bribed the ARVN gunners, or maybe the two sides agreed to avoid attacking each other in certain situations. It was a mystery I never solved.

When did Viet Cong supporters go to bed? The entertainment continued past midnight without a hint of ending, and nobody looked tired except us. Oanh said Viet Cong supporters simply didn't sleep much, and when I considered that most Viet Cong attacks were at night, I figured he must be right. We hadn't even completed the evening itinerary: one of our guides said it was time to leave the gathering so that we could meet some high-ranking Viet Cong officials. This news unloosed another jab of adrenalin: we got too excited to feel fatigue. We said goodbye to Oanh and left.

Our next trek was shorter, a mere fifteen minutes, but I'd lost all sense of direction, and felt like Theseus in the maze. It was nearly one a.m. when we reached the officials' lair: we thought we were entering the innermost circle, yet all we found was another conundrum, an enigma at the heart of Viet Cong hearts. Two officials greeted us, breathing daggers of icy disdain. They didn't tell us their names: we gathered from everyone else's deferential manner that they held high positions. One man was dressed in white, the other was dressed in black, and everything they said was black-and-white: to me they were the black-and-white men. "As you know, the ceasefire has been in effect," one said. "However, the sound of firing has not stopped because Saigon has not seriously executed the ceasefire. We know that you came here to find truth and justice, so we are very happy to welcome you."

Véronique and I tried to begin an interview, but the men first had a question of their own. "The Saigon government claims that it controls 90 percent of the territory and 95 percent of the population" of South Vietnam, the man in white said. "When you write a story, do you report this statistic as fact?" I said we gave the sources for such information and tried to determine whether it was true.

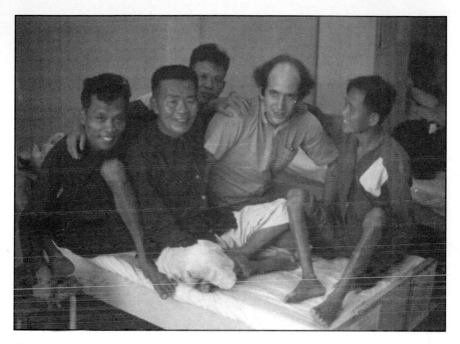

Tiger cage prisoners with author. Photo by Jacques Leslie.

U.S. Embassy Economics Affairs Counselor Charles Cooper, Hoang Duc Nha, and author. Photo by Jacques Leslie.

Ron Moreau. Photo by Jacques Leslie.

Interpreter Phan Phi Long. Photo by Jacques Leslie.

Big Red One insignia carved out of the forest. Photo by Jacques Leslie.

Veronique Decoudu. Photo by Matt Franjola.

The view from my boat on the Perfume River. Photo by Jacques Leslie.

Martin Woollacott. Photo by Jacques Leslie.

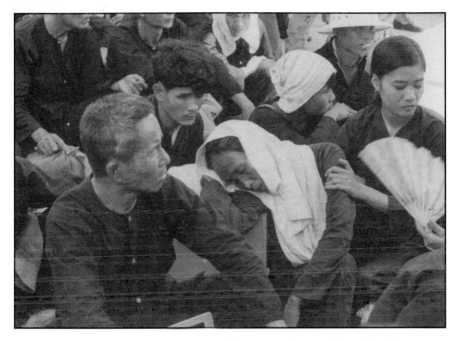

Pro-Communist prisoners waiting in the sun at the Bien Hoa Air Base to be returned to Viet Cong territory. Photo by Jacques Leslie.

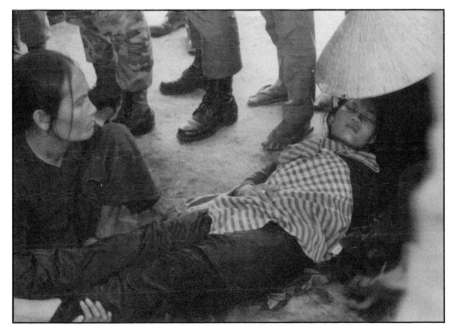

A prisoner suffers "epilepsy." Photo by Jacques Leslie.

Viet Cong press conference at Tan Son Nhut airbase in Saigon. Photo by Jacques Leslie.

Rubble at Quang Tri. Photo by Jacques Leslie.

Sydney Schanberg, Matt Franjola, and Beth Becker. Photo by Jacques Leslie.

Peter Arnett and companion. Photo by Jacques Leslie.

Aboard an LST with Cambodian soldiers, awaiting its departure for the Battle of Kampong Cham. Photo by Jacques Leslie.

James Fenton. Photo by Jacques Leslie.

Neil Davis. Photo by Jacques Leslie.

President Lon Nohl and Information Minister Chhang Song, on a stroll.
Photo by Jacques Leslie.

Preah Vihear. Photo by Jacques Leslie.

Preah Vihear and the Cambodian plain below. Photo by Jacques Leslie.

An area between Phnom Penh and Kampong Cham, from the air, during the rainy season. The Mekong River is in the distance. Photo by Jacques Leslie.

Cambodian children. Photo by Jacques Leslie.

Cambodian soldiers. Photo by Jacques Leslie.

The man didn't look mollified, but he said we could proceed — of course, he said, we'd have to remember that some of
our questions probably couldn't be answered for security reasons. Véronique tried an easy one: how was the village organized? The man in black said the village N.L.F. unit represented
"all classes of people" and left it at that. "In this capacity, we
would like to tell you that the fighting continues tonight, when
it was supposed to be stopped two days ago. We would like to
tell you to make the people of the world understand the situation of our people."

For the next two hours we politely sparred: we weren't
interested in reporting their rhetoric, and they evaded our questions. At last they broke off the interview and commanded that
we be served yet another meal. At different times in the Viet
Cong zone we'd been given coconut milk, iced tea, hot tea,
water, cookies, and now our second dinner. "In liberated areas
you must eat plenty so you can run from the shellings," the man
in black said unsmilingly.

We embarked on another journey, this one mostly by
motorized sampan. I was glad to be back with our young guides:
one of them sang to himself as we puttered through the water. I
was frightened that an ARVN sentry would see us, especially
because the guide used a flashlight to check the boat's distance
from the bank, but even Long said not to worry: even though we
were visible from both shores, we apparently weren't in danger.
Viet Cong control of the region appeared total.

Our destination was a family residence where we were
to sleep for an hour, then arise before dawn to sneak back to the
government side. As soon as we arrived, an old woman handed
us hot milk — I felt like a child on my way to bed — and led us
to wooden sleeping platforms draped in mosquito netting. I took
off my boots and lay down, but I was too excited to sleep. Sleep
was superfluous anyway: it would have been like a dream within a dream. In fifteen hours I'd fulfilled a lifetime's quota of

dreams; now we had only to make the crossing in order to claim one of the great stories of the war, yet the crossing might be dangerous, particularly since we'd been told that South Vietnamese policemen towed away our car. I thought of a million worrisome things. Were the police looking for us? If they caught us, would they arrest us, imprison us, shoot us? Had another journalist already emerged from some other Viet Cong zone, beating us to the story? Would we be allowed to file? And would the *Times* publish the story, or would it be vetoed on grounds of disbelief?

I lay wide awake on the mat for much longer than an hour, waiting for our Viet Cong guides to start us on our journey back into Saigon territory, but no one made a move. How could Véronique and Long sleep? Had the guides overslept, or had they changed plans on us? I would have preferred that someone else be the one to startle a Viet Cong soldier out of sleep, but at 5:20, twenty minutes after we were supposed to arise, I felt I had no choice. I found a soldier outside the door; he looked as disoriented as any other mortal when shaken awake.

By the time we were prepared to leave, it was 5:40, and the sun was nearly up. Our success depended on crossing in semi-darkness, before the curfew ended at six: after that other people would be circulating, and would notice us in a place where Westerners didn't usually appear. Our plan was to cross zones on the water: an old woman would take us in a sampan, maneuvering through canals and a river past four government checkpoints, until we reached a landing near a marketplace. She'd walk ahead of us, carrying a basket as if on the way to market, leading us past the last government checkpoint; then she'd disappear into the crowd. In case of trouble, she carried a government identity card, and we were to act self-assured, as if our presence was appropriate; our countenances might determine whether we got by.

The three of us sat in the front of the sampan; the old woman was in back, next to the motor. She looked game for the adventure and reasonably spry, but she unfortunately wasn't strong: we sat motionless in the water for 15 minutes while she tried in vain to yank the drawstring hard enough to start the engine. I half-hoped we'd give up the attempt and make the crossing the next morning, but the Viet Cong soldiers were determined to send us back now.

At last one of them got the engine started, and we began down the river. I slumped down in my poncho liner, and Véronique pulled a floppy hat over her head: striving for invisibility, we would happily have settled for looking small and Vietnamese. A thick mist clung to the water, hiding not just us but a fish net in which our boat promptly got fouled. Now we were in trouble: surely the old woman wouldn't be able to restart the engine. But she did, on her first try. We took deep breaths. Then, more trouble: the propeller got caught in floating plants, and the engine died again. We were so desperate we paddled with our hands until the woman started the engine yet again. Long, the former naval officer, struck a pose at the fore as if recommissioned, trying to keep us away from the plants, but we still ran into them again and stalled. By now fairly proficient, the woman got the engine started once more. Had we wasted too much time? It was after six, the mist was lifting, and another boat was on the water. It caught up to us, and a Vietnamese man and woman looked Véronique and me in the eye. They didn't even change expression; they just kept on going.

We reached the shore. The woman left with her basket. We let her get 10 or 15 yards in front of us. As we passed the last checkpoint, we practically strutted. The soldiers never moved. The woman vanished.

We couldn't relax yet; we had to get out of the town first. We walked to the highway and found a bus bound for Saigon, but it wasn't leaving for half an hour. We sat in the rear, and Véronique and I tried to look as inconspicuous as two Westerners on a bus usually ridden only by Vietnamese could be. Two policemen approached, and struck up a conversation with a hawker just outside our window. Were they looking for us? The driver started his engine, but he didn't leave: it was as if he were teasing us. At last the bus pulled away: now we were home free.

Despite everything the journey had been easy; the Red Sea had opened for us. Only one thing was dispiriting: I discovered that my camera hadn't worked. It was new, and I wasn't used to it: when I tried to rewind the film, I realized that the spool hadn't caught when I loaded it — the film hadn't been exposed. The discovery was painful but endurable, like being socked in the stomach after winning the Olympics marathon.

We arrived at the bus station at 10 a.m.— Saigon never looked so inviting. Our first thought was to tell McArthur and Bolo what happened. We raced to McArthur's house and gave him a rundown. McArthur was calm and professional: he told us not to worry about the car, and instructed me to write every detail I could think of. As we left, I asked him if he'd heard of any other journalists getting into Viet Cong territory before us. He said he hadn't. It was the answer I longed to hear. I started to raise my arms in triumph, then thought better of it: McArthur was squinting at me out of the corner of his eye. He was 47, a bit too old for adventures like ours. I spared him my glee.

The three of us split up for showers, then regrouped at my villa half an hour later. Long filled us in on the information he'd gathered but hadn't been able to tell us, and then we broke up to write our stories. For once I had no trouble writing a lead— I felt that at last I was writing the story I had always wanted to write, that I had always known how to write. I was still writing late that night when Jack Foisie, the *Times'* Bangkok correspondent who was in Saigon to help with ceasefire coverage, offered his help. Bald with fringes of white hair, Foisie had a pixieish appearance and a perennially jovial manner to match. Though he'd been covering combat since World War II, he now cheerfully acted as my aide. He plied me with coffee when fatigue began to overwhelm me, edited the story, and, in a gesture that reflected true generosity, retyped it for me as I sat slumped in a chair. We finished at 2:30 in the morning.

I lay in bed for five hours but slept only fitfully: I couldn't relax until I knew what happened to the story. What if it so appalled the Vietnamese cable transmitter that he refused to send it to L.A.? Or what if it offended Gibson, what if he thought it wasn't "professional"? I hated the suspense: at 8 a.m. I called Gibson up. I knew immediately that he was pleased: I could hear the exuberance in his voice. The story excited him so much he'd phoned my parents to tell them about it. He said the story—"every word of it"— would run on the next day's front page.

The story received fabulous play. It ran across the top of the page, above the masthead. Apparently to distinguish me from such deceased adventurers as Shimkin, a box stated that I was "the first American correspondent to have entered and returned from Viet Cong territory in South Vietnam." The Washington *Post* and many other papers carried the story. U.P.I. distributed a summary leading with Oanh's remark about Jane Fonda and Martin Luther King, and the New York *Times* ran that.

In Saigon the word got around quickly: I was very well-known for a week or two. Everyone tried to duplicate the feat, but it was ten days before anyone succeeded, and then in quick succession half a dozen people did it, just as we did, by walking into Binh Phu village in Dinh Tuong. I noticed that all those who tried harbored at least some sympathy for the Viet Cong, as if only hawks still couldn't believe they could enter Viet Cong territory without being shot. Oanh finally told the journalists to stop coming, as he had other things to do. Somebody told me he asked after Véronique and me; we were still the pioneers.

Even the South Vietnamese government didn't appear disturbed, at least not at first. The regime announced that journalists were banned from visiting Viet Cong territory, but this seemed no more than a face-saving gesture, which deterred no one from going; as if to demonstrate its lack of concern, the government renewed my press accreditation soon afterwards. McArthur figured the regime was more likely to seek retribution against its own citizens than foreigners, and so advised Long to lie low for a week or two. I didn't realize how prescient this was until I tried to retrieve my rented car, which had been towed to the district police headquarters a few miles down the highway from Binh Phu. A week after our journey, I hired a car and driver and returned to Dinh Tuong; I recognized the car, minus headlights and a few lesser parts, as soon as we pulled into the police compound. The police chief was affable at first. He said he'd be happy to return the car to me, as long as I'd answer a few questions. He looked like a Vietnamese version of Edward G. Robinson, except that his ears were as big as air raid sirens. The congeniality ceased on about his third question: who, he wanted to know, was the interpreter on our trip to the other side? I'd decided to tell him whatever appeared in the story, nothing more; I therefore wouldn't answer the question. Was the interpreter Vietnamese? I wouldn't respond. He threatened arrest. I said in that case I'd have to call the U.S. Embassy. I could tell he didn't know I was bluffing; for all I knew, embassy officials might have considered my arrest just deserts. The chief bided his time, while I did my best to look recalcitrant. After an hour he said I could leave, without the car.

It was typical of the South Vietnamese government: Long was known to work for the Los Angeles *Times*, and it would have taken no great investigative talent to determine whether he'd been our interpreter. The authorities, however, stayed too much in character: they relied on intimidation, and the technique didn't even work.

Something still was missing: as exciting as my story was, the acclaim I yearned for didn't quite materialize. It seemed to me that I'd explored the outer reaches of the solar system and come back, and still I heard a familiar voice saying, *I'm not satisfied*. I'd been a newspaper reporter for 13 months, and now I was calculating how long I'd have to wait to find out if I'd won a Pulitzer Prize: *then* I'd feel satisfied. Riding her own crest of glory, Véronique left Vietnam for good ten days after our story, and I barely noticed — I didn't notice anything other than journalism. I pasted my clippings in my scrapbook and reviewed them again and again. I was no cub reporter now: even McArthur acknowledged that, by passing me a note saying he'd burned the file of his correspondence with Gibson regarding my progress. I thought I was ready to perform reportorial miracles on a regular basis. The truth, however, is that although I was only 25 years old, with big stories yet to cover, at the moment I returned from Viet Cong territory, I started dying as a reporter.

What was born in me took many more years to fathom. Before I entered Viet Cong territory I hadn't believed that triumph was possible. To live meant to suffer; to live nobly meant to achieve tragedy. Now, however, I'd stumbled into a realm that confounded my assumptions: I'd located something astonishing without having to pay for it. Immediately afterwards I thought this meant only that if I kept searching, I'd find other secret domains, but I still assumed that the realms were exterior to me. Then, over years, something flipped: time deprived Viet Cong territory of its concrete form and turned it into a symbol signifying the existence of an exquisite zone inside my head. To reach the other side, I'd first had to imagine the feat, and then I'd had to believe that I could accomplish it. The prerequisite of satisfaction was acknowledging its source inside me. I could no longer convince myself that suffering was my inevitable fate. I contained the possibility of fulfillment.

CRUISING
Chapter

5

If the Viet Cong trip suggested the existence of other modes of being, it was still true that I'd merely had a taste of them: I lacked the means of more permanently inhabiting such terrain. In the Viet Cong zone I'd been something like a prisoner on furlough; now, in Saigon, I was back in jail with a deepened awareness of my bondage. And just as if I'd set out to conduct a study of my confinement, I now found myself writing again and again about prisoners.

The first prisoner story I covered provoked Pavlovian drools of anticipation in most American journalists, but it left me indifferent: the POWs were coming home. I hated being a cog in the POW publicity machine, for it seemed to me that their welfare had taken precedence over the greater suffering of the Vietnamese. The POWs were the props on which American policy was based; we'd traded in the war for them. They were 500 men on one side of an equation that on the other side comprised hundreds of thousands of lives, all expended so that they could be freed. They were said to have suffered horribly, to have been tortured, but so many of the stories I read about them confused Vietnamese torture with American culture shock, with the American incapacity to believe that fish and rice was the diet of a significant portion of the world's people, not just of POWs, that I was skeptical of the claims. Anyway, weren't the POWs military men who accepted capture as a risk of their profession,

weren't most of them officers caught bombing the North? What
did they expect? They were the American fig leaf, obscuring our
lack of purpose in Vietnam.

The prisoner release in Saigon was a spectator event, a
ceremony, a scene in the re-enactment of the myth of the prisoner, who returns after living in the underworld and is wise for
having suffered. Yet here the ceremony was in service of policy,
not wisdom. It was bizarre: we treated the POWs like conquering heroes when all they'd done was survive. Even though the
event occurred on Vietnamese ground, virtually all the onlookers were Americans — journalists, diplomats, officers, even a
hawkish journalist's wife — who looked as if they awaited
Lindberg's landing or a space vehicle's splashdown. In the cor-
doned area of Tan Son Nhut Airport to which we were confined,
a battery of television cameras was poised to record the arrival,
and every hour wire service reporters filed speculation on the
exact time when the POWs would be freed. The prisoner
exchange was supposed to occur at 8:30 that morning in Loc
Ninh, 75 miles from Saigon, and then the prisoners would be
brought to Tan Son Nhut in American helicopters, but something
went wrong. By the time the helicopters' red and green flashing
lights were visible in the distant sky, it was past dusk, and the
prisoner exchange in its prolongment had become a metaphor
for the war itself. Milking the moment for its dramatic effect, the
helicopters came in single file. Even the journalists applauded.
The journalist's wife jumped up and down. One by one the prisoners debarked from the helicopters, waved, shook Ambassador
Bunker's hand, and climbed into a hospital plane bound for the
Philippines. That was it. We were too far from the prisoners to
ask questions; all we heard from them was this, as reported to us
afterwards by Bunker: "They all said, 'It's great to be back,' and
I said, 'It's great to have you back.' It's a great day for all of us."
The message was telling precisely because of its inadequacy:
leery of the underworld, we refused to allow its tidings to be dis-
seminated.

By contrast, the release of imprisoned ARVN soldiers was barely acknowledged, even by the South Vietnamese government; that was one reason I felt more sympathy for them than for the American POWs. Two days after the ceremony at Tan Son Nhut, I drove out to Bien Hoa to interview them. They'd been released by the Communists at the same time as the Americans, but nobody confused these men with heroes: their return evoked virtually no press coverage, foreign or Vietnamese, and their own officers regarded them as nuisances, men who should have died. The ARVN command didn't know what to do with them: they'd been exposed to Communist indoctrination (with the result that 20 percent changed allegiances, according to one of them), so it didn't want to release them, but it also didn't want to hold onto them indefinitely because of the drain on its resources. The solution was to subject them to more indoctrination, this time *anti*-Communist. Instead of being allowed to rejoin their families, they were still held captive, this time by their own army. Eventually they'd receive a short home leave and then they'd be sent back into battle, presumably knowing better than to let themselves get captured again. They were given no cars, no book advances, no medals or raises. Many of them suffered from malaria or jungle skin diseases; their captors lacked the medicine (and the inclination) to treat them. I talked to a man with malaria: though standing in sunlight on a hot day, he was wrapped in a blanket, shivering. He said his wife was killed the day he was captured, his father had been abducted, his mother was dead, and his only son lived with relatives, who didn't know he'd returned. Here was abandonment personified, all the more compelling because neither he nor anyone else tried to conceal his demoralization. To be a prisoner is to be not a hero but a victim.

A military band struck up a tune, and I wondered if the prisoners were being honored in the American fashion after all. Far from it: the band was playing for two arriving ARVN gener-

als, whose rank was deemed sufficient reason for the tribute. The
POWs rose languidly from the dusty barracks floor, politely
applauded the   generals, and listened listlessly to a lecture on
anti-Communism. Then the generals led the POWs in a chant:
"Overthrow the Communists! Overthrow the Communists! The
Republic of Vietnam forever! The Republic of Vietnam forever!"
It sounded like a dirge.

A few days later Gibson requested a story on political
prisoners held by the Thieu regime, and I jumped at it. Most stories on political prisoners — people imprisoned for their political beliefs rather than for the commission of a crime — focused
on whether there were hundreds of thousands of them, as
Thieu's opponents extravagantly claimed, or none, as Thieu just
as preposterously asserted. I gathered that 40,000 to 70,000 was a
reasonable estimate, but I found the debate unilluminating, as if
accountants had defined its terms. The Thieu government
unquestionably held thousands of people without trials or sen-
tences, and, according to some claims, tortured many of them.
The problem for journalists was that descriptions of prison life
were invariably based on secondhand accounts. I wanted to do
better. I talked to everyone I could think of who might know
something about political prisoners, until I tripped over this bit
of intelligence: two American Quaker volunteer workers in
Quang Ngai province had regular contact with patients in a hospital prison ward and might be able to smuggle me inside it.
Quang Ngai was reputedly so embittered a place that I preferred
not to visit it alone, so I asked Martin Woollacott, the *Guardian's*
highly competent Asia correspondent, to join me. We flew there
together.

Sure enough, Quang Ngai was mean; even in the
province capital I didn't feel safe. Most territory outside the capital belonged to the Viet Cong; inside it, antagonism towards
Americans was such that Vietnamese occasionally threw rocks at
them as they walked down the street. The Americans used the

full brunt of their military prowess to undermine the Viet Cong's authority, with the result that Quang Ngai was perhaps the country's most embattled province. Emblematic of that distinction, the My Lai massacre occurred a few miles from the capital.

I thought the two Quakers, Jane and David Barton, were courageous simply for living in a place where rifle exchanges outside their house were regular nighttime occurrences. They ran a medical dispensary established and supplied by the American Friends Service Committee; their medical mission gave them entry into the prison ward. Woollacott and I went to Quang Ngai without assurance that they'd help us, but they quickly agreed to: they were anxious to spread word of the evidence of torture they'd discovered. According to them, many of the prison ward's patients had been tortured during interrogations by the South Vietnamese police; more than half were being treated for injuries caused by torture. A favorite police technique was to attach electrodes to a suspect's hands, feet, or nipples and run an electric current.

The next morning the Bartons took us to the prison ward and told the guard we were their helpers. That was all it took: we were allowed to follow the Bartons inside the ward. The room contained men and women, young and old, innocent and guilty, even two infants born in prison in the previous three weeks. The ward's 24 residents shared 14 beds, two of which lacked mattresses, and the beds were packed so closely together that their frames nearly touched. The ward looked miserable, but unexceptionally so: it was only slightly more disheveled than other rooms of the moldering, ramshackle hospital. What disturbed me more than the physical conditions was something I didn't perceive until a few minutes passed: the ward exuded anarchy, a hint of asylum. I watched a cadaverous one-legged Buddhist monk, himself a prisoner with advanced tuberculosis, jab a hypodermic needle into the hip of a female patient: while she twisted in pain, he looked off, with a gleam in his eye that bespoke crazed elation. What was in the syringe? Why was a patient administering the injection?

We accompanied Jane as she made her rounds. After checking on a patient's medical problems, she explained that Martin and I were journalists and acted as our interpreter. All the prisoners were "political" — they were arrested because they were suspected of supporting the Viet Cong. Judging by what the prisoners said, we gathered that sometimes the police's suspicions were right, sometimes not. Since the Viet Cong were so popular in Quang Ngai, and contact with them outside the main towns was unavoidable, the police frequently construed innocent acts as collaboration. A 17-year-old boy told us he was arrested while fishing at night; during his interrogation the police tortured him until he "was on the point of dying." A 19-year-old girl said that three years earlier she was carrying produce to market when police stopped her and accused her of transporting food for the Viet Cong. When she denied guilt, she was beaten and tortured with electricity, then put in solitary confinement for two months. She broke her arm during a seizure induced by the torture, and now, typical of the curious combination of humane and inhumane treatment given the prisoners, she was getting the broken bone set in the prison ward. "When I was captured, I was really frightened," she said. "But now that I've been beaten, I am no longer afraid. I know what it is."

The Bartons had already warned us about the seizures, which oddly occurred only among the women. Though tortured months or even years earlier, many of the women suffered residual seizures as often as several times a day. During the seizures they seemed to relive their interrogations, sometimes yelling out answers to questions posed while they were being tortured. Suddenly a woman who'd been listening to our conversation began moaning and writhing and furiously pounding her bed with her fists and legs — the talk about torture had itself induced a seizure. The other patients didn't look surprised: using cloth strips already attached to the four corners of the bed, they tied down the woman's limbs so she couldn't hurt herself. She writhed until she slipped off the bed and hung appallingly at its side; after the other prisoners righted her, she arched her back until only her head, arms, and feet touched the bed. "You don't have to hit me," she said frenziedly. "I don't know anything." She was apparently talking to her interrogators.

Like a grenade lobbed into an ammo dump, the first seizure induced another one, and another, and another. Martin and I stared dumbfounded as everyone else in the room soon either was in convulsions or was calling for someone who was. Five or ten minutes passed before all the seizures subsided. As we left, Jane said, "You can't imagine bedlam being any worse."

We talked later to one of the ward's patients as she lay on a stretcher outside. Eighteen years old, she had a gaze so deep I could see miles into her eyes. She fought for the Viet Cong— she said so. Ten months earlier she'd been on a military operation with four female comrades, she said; they walked into an ambush in which two of them were killed, and she was wounded and captured. For 23 days she was alternately beaten, interrogated, and given anti-Communist lectures. She said the beatings were so fierce "I didn't know pain any more — I was already dead." Considering that she knew I was an American, and that Americans were widely known to condone and even participate in torture sessions like those the girl had undergone, I was amazed by her candor.

A policeman strolled by, and Jane pretended to resume the girl's medical treatment, as she wasn't supposed to talk politics with the patients. From her stretcher the girl saw the policeman and said to Jane, "Are you afraid? I'm never afraid." It sounded less like a boast than a simple statement of fact. At the end of the interview I asked her which side she thought would win the war, and knew the answer before she provided it: "The National Liberation Front will win," she said evenly. I knew I'd touched something solid. Here was a prisoner who'd transcended victimization, who'd somehow emerged stronger because of her confinement.

Martin and I tried to get back to Saigon by jumping aboard a nearly empty South Vietnamese Air Force cargo plane as it was revving its engines on the Quang Ngai airstrip. Most South Vietnamese Air Force officers were less kindly disposed towards journalists than their American counterparts were, but we figured all we risked was being kicked off the plane. Sure enough, the pilot walked back from the cockpit and ordered us to debark. I was ready to oblige him, but Martin, not easily cowed, whispered that we should hold our ground: he didn't want to waste an extra day in Quang Ngai waiting for a civilian flight if he could possibly avoid it. First we pretended not to understand the pilot; then, when his meaning was all too obvious, we ignored him. He stood in front of us, becoming angrier by the moment, finally gesticulating wildly, and still we didn't move. Martin had suspected from the beginning that the pilot wouldn't dare to use force to remove us from the plane, and he was right: we'd called the pilot's bluff. Humiliated, he turned on his heel, retreated to the cockpit, and started the plane down the runway.

My confidence in South Vietnamese air force pilots had not been boundless to begin with. Now the plane quivered violently as it ascended at an angle far closer to vertical than looked safe to me, and an ARVN soldier across from me sat with gritted teeth and eyes bulging in terror, as if he were convinced that the plane would soon drop out of the sky. His fear was contagious. How much longer, I wondered, would I have to risk my life on rickety planes like these? I'd been in Vietnam for fourteen months now, longer than any GI's tour. Wasn't thirteen months when Gloria Emerson said the serious symptoms started to set in? It was the first time I'd thought of myself as a short-timer.

Back in Saigon, Martin and I settled in to write our pieces. Comparing notes on the phone, we found ourselves arguing. I thought the story was simple: torture. Martin disagreed. He said both sides committed torture, so it was unfair to single out the South Vietnamese. He was going to write about "little people caught in the big war," such as the boy who'd gone fishing and ended up beaten and jailed. Our dispute was civil, but I was stunned: how could a journalist play down torture? Perhaps with his country's colonial era safely tucked into the past, a cool Brit could see the Quang Ngai prisoners as players in a blameless tragedy, but I couldn't. In the name of freedom the United States gave license to torture, a fact which surely many Americans were not prepared to face. We had to know what we were capable of, we had to know the misery we caused. Martin argued that the Viet Cong's commission of torture cancelled out the ARVN's, but I thought we were responsible for our actions, regardless of what the Viet Cong did. My story was about torture.

Sometimes it was like writing shorthand. Did readers notice the difference between "some observers" and "many observers," between "possible" and "probable," between "regime" and "government"? So many clues, intuitions, judgments of others' honesty and perspicacity had to be packed into 800 or 1,500 words, so many avenues of thought hinted at, facts alluded to, so much left out. What the stories lacked most of all was feeling: the feeling of an event, the feeling a political actor evoked, the feeling that ran through my head and led me to choose this word instead of that, this story instead of that. Gibson lobbied endlessly for "objectivity," but the term was more elusive than mercury — after all, his model of objectivity was McArthur. I thought objectivity was impossible — a refuge for the meek, who'd rather omit what was least tangible, which is surely where truth lies. My standard of good journalism was honesty, which meant facing the truth, following it down its own path, not sculpting an idealized image of it, all clean and sparkling with bogus ideology. I knew no objective journalists, but I knew some honest ones.

I still wasn't done with prisoners. Before going to Quang Ngai I'd met Chan Tin, a Roman Catholic priest in Saigon who made it his avocation, his discreet passion, to keep track of the political prisoners in South Vietnam's jails. Chan Tin's manner betrayed none of the grimness of his task: he was soft-spoken, with at least the hint of a smile often on his lips, and his rotund appearance suggested that he enjoyed a good meal. It's possible, even likely, that he worked for the Viet Cong, but I never knew for sure. All I was certain of was that his mild exterior concealed a gambler's heart, for the threat of his arrest was almost certainly constant. It amazed me that despite operating so openly he remained free. The only explanation I heard that sounded even remotely plausible was that Thieu owed too much to South Vietnam's Catholics, most of whom were staunchly anti-Communist, to risk provoking them by arresting a priest. Chan Tin's objective was to prevent detained dissidents from disappearing inside the prison system, as so frequently happened. He compiled a list of political prisoners, broken down jail by jail, and gave me a mimeographed copy, but it was useless to me without meatier information. He promised to contact me if he uncovered something notable, but I couldn't imagine what that could be and didn't put much stock in his pledge. Nevertheless, after returning from Quang Ngai I saw Chan Tin again. He told me to expect a phone call sometime in the next week, at which time I'd be instructed on how to meet some recently released prisoners. A few days later I got the call which led to my meeting with the tiger cage prisoners.

The biggest mystery to me was why the men were set free. For one thing, they clearly supported the Viet Cong. The Con Son prison was known to house South Vietnam's most "recalcitrant" inmates, and indeed the men spoke of refusing to salute the government flag despite facing drastic punishment for their inaction. The men's leader said they were all arrested for "demanding the right to live and the right to peace," which surely was a cryptic way of saying they supported the Viet Cong. The oldest man, an ethnic Chinese with whom I briefly spoke Mandarin, was bluntest: when I asked why he was arrested, he glanced quickly around the room and said in a hushed voice that he had been smuggling arms into Saigon. The implicit trust in his confession startled me.

True enough, with the onset of the ceasefire, international pressure had grown for an inspection of South Vietnam's prisons, particularly Con Son. It was likely that South Vietnamese officials wanted to empty the tiger cages before the Con Son prison was put on display, at which time the officials would allege that the cages weren't even used. But if this was their objective, why, after torturing the prisoners and causing so many of them to die, did they free the survivors, whose physical condition alone would belie the authorities' claims of humane prison conditions? Why, for that matter, weren't the survivors killed, like others at Con Son? The leader of the thirteen men said they were part of a contingent of 124 recently transferred from Con Son to other prisons throughout South Vietnam, a bit of information that jibed with something I'd heard from the female Viet Cong soldier in Quang Ngai. She said that 20 or 25 men, all paralyzed below the waist, had recently been transferred to the Quang Ngai prison from Con Son — thus I had independent corroboration of part of the men's story. Their leader said they'd been released at Bien Hoa, 15 miles from Saigon, on condition that they reported to police every ten days and that they didn't visit Saigon or talk with foreign correspondents. Maybe the Viet Cong paid a bribe to get them released, or maybe they'd gotten help from Viet Cong supporters within the prison bureaucracy — one prisoner seemed to imply as much when he said, "The only reason we got out of Bien Hoa is that we knew people." In any event, the police surely underestimated the men's fearlessness, for here they were, a mile or two from Saigon if not in the city proper, talking to the journalists they'd been ordered to avoid.

I knew no theory to explain the transcendental quality of the men's experience. I was aware only of feeling humility, even awe. I felt I had a mission to report their story, and tried to buttress their claims with as much supporting evidence as possible. I found an American doctor, John Champlin, who'd already examined the prisoners and was willing to make his findings public. Champlin, a former employee of the charity organization that funded the Barsky Unit, was sympathetic to the men, perhaps even as moved by them as I was, but his statement hedged slightly. "The prisoners are not only paralyzed below the waist," he said, "but they are also insensate below mid-thigh level. I think their leg problems are due to disease, atrophy, and malnutrition. A number of them have deep scars around their ankles which they said came from leg irons.... Nothing they said flatly contradicted the results of my examination." I disliked the words "I think" and "flatly"; nevertheless, I was grateful to have virtual confirmation of the prisoners' allegations from a source whom Americans would regard as more credible than the prisoners themselves.

Now time sped up again. I was back in that heady adrenalin vortex I'd entered after I returned from Viet Cong territory. I rushed to write the story, as if it might otherwise disappear, and filed it at night. Once more I couldn't sleep, and the next morning I called L.A. One of the desk men got on the line. My spirits dropped as soon as I heard the tone in his voice: he sounded as if he were suppressing a yawn. Yes, he said, the paper had run the story on the front page, but only because it had previously carried American POWs' charges of torture there — it was a balancing act, as if the two stories somehow justified each other, then canceled each other out. "This is news!" I wanted to yell. "These men faced death, they suffered unimaginably, and somehow they are happy!" Flying high, I'd been intercepted, for I couldn't even get the point across to my editors.

As it turned out, I was fortunate that the *Times* ran the tiger cage story on the front page. The New York *Times* carried its reporter's piece on page seven, and though Ron wrote a story for *Newsweek*, the magazine didn't even use it. Of major American publications, only *Time* ran a display comparable to mine. On the other hand, several days later the Associated Press, whose reporters never saw the prisoners, carried a story refuting mine. It cited "U.S. sources" who said that two years earlier American doctors had examined 116 political prisoners claiming to be paralyzed as a result of maltreatment and concluded that all "were either faking or victims of hysteria." According to the A.P., the team "found no evidence among the prisoners of physical paralysis, or of malnutrition or organic disease that could cause it. Muscle atrophy and nervous system damage also were ruled out."

The A.P. was acting according to the hallowed journalistic axiom advising that if a competitor beats you to a story, then at least try to discredit it. Infuriated, I felt as if my judgment were being challenged, as if the assessment of American officials, who, after all, bore some responsibility for the prisoners' treatment, was trusted more than the overwhelming evidence of torture the men displayed. I worried that the A.P. story would undermine my credibility, that Gibson might believe the A.P. instead of me, and I half-expected him to charge me once more with being "unprofessional." The fact that the accusatory cable never came didn't entirely mollify me, for it felt to me that my sacred vessel, journalism, had already betrayed me.

I did one more prisoner story, involving an exchange between the South Vietnamese government and the Viet Cong. About 100 pro-Communist prisoners were to be flown from Bien Hoa Air Base to an air strip in Viet Cong control, where they'd be released. When I arrived at Bien Hoa, I found them squatting in the shadow of their plane, surrounded by South Vietnamese policemen. The prisoners had been poised for their departure for more than a day, while Saigon officials awaited word that another group of pro-government prisoners held by the Communists at Loc Ninh was ready to board a plane bound for Bien Hoa; once that happened, both groups would be allowed to depart.

The heat was oppressive. Most of the prisoners used small towels to shield themselves from the sun, and a few fortunate ones wore conical hats. Apparently depleted by the heat, a woman prisoner collapsed, and a doctor from the South Vietnamese Ministry of Social Welfare, apparently present to convey the image of a government concerned even about its enemy prisoners, gave her an injection. A few minutes later another woman prisoner began to convulse, in a manner I found all too familiar. "Take off the chains," she screamed as she twisted and kicked. "Let me free.... Give me back my clothes. Uncover my face. Oh, my God, I'm dying, I'm dying." The other prisoners recognized the phenomenon, too: they quickly grabbed the woman's limbs and held her tightly so she wouldn't hurt herself. After fifteen minutes she calmed down, and the doctor gave her, too, an injection.

"Epilepsy," the doctor said, but I knew what the woman was suffering from, and began quietly circulating among my colleagues with the news. "The woman was tortured by electricity," I said. "I've seen this happen before — it's a well-known phenomenon." Some of the journalists looked at me blankly, as if I were as partisan as the doctor or the woman herself. None of them appeared moved, or even particularly interested. I tasted the familiar bitterness of my impotence.

It seemed to me that I was incapable of communicating what I knew was true. My story about the tiger cage prisoners, for example, prompted a letter from a reader. Such letters were scarce: I had the feeling that most Americans long ago had grown tired of Vietnam, or else had suffered too much because of it, and so stuffed it into the deepest recesses of their consciousnesses, hoping to forget it. Desperate for evidence that I could leap across that divide, I looked forward to readers' letters, but most were disappointing. Someone wanted to find out how to support a charity in Vietnam, or needed a fact for a term paper, or had taken it upon himself to warn me of the Apocalypse — I think religious zealots wrote me more letters than anyone else. Still, even by the zealots' standards of craziness the letter I received about the tiger cage prisoners was special. The reader had misread my piece and assumed that the prisoners I described were American POWs. He read this sentence— "Although it is possible that the prisoners exaggerated the severity of their experiences in confinement, their physical condition alone seemed to verify much of what they said" — and was outraged: he thought I was questioning American POWs' honesty. He enclosed a letter he'd sent to the *Times'* editor-in-chief, which said, among other things:

> The L.A. *Times* had a LOT of GUTS to publish
> such a DISGRACEFUL Statement as that. Now
> the Only HONORABLE thing YOU can (and
> Sure SHOULD) DO, is to PUBLICLY censor the
> "STAFF Writer" and APOLOGIZE to our
> Honorable (Truth-Telling) P.O.W.s for YOUR
> GOOFING in publishing YOUR Insult to Our
> American P.O.Ws. (Do YOU have the GUTS to
> do it? It remains to be seen, whether or NOT
> you DO.)...

The author was demented but it didn't matter. It was clear to me that once a story left my typewriter, the meaning I invested in it became less and less firmly attached, until by the time it was transmitted through the air, edited and reedited and given a headline, transposed into type, printed, and distributed as part of the newspaper, my meaning was all but obliterated, fragmented into as many pieces as the *Times* had readers. I was a correspondent and I felt mute.

At least I got the attention of Saigon government officials: they turned down my routine application for an extension of my press credentials and said they were considering expelling me. The government spokesman said my stories were "un-Vietnamese," whatever that meant, and called the tiger cage story an "invention." It was an insult and it was a grand compliment; I hated the Saigon government and I loved it. I was a celebrity, a villain, a hero, something: thanks to Vietnam my existence made a difference in the world. I wanted to cuddle around all the intensity, suckle it, feel its nurturance: in the presence of all that heat, I knew I was alive. Until I lived in Vietnam, I thought, I'd existed dimly, like a snail; now my acquaintances were torture victims and their torturers, rebel village chiefs and their pursuers, pimps and whores, beggars, bombers, pickpockets, sappers. Vietnam fed me front-page stories, glory, the world's best grass — could the country now betray me, could it shove me aside? *Let the government expel me!*, I thought — *that would be the greatest compliment of all!* — *and yet, don't make me leave, I can't live anywhere else.*

For two days I hung in limbo, and then the government said sorry, our mistake, and gave me a new press card. I was happy and I was disappointed: in the end Vietnam hadn't let me down, and yet it had, it had.

After that I took an R & R, but leaving the country still wasn't easy, even though I called upon our Vietnamese "fixer" to procure my exit visa. McArthur employed the man to run the gauntlet of the South Vietnamese bureaucracy, by legal means if possible, by illegal means if not. I imagine that every country in the world breeds men like our fixer — he wore dark sunglasses and greased his hair and seemed to have learned his mannerisms by aping Jimmy Cagney in his tougher roles. He had no trouble producing documents like the forged international driver's license I once asked him to get me, yet when he tried to obtain my exit visa, he encountered surprising difficulty.

The reason, it turned out, was related to the rented car I'd left in the Cai Lay police compound. A month after my unsuccessful attempt to retrieve the car, Louis Mazeyrat, the Corsican owner of the rental agency, engineered its recovery himself, minus a hundred   dollars' worth of stolen parts. According to conventional wisdom, all male Corsicans with longtime residence in Vietnam were small-time racketeers capitalizing on well-oiled connections inside the Saigon government, and Mazeyrat's ease in regaining the car did nothing to contradict the stereotype. On behalf of the *Times*, I offered to pay him for the missing parts plus a month's rental fee to cover the police's term of possession. Mazeyrat accepted cordially, and I thought that was the end of the matter, but it apparently wasn't. While the car was rusting in the police compound, Mazeyrat must have felt sufficiently unsure of recovering it to use his government connections to prevent issuance of an exit visa to me: I assume he figured that if he couldn't get the car back, I'd be forced to reimburse him for its full value before I could leave the country. Once he retrieved the car, however, he neglected to retract the whammy. The fixer said he'd never met an obstacle like that before, but he still got me the exit visa. His connections were better than Mazeyrat's.

I was alternately enthralled and appalled by Bangkok, the sunken, lascivious, switchblade-cold city where I spent my R & R. It was like an extreme version of Los Angeles. Cars moved around in anxious, volatile swarms; submitting to the whims of a Bangkok taxi driver evoked the same feelings of vulnerability as exposing oneself to hostile fire. Like L.A., Bangkok was coated with a shiny, metallic veneer, but here it was less convincing and pervasive; tall steel-and-glass hotels rose up from the uncertain landscape as if they were sanctified, beckoning an ambivalent populace to embrace modernity. Far too many peasant off-spring did: huge numbers of them abandoned the countryside for Bangkok's alleged charms, and then, not finding more savory work, became prostitutes, massage girls, and petty criminals. Thai authorities tried to turn this development to their advantage, luring American GIs and other foreign tourists by proclaiming Bangkok the sex capital of Asia.

I prowled around the sex emporia, and was amazed by the antiseptic glaze of efficiency the Thais wrapped sex in. The darkened lobby of one massage parlor I entered was adorned with imitations of nude Roman sculptures. A slick attendant apprized me of the wide range of sexual services the place offered, then directed my attention to a glass partition. Through it I stared at a dozen prospective "masseuses," each of whom wore a number — I'd stumbled into an erotica aquarium. I read in a Bangkok newspaper that the windows were formerly transparent on the patrons' side only, but the women had successfully argued for the right to look back at their potential customers, a triumph the article attributed to the influence of the women's liberation movement. Talk about a hollow victory: the women appeared to take no notice of my existence, and instead stared impassively at a television set installed above the partition. Everything was available here except enthusiasm; the women all wore mask-like expressions, accentuated by uniformly thick makeup. At last I told the attendant that I'd chosen "19." He announced the number through an intercom, and "19" rose unenthusiastically from her seat. Wordlessly — for she didn't speak English — she led me to a cubicle whose most prominent feature was a bathtub. She pointed to it, and I stripped and got in it, and she washed me and massaged me and mechanically brought me to orgasm. I felt like a semen-producing machine. Even after I left the place, I couldn't shake my grief.

I enjoyed myself most in Bangkok on the evening I inadvertently dined with a roomful of fellow journalists. I'd felt like eating sukiyaki, and instructed a taxi driver to deposit me at the best Japanese restaurant he knew. He left me at a small establishment whose only patrons were Japanese; some of them graciously struggled in halting English to strike up a conversation with me. I soon learned that the restaurant was a Japanese journalists' hangout, of all things, and that the man telling me this, a journalist himself, was about to be transferred to Vietnam. Heartened by the coincidence, I assured the man that we'd soon eat together in Saigon.

I ended the R & R relieved that I could go back to the war now. It was still a war, by the way. As anticipated, the most significant change set in motion by the ceasefire was to remove American soldiers from direct involvement, but without them, combat continued to flourish; indeed, casualties among Communist and ARVN troops were significantly higher during the first two months of the ceasefire than during the comparable period of the previous year, when no ceasefire was in effect. This fact appeared to matter little to the news editors of America, who reasoned that if Americans weren't fighting, the war wasn't worth covering, or at least not to the same extent, anyway. The Associated Press' Saigon bureau was being reduced from seven reporters to four, the New York *Times* was down to three, and other news organizations planned similar cuts. I considered these reductions more evidence of American ethnocentrism, and responded in virtually Vietnamese fashion: I felt abandoned.

Equally disturbing, some of the reporters being rotated into Saigon struck me as woefully inept. At the top of that list was Lloyd Norman, who'd replaced Nick as *Newsweek's* bureau chief. I never understood what persuaded Lloyd and his wife Dorothy to give up Washington, where he'd been the magazine's Pentagon correspondent, for Saigon: it could not have been love of adventure. Lloyd and Dorothy said *Newsweek's* editors convinced them that Saigon was a garden spot, that Lloyd would be covering the onset of peace, and, astonishingly, the Normans bought that transparent line: that alone should have disqualified Lloyd from membership in any press corps. Nick suspected that the editors wanted a younger reporter covering the Pentagon, so they forced poor Lloyd out. Not holding foreign news in particularly high esteem, they offered him Saigon as a sop.

Both Normans were in their fifties and exuded fear: they showed me how far I'd come. Dorothy, gaunt and silver-haired, looked as if worry were her chief occupation. The first time she was greeted by a Vietnamese, a venerable *Newsweek* assistant named Cao Giao, she took one step backwards for each step he advanced towards her; they met practically against the wall, where he politely shook her hand. In time Dorothy decided that Cao Giao was at least preferable to the uncivilized Vietnamese who strode down Saigon's streets. The *Newsweek* bureau became her refuge; she spent hours standing at its second-story window, staring down at Tu Do Street in horrified amazement.

Compared to her, Lloyd appeared almost calm. He was short and round and convincingly self-deprecatory. Obsequiousness was his most obvious character trait: all officialdom seemed to impress him. He moved and reported stiffly, without a trace of suppleness, constantly filing meaningless scraps of information culled from U.S. embassy briefings and Vietnam Press, the laughable Saigon government news agency. He knew he was out of his element, and must have figured that if he couldn't understand Vietnam, he could at least write a lot about it. He put in long, long hours, but *Newsweek* rarely used his reports. Sometimes he'd acknowledge that he needed to see the country, and he'd listen attentively as Ron, technically his subordinate, patiently explained the war to him over and over again. Nevertheless, he seemed never to grasp that understanding Vietnam required getting out of the cocoon American officials were glad to fashion for him in Saigon. Once when I walked into the *Newsweek* office and asked where Ron was, Lloyd replied, "He went to Tay Ninh." Lloyd apparently didn't realize that what Ron was doing in Tay Ninh, an embattled province a couple of hours' drive from Saigon, was reporting, for he added, "I guess he felt like taking the day off."

One minor disaster after another befell the Normans:

they attracted abuse. They were so frightened of walking on Saigon streets that they took taxis to traverse the three blocks between the *Newsweek* office and villa. Sensing their helplessness, one cab driver took them home via the airport, half an hour out of the way; when at last they espied their front gate, they were so grateful that they paid the full fare without complaint. On the occasion when Lloyd was held up in front of the villa by a man who appeared to hold a gun in his coat pocket, Lloyd hastened to turn over his money, watch, everything. Following another attempted holdup, the culprit was arrested, and his *modus operandi* was revealed: all he held in his pocket, it turned out, was his pointed finger.

Once I was with Dorothy when she saw a beggar, and, horrified, exclaimed, "Doesn't this country have a welfare program?" Annoyed, I told her the country was the welfare program. What sympathy I harbored for her was tempered by her almost willful ignorance of Vietnam and her expectation that she was owed precisely the same creature comforts she'd enjoyed in Washington. Her most frequent complaint, one I found particularly offensive, was that Saigon possessed only one English-language television station, and it showed reruns. Considering that, I was not entirely displeased when, with the completion of the American military withdrawal, the station closed down.

Four months passed before the Normans gave up: then Lloyd called his editor and said they couldn't take Vietnam any more. Eventually he was restored to the Washington bureau, though he didn't get his old job back. On their last day in Vietnam, I went to the *Newsweek* villa to say goodbye. The Normans were jittery, still unconvinced that a clean escape from Vietnam was to be their destiny. The last words I heard Lloyd utter were, "Does the car have enough gas to get us to the airport?"

Compared to some other departures, the Normans' was dignified. Sylvan Fox was a longtime desk man and local reporter for the New York *Times* before he was surprisingly designated the *Times'* Saigon bureau chief. He arrived in Vietnam at

about the same time as the Normans, and for a few months func-
tioned with competence if not enthusiasm. He, Lloyd, and
Dorothy became friends; they must have fed one another's dis-
satisfaction with Vietnam. One day Fox disappeared. After surfacing a few days later, as I remember in Hong Kong, he
informed the *Times* that he wasn't just resigning as Saigon
bureau chief — he was quitting journalism altogether.

I was moving in the other direction, becoming more settled in Vietnam's prickly embrace. To that end I fired Sinh, my
Chinese maid, and replaced her with a far more congenial
Vietnamese named Chi Ba. Sinh was so uncommunicative that
I'd long ago abandoned hope of practicing Chinese with her, and
her dour presence was ceaselessly unsettling. We finally had an
argument and I seized the opportunity by asking her to leave.
She said I'd misunderstood her but she wouldn't explain: all she
did was go. I felt guilty about casting her into the sea of unem-
ployed, but on the other hand she left so quickly I didn't have a
chance to find her another job.

Once Chi Ba started work, I felt relaxed in my villa for
the first time: it was as if another layer of my resistance to
Vietnam had been stripped away. Chi Ba was industrious, curious, earthy, and, in a minor way, unscrupulous. It didn't take
long before I discovered that she was stealing small amounts of
food and cash from me, and I actually took comfort in the revelation. Her thefts had a kind of directness to them which laid
bare the terms of her employment. Compared to her, the right-
eous Vietnamese were the scary ones.

Of an indeterminate middle age, Chi Ba was canny and
innocent at the same time. One reason I liked her is that even
after she'd worked for me for a few months, she still thought I
was French. Whether she concluded that from my first name,
which my parents conferred on me even though my ancestors
lacked even a trace of French blood, or the fact that we conversed
in rudimentary French, I wasn't sure, but I didn't have the heart

to tell her I was an American: she considered herself more distinguished for working for a Frenchman. Often she'd ask me
whether some food she'd bought in the market was sold in Paris,
and, not knowing the answer, I'd respond according to its availability in Los Angeles.

Another time Chi Ba told me she was Catholic, and
asked if I was. I said no, and was about to tell her I was Jewish,
but she spoke first. "Oh," she said, "then you're Buddhist." This
suddenly formed conviction withstood all my efforts to dispel; if
I wasn't Buddhist, she seemed to imply, I ought to be. In truth, it
didn't strike me as a bad idea.

I was looking for the warm heart at the heart of Vietnam:
I suspect that's one reason I kept making stabs at returning to
Viet Cong territory for longer stays. Immediately after my first
trip, I began phoning the press officials of the Communist delegation stationed under provisions of the ceasefire agreement at
Ton Son Nhut, and, struggling with my French and theirs, did
my best to ingratiate myself with them. Eventually the
Communist officials were allowed to hold a press conference
which, to their chagrin, foreign but not Vietnamese journalists
could attend. We were taken by bus to the Communist compound, past the barbed wire barriers that kept the delegation
sequestered, and led to a conference room prominently featuring
a banner depicting Ho Chi Minh. Ho Chi Minh at the core of the
South Vietnamese war machine! — that irony alone was sufficient to justify attending the conference. Unfortunately, the content of the press conference presented no such justification. For
an hour or two we listened straight-faced to a Viet Cong
colonel's dreary propaganda harangue, translated into English
by a monotoned North Vietnamese soldier, until at last we were
handed soft drinks and invited to chat with the officers. I gave
them my written request to return to Viet Cong territory and
enclosed copies of my Dinh Tuong stories.

At another press conference weeks later, I got my

answer: my proposal was approved. The delegation's information officer gave me a letter instructing me to appear on a specified afternoon at a canal in the Delta province of Kien Tuong, where an intermediary would guide me to nearby Viet Cong territory. It made no sense to jeopardize Long on another Viet Cong journey, so I cabled Dave Elliott, who'd expressed enthusiasm about interpreting on such a trip, and he flew in from Hong Kong.

On the scheduled day Dave and I drove to Kien Tuong only to discover that the directions in the letter were maddeningly vague. For hours we searched along the canal for our intermediary, all the while wondering if we were already in Viet Cong territory and therefore risking arrest. We even crossed the designated canal by boat to look for the intermediary on the other bank, but we found no one. As our frustration increased, the questions Dave asked villagers became more and more blunt, until we were all but stating outright our desire to enter Viet Cong territory. We finally gave up and returned to Saigon.

I phoned the Viet Cong information officer and told him what had happened. He was apologetic, and said I'd be given another letter at the next press conference. This time our instructions were to go to An Xuyen province, at the southern tip of Vietnam, so far from Saigon we'd have to fly. Ten days after the Kien Tuong fiasco we took an almost empty Air Vietnam plane to Quan Long, An Xuyen's tiny province capital. Quan Long was so small it lacked taxis, so we hired motorcycle drivers. Uncomfortably perched on the motorcycles' rear wheel fenders, we headed down a bumpy, unpaved road towards our designation. Again the directions were vague. Worse, we could see that a battle was taking place near the apparent rendezvous area. We continued on, passing a few wounded ARVN soldiers and a unit firing mortars at Viet Cong troops. The ARVN troops must have doubted our sanity, and as we grew more conscious of the danger we faced, we began to doubt it, too. We found no evidence that Viet Cong soldiers had been told to look out for us, which meant that if they did find us, they might regard us as their enemy and kill us. Furthermore, even if we surmounted that hazard, gaining entry into Viet Cong territory might signify only that we'd earned the distinction of being ARVN targets. We spent several hours trying to reach the zone without losing our lives in the process, and then, once more, gave up.

Were the Communist officials in Saigon too unfamiliar with the Delta to provide accurate directions? Had their instructions to local cadres been delayed or intercepted? Or had they never been serious about helping us? After returning to Saigon, Dave wrote a letter to the Tan Son Nhut delegation in Vietnamese, explaining the foul-ups and requesting one more attempt at a liaison. I delivered the letter at the next press conference, and never got a reply.

Looking back, I consider my failure to return to Viet Cong territory a blessing in disguise. The day after our attempt in An Xuyen, Ron, who unbeknownst to us had been prowling around the same terrain, made contact with Viet Cong soldiers there and spent eleven days with them. His experience, however, was considerably less exhilarating than mine: the soldiers he accompanied were surly, verging on brutal, possessing nothing like the grace of Oanh. My quest was for something beyond politics, and my Dinh Tuong journey helped fulfill it. An experience like Ron's would not have furthered my search.

I was up, I was down; my emotions were hostage to my journalistic fortunes on a daily basis. What rescued me next was a contact I'd made in Washington in late 1971, just after the *Times* hired me. I'd gone back to Washington to close my apartment and to make courtesy calls on officials who dealt with Vietnam. One of them was Richard Moose, a staff member of the U.S. Senate Foreign Relations Committee. The committee's chairman was Sen. William J. Fulbright, a notable opponent of American involvement in the war, and Moose adhered to his mentor's views. What made Moose's role interesting was that his quasi-official status gave him access to classified data, and the assessments he periodically co-authored for the committee comprised perhaps the only dovish analysis of such information emanating from the government. Now I heard that Moose was in Saigon to gather information for a new assessment, and I arranged to see him again. During our conversation Moose mentioned that he'd been given a stack of monthly reports written by Province Senior Advisers, the top civilian U.S. advisers in South Vietnam's 44 provinces, and that he was struck by the frequency of references to to the corruption of South Vietnamese officials. I asked to see the reports. Moose thought for a moment, then agreed; the reports weren't classified, he said, so there was no reason why I shouldn't have a look.

A day or two later he handed them over; I made copies, returned the originals, and rushed back to my villa to see what they said. Moose had given me 27 monthly reports, each two to ten pages long, covering half of South Vietnam's provinces. In contrast to the dreamily Pollyanna-ish statements that the PSAs so often made to journalists, their written reports were refreshingly factual. My favorite selection described corruption in a province where, the local PSA wrote, "Officials in areas of doubtful security appear to be stepping up their level of corruption and alienating the population. In reaction to this, the province chief has ordered complete investigations, not of those accused, but of the accusers!" The PSAs referred again and again to South Vietnamese officials' corruption, complained of their falsification of a computerized survey of the government's political strength, and described how that strength was augmented, in violation of the ceasefire, by forcing villagers to resettle in government-controlled territory.

Under the headline, "U.S. Advisers Tell of Viet Corruption," my story led the next day's paper. Considering my visit to Viet Cong territory, the torture pieces, and now this, I figured I was on a hot streak.

Moose left Vietnam soon afterwards, and so couldn't

give me ensuing editions of PSA reports, but Banks, the disaffected bureaucrat, could: now at last I knew of useful documents
he was likely to have access to. I waited until the next month's
reports should have been issued, then asked Banks if he could
get them for me. He looked surprised, as if he considered the
reports too inconsequential to be of interest (unlike, say, his
sedan statistics), but he said he'd get them.

In the meantime, he said, he had a tip: the U.S. was
planning to make a $45 million loan to the South Vietnamese
government, with extremely soft repayment terms, to make up
for the decline in spending by American troops in Vietnam as a
result of the military withdrawal. According to Banks, the loan
had several unusual features which suggested that American
officials were perpetrating a deception: Congress originally had
approved the $45 million for another use, but since the appro-
priating legislation didn't specify that use, the Nixon
Administration felt free to divert it to Vietnam; the fund from
which the money was drawn had not been used to support
South Vietnam in nine years, and previous allocations from it
were no more than $10 million; and, despite Congressional lead-
ers' Watergate-inspired complaints that the Nixon
Administration ignored them, U.S. officials were not planning
on informing Congress of the loan proposal for another ten days.
When I called up another USAID official to confirm the report,
he expressed surprise that I knew about the loan, but he agreed
to give me more information to ensure the story's accuracy.

The next day the *Times* ran the story on the front page. A
day or two after that Banks summoned me to his apartment. He
had just attended a USAID staff meeting, he said, at which
USAID's Saigon director expressed outrage about the story and
instructed USAID employees to stop talking to journalists. Banks
was amused. The fact that he was now talking to me showed
what he thought of the director's order. I was pleased: the story
had gotten attention.

Banks had another reason for meeting me: he handed
me an envelope containing 140 pages of documents, the collect-

ed April PSA reports. It turned out that the information in them
wasn't as startling as the previous month's revelations about corruption, though I found grist for a story about Vietnamese
usurpation of Montagnard land. I enjoyed the story less for its
contents than for its likely impact on embassy officials: they
probably had deduced that I'd gotten the March reports from
Moose, but he was back in Washington and I was quoting the
April reports. What did they think now?

   A few days later Banks had more documents for me. Not
only did he provide unclassified monthly reports compiled at
the four American consulates in South Vietnam, but he added a
spectacular bonus: 60 pages of classified U.S. Embassy documents called "situation reports," summaries of notable events
dispatched daily from the embassy to the State Department in
Washington. I was startled when I saw the word "CLASSIFIED"
written across the top and bottom of each page, but Banks was
nonchalant. "I thought you might be interested in these," he
said, while I struggled to contain my excitement.
   In contrast to the Nixon Administration's public claims
that only the Communists were violating the ceasefire, the
"sitreps" provided detailed descriptions of major violations by
both the Communists and the South Vietnamese, and even a
minor one committed by the Americans. Statistics in the documents showed that in one region South Vietnamese forces fired
more than six artillery rounds for every round of the less lethal
mortars launched by the Communists. The documents
bemoaned the ARVN's penchant for indulging in petty corruption: they cited instances in which soldiers extorted money and
goods from civilians, demanded tribute payments for passage on
rural roads, and engaged in illegal trade with Communist forces.
   My favorite passage described an incident in which
South Vietnamese officials were discovered lying to the
Americans. The Americans first reported that in Binh Dinh, one
of the most embattled provinces in the country, a company in the

ARVN 23rd Division "was on patrol...when contact was made with an unidentified Viet Cong force." In the ensuing battle, 53 Communist soldiers were reported killed, while the South Vietnamese suffered only two casualties, neither fatal. Later in the day other ARVN units joined in, killing 29 more Communist soldiers while only one ARVN soldier was killed and one was wounded. Made suspicious by the overwhelming casualty ratio, the report's author dryly speculated that ARVN troops may not have found the Communist unit unexpectedly, but rather "may have launched a preemptive operation," a flagrant ceasefire violation.

That suspicion turned out to be correct, as the next day's sitrep explained. It said that South Vietnamese officials "disclosed today that patrolling company...which killed 53 V.C. on May 16...was actually not on patrol. According to most recent [South Vietnamese] version of incident, 23rd ARVN Division...received firm intelligence on location of V.C. battalion-sized training center..., picked best company... for action, and made detailed plan for raid." Predictably, this account wasn't the one made public. Looking back through the South Vietnamese military spokesman's public statements concerning the day of the battle, I found this: "This morning...an element from the 22nd Division, while securing its defensive position, detected an enemy transportation unit moving a large number of weapons and munitions.... The infantrymen were engaged by the Communists. Initial reports indicate 49 enemy killed and 104 assorted weapons along with a quantity of munitions were seized. Two infantrymen were wounded in the action." The statement didn't even correctly identify the ARVN division involved.

I wrote three stories based on the documents. Once word of them got back to Saigon, some of my sources got upset. The director of the South Vietnamese government press center yelled at me over the phone, "You are not a fair journalist!" and hung up. The U.S. Consul-General in Danang, whom I'd once interviewed, told an acquaintance that my stories had ruined his relationship with the top South Vietnamese general in the region, and as a result he would never again "give me the time of day." A USAID economist who'd given me several useful background briefings on the South Vietnamese economy told me I'd gone too far by using classified documents, and said he'd no longer talk to me. I didn't mind. I didn't enjoy seeing my sources dry up, but I knew I'd take Banks' documents over the officials' briefings any time. As for Banks, he said he'd have to forego giving me documents temporarily, as the embassy was trying to figure out who my source was. He'd even been questioned by embassy security officers, he said, but so had everyone else with access to the documents, and he wasn't worried. I was amazed by his casualness, but he apparently knew what he was doing, for he didn't get caught.

Banks had one other tidbit for me, which reflected his sexual obsession: Saigon was now graced by a restaurant whose waitresses went topless for Sunday brunches. A topless restaurant was a first for Saigon, so I figured I might be on to another, albeit minor, story. According to Banks, the place was striving to be "high-class": this meant, among other things, that Vietnamese weren't allowed to enter except as employees. The restaurant didn't even have a name, just a street number, as if it were a kind of secret code.

Dave Elliott and I went there on a Sunday morning. We walked in and nearly disappeared: thick clouds of cigarette smoke and a shortage of windows obliterated the day. It was like entering a seedy cocktail lounge: the walls were covered with bordello-red wallpaper, and the waitresses were topless, as billed. They didn't look happy about it, though: one had long hair which she arranged to cover her modest breasts. The customers were the sort of men Banks would have been comfortable with, most of them paunchy or aging or both, attracted to Saigon because it satisfied a lifetime of lustful longing. A fat man with a tattoo on one arm pinched one of the waitresses as she walked by, then told her to remove her panties — that was all she had left to take off. She smiled wanly and tried to ignore him. Food was clearly a secondary consideration, both to the proprietor and the patrons: my pancakes had the texture of wall insulation, and the sausages brought petroleum to mind.

Even if our waitress lived in Saigon, she was far, far from home now, and when Dave said something to her in Vietnamese, she looked startled. From then on she treated us as her allies, members of an ill-defined Resistance, and she gave us a summary of her life story. Twenty-two years old, she'd moved to Saigon from the Delta three years earlier hoping to make money to support her family. At some point, probably soon after her arrival, she fell into prostitution — all she would say was, "If I meet someone I like, I'll go home with him." Now she longed to return to the Delta, but she was afraid to: she'd disgraced herself, and she hadn't even saved any money. As she contemplated her ignominy, she began to cry. Here was the underside of the American strategy of luring Vietnamese into the cities: as a result of the American withdrawal, thousands and thousands of Vietnamese women now had stories like the waitress'.

Later I interviewed the owner, a goateed ex-GI who boasted of his accomplishments, licit and otherwise, as if he considered himself a model of American free enterprise. I took notes, but it didn't stop him. He said he paid "a lot of bribes" to get a restaurant license; then, during a time of flagging business, he showed pornographic movies on Sunday afternoons even though the practice was illegal. Using topless waitresses was also illegal, he said, but he didn't think he'd be caught: the police "have got to catch me in the act, and I'm slippery." He routinely stationed teenaged sentries outside the restaurant, he said; if the police raided it, the sentries would trip an alarm, giving the waitresses time to dress. The waitresses were rounded up by "impresarios" (including the owner's Vietnamese wife, according to our waitress), and were rotated each week to give the customers "a change of scenery." They got ten dollars plus tips for four hours of work. "I'm not training them as waitresses," he said. "They're just there for entertainment."

A topless restaurant wasn't exactly vital news, so I felt free to take more liberties than usual in writing the story. This was the lead:

> SAIGON— The Americans, whose past contributions to Vietnamese culture include air horns, motorcycles, and silicone bustlines, have now given Saigon its first topless restaurant.

The paper buried the story deep inside the paper, which for once was fine with me: editors were less likely to tamper with it that way. As it turned out, only one word of the story was changed, but what an interesting change it was. As edited, the passage read:

> The clientele seemed to represent Saigon's seamy civilian underworld. But Greenawalt said his customers included construction workers, AID and Defense Department employees and even a few embassy officials.

An editor added "But." He apparently couldn't believe that construction workers, AID and Defense Department employees, and embassy officials *were* the underworld.

Later on, the owner passed word that if I ever appeared on the premises again, he'd kill me.

I ran into the journalist I'd met in the Japanese restaurant in Bangkok, and invited him for lunch at my villa. His English was even poorer than I'd remembered, so that our conversation often broke down, but he did communicate one bizarre fact: two months earlier the Japanese manager of the local office of Mitsubishi, the giant trading corporation, had been arrested and imprisoned in Saigon. The journalist said the reason for the detention was a mystery, and then he dropped the subject. It sounded like something I ought to look into.

I was in no hurry. First I wrote a story about what I thought was an unrelated development: the imprisonment of Nguyen Tan Doi, the owner of South Vietnam's biggest bank and one of the wealthiest men in the country. Six weeks earlier, South Vietnamese police had arrested Doi and summarily closed all 33 of his bank's branches, creating vast inconveniences for the bank's 200,000 stranded depositors. Although Doi was eventually convicted of engaging in many illegal banking practices, few people familiar with Saigon politics thought that explained his detention. In a country where corruption was generally winked at, they argued, the authorities would not have reacted so sternly unless Doi had committed some other offense, most likely political. The most popular theory was that Doi, who'd befriended many ARVN generals and was often observed flying in helicopters with them, intended to supplant Nguyen Van Thieu as South Vietnam's president, and that Thieu arrested him to prevent any possibility of his becoming a rival. I framed my piece to suggest that Doi's arrest was an intriguing unsolved mystery.

And then, a week after the meal with the Japanese journalist, I got around to making phone calls about the Mitsubishi man's arrest. I started in the morning; by the afternoon I'd learned that the man, named Tokuji Ishimura, had become involved, perhaps unwittingly, in smuggling scrap brass out of South Vietnam. That was about all I could find out; most of my questions led to dead ends. Oddly, Ishimura's colleagues at Mitsubishi didn't seem overwrought about his detention. Prison, one said, is "not so bad. He has money, so the food is comparatively good, there are no telephone calls and no business matters."

I almost wrote a story that evening about Ishimura's

plight, but opted instead for developing the story further. For the next couple of days all I did was ask questions. The people I talked to spoke of brass circumspectly: until five years earlier it had been the chief ingredient in American artillery shell casings, and was extremely valuable. Used casings were strewn across the Vietnamese landscape; anyone who could round them up and ship them out of Vietnam would make a fortune. Apparently someone was trying to do exactly that: I learned that Ishimura had been offered a chance to buy scrap brass, and was shown a permit to export it from South Vietnam. Skeptical of the permit's authenticity, Ishimura showed it to the South Vietnamese authorities. Their response suggested that Ishimura was prescient in questioning the document's validity, less so in sharing his suspicions with the government. First the officials asked him who gave him the permit; then, when he wouldn't answer, presumably because he was a discreet businessman, they threw him and two intermediaries in prison. The two intermediaries, also Japanese, were eventually released, but Ishimura remained there.

For every question about the case I resolved, I developed several unanswered ones. The biggest one was the identity of the smugglers, which of course the South Vietnamese government didn't know either. Why were the authorities so interested in the answer that they risked a diplomatic incident with Japan by detaining an influential and apparently innocent businessman? I heard speculation that ARVN officers were involved; considering that they had easiest access to the shell casings, that at least made sense. And how much were all the casings worth? Emil Sasse, the head of the U.S. embassy "property disposal branch," was the only man with authority to tell me, but when I asked the U.S. embassy spokesman for permission to interview him, I was turned down. An official at the Japanese embassy at least agreed to a meeting, but only, it turned out, to find out how much I knew. I answered his questions in hopes that he would answer mine, but he didn't even make a pretense of giving any information in return. He advised me to drop the story; if I didn't, he said, I'd be endangering Ishimura's life. He shouldn't have said that: now I knew the story was important.

Why weren't Japanese journalists digging into the affair? — after all, it was of more immediate interest in Japan than in the U.S. They had a reputation for timidity, for working in a pack, and I could only surmise that if their embassy waved them off a story, they wouldn't touch it. Still, it was eerie. The case had been going on for more than two months, yet it had drawn virtually no press attention, in Saigon or abroad, and representatives of three governments were behaving as if I were probing the secret of the H-bomb. I did pick up one tidbit which whetted my appetite for more: six months earlier, without fanfare, the U.S, which was the legal owner of all military scrap metals, agreed to turn over title to the scrap to the South Vietnamese government as supplemental military assistance. At the very least the deal provided a modest boost to the declining South Vietnamese economy in the form of $10 million worth of scrap iron and steel already accessible to authorities. But if the authorities could also cash in on the far more valuable brass, the deal would amount to a windfall amounting to as much as the equivalent of a year's worth of American economic aid. The catch, of course, was that the South Vietnamese government would have to collect and export the brass in order to cash in on it. Instead, someone was trying to smuggle it out.

Just when I felt stymied, I got a phone call. The man on the other end wouldn't identify himself; he just said he wanted to talk about brass. His voice was funereal, barely audible. He said he'd meet me at my villa.

When I answered my doorbell, two Americans were standing at the entrance. They all but shoved me aside in their haste to get inside. What were they hiding from? They looked like the Laurel and Hardy of scrap brass: one man was fat, with a tattoo showing above one of his gnarled elbows; the other was thin and jumpy and grayer than rain clouds. I knew without asking that the thin man had called me: to be in his company was like being continually reminded that life is a somber business

ending in death. Even in broad daylight he seemed to creep, and
he hid behind a pillar when he saw Chi Ba coming. Neither man
would tell me his name; they just opened their wallets and, holding their thumbs over their names, showed me official-looking
identification cards. They were police, or investigators, or spies,
double- or triple-agents; at the very least they were spooked
spooks. They'd been investigating the brass case, they said, but
the authorities wouldn't act on their evidence. When they found
out I was looking into it, they decided in desperation to give me
their information; their last hope, they said, was that making the
case public would bring about action. They knew whom I'd
interviewed, how much of the story I'd pieced together. I'd
found out a lot, they said, but I lacked their larger perspective,
which they promised to relate. Not all at once, however; the
story was too complicated to be communicated in one sitting.
Meanwhile, they said, I should continue interviewing other people, as openly as possible, so that they wouldn't be suspected of
being my sources. We agreed on a time when they'd return the
next day. As they left, they added one more thing: *your phone is
tapped*, they said. *Your life is in danger.*

Did I dare believe them? Did I dare not to? As much as
those words frightened me, they gratified me, too. I was a character in a John LeCarré novel now; I was the hunter and the
hunted.

When the men returned, they were accompanied by a
Vietnamese colleague whom they said understood some aspects
of the case better than they did. Unfortunately, his English was
so poor and his command of chronology so shaky that I often got
mired in detail. One moment I believed I possessed information
so startling that Nixon himself would have to take notice; the
next moment, puzzling over the dreadful trivia that is the stuff
of investigations, I wondered if I knew anything at all.

The gist of what the men told me was that a syndicate of
ARVN generals was trying to smuggle brass out of South
Vietnam — no wonder their investigation had come to a stand-
still. In addition to the three Japanese, two Americans and a

Vietnamese had been arrested, and two people with French passports had disappeared. One of the arrested Americans had
worked in the U.S. embassy's property disposal branch, where
he'd apparently forged export permits in return for payoffs from
the syndicate. The Mitsubishi manager had been arrested for
possessing such a permit.

The more the men told me, the more excited I became,
for what they were effectively saying was that many ARVN generals, the regime's "defenders of democracy," were in fact war
profiteers. Corruption in Vietnam was an old, old story, but the
scale of this smuggling set it apart: by holding on to the brass,
the generals seemed to be trying to assure their own private fortunes while jeopardizing the future of their government.

To accept information from men who wouldn't identify
themselves was unorthodox journalistic practice, to say the least.
Yet I felt sure the men were telling the truth: not only did their
information jibe with what I'd learned elsewhere, but they did-
n't act like liars. After the men left, I told McArthur about them.
To my relief, he supported my inclination to trust them.

After the second rendezvous at my house the men
wouldn't return: they said meeting there was too dangerous.
From then on I had contact only with the thin man. The next time
we met, he picked me up at a street corner, then drove around in
circles for ten or fifteen minutes while constantly looking in his
rearview mirror. "You can't be too careful," he muttered, and I
imagined someone following us, even training a gun on us. At
last he was satisfied that we weren't being tailed, and he pulled
into a parking lot. We talked for ten minutes without leaving the
car. Then he drove in circles again, and dropped me at another
corner.

He left me at the *Newsweek* villa, where Ron was now
living. I stopped by, for reassurance as much as anything else. I
decided not to tell Ron anything about the content of my story—
I was afraid he'd steal it — but I told him I was onto something
big. I described being driven around in circles, being warned
that my life was in danger. "Oh, sure," Ron said disbelievingly.

One reason I loved journalism was that I assumed truth was built into it: when it was practiced as it should be, truth, or at least the vulgar version of truth called fact, actually became the object. The best journalists, I believed, were on quests to uncover fact, to reach far down and grasp it and see it glistening in the hand. The danger we courted was possessiveness: we were more possessive with exclusives than with wives or girlfriends. Like lovers, we succumbed to the illusion that what we possessed was something material, permanent, until ultimately the content of our stories lost significance: the goal became the continual, indiscriminate discovery of noteworthy or provocative fact. I understood that readers didn't know or care which stories were exclusives, but that just made me rue readers' benightedness. I adored exclusives' feel. More and more I'd been prefacing dispatches to L.A. with notes saying this or that fact was exclusive; perhaps occasionally a story got a front page display as a result, but good play wasn't the sole aim of the exercise. "Look at me!" the notes announced. "Look at what I've found!"

And now I was onto what seemed like my biggest exclusive of all.

I couldn't sleep. I lay in bed, mulling over such paradoxes as why generals who presided over a war in which a million people had died would hesitate to kill just one person more, a reporter, who happened to threaten their interests. Trivial acts now seemed fraught with consequence. If I turned on the air conditioner, for instance, would I be able to hear the syndicate men coming to kill me? For a while I left the air conditioner off, and jumped up every few minutes to check the source of this or that strange sound — the world outside my window seemed to simmer with menace. Eventually, though, I wore myself out, and finally turned the machine back on: I figured that if I were going to die, I might as well do so in the soothing embrace of cool air. When I awoke in the morning, I took notice of my continued existence with an iota of surprise.

I called up the U.S. embassy spokesman to make one more plea for an interview with Sasse, the head of the property disposal branch. I said I already had enough information to write an explosive story about scrap brass, and it was therefore in the embassy's interests to help ensure that the story was accurate. The argument worked, for I finally got the interview. Sasse was nervous, and insisted on recording our conversation; I couldn't tell whether he was trying to protect himself or intimidate me or both. He launched into a lecture, complete with slide projector and darkened room, on the role of the property disposal branch in Vietnam, meanwhile brushing off my questions about brass, but I figured I could wait him out, and did: the interview lasted two and a half hours. Yet Sasse wouldn't discuss the details of the case, and he never did give me an estimate on the value of the scrap brass left in Vietnam. His most notable revelation was inadvertent: he said American "customs advisers" were working with South Vietnamese police on an investigation of the brass case, thus seeming to identify my anonymous sources.

In the end I took the story beyond what the anonymous sources told me. The only other person besides McArthur and my various sources with whom I discussed the story was Dave Elliott, who happened to trip over another key to the puzzle. He said a Saigon judge had told a Vietnamese friend of his that among those involved with the syndicate were Prime Minister Tran Thien Khiem, the second most powerful man in the government, and Nguyen Tan Doi, the imprisoned banker. Not only was Doi said to be the banker for the brass syndicate, but he also owned a factory where scrap brass could be made into copper wire. As it happened, my anonymous sources had told me about a forged export document for 4,550 tons of copper wire: in this and other respects, the accounts confirmed each other. I seemed to have solved two mysteries at once: brass explained why Doi had been arrested, and Khiem's involvement explained why the investigation had reached an impasse.

I thought this was Vietnam's Watergate, and I was Woodward and Bernstein; my story was the "smoking gun" that showed the folly of American support for a regime that diverted hundreds of millions of dollars into its own officials' pockets. I wondered whether the syndicate might respond to the story's publication by killing me. I was so scared I considered flying to Hong Kong to file. The South Vietnamese government might not let me return, I knew, but it would be an impressive departure, almost like being expelled, and at least in Hong Kong I wouldn't have to worry about being killed. McArthur talked me out of the idea. He said that once the story was published, the damage would be done, and the syndicate would lack a motive. I hoped the syndicate was as logical as McArthur.

The *Times* didn't carry the piece the first day after I filed it, nor the second day — the editors were waiting for a slow news day so that they could use it as the lead story. By now I didn't care whether the piece led the paper or not — I just wanted it in print. What if some other journalist stumbled on to the story and beat me to publication? I knew that none of my colleagues had access to my sources, and that it would take anyone a week or two to turn up as much information as I had, but that didn't placate me — I was just frantic.

And then the story ran. The Washington *Post* picked it up, so it appeared in the capital, and *Stars & Stripes*, the armed forces newspaper, used it. That was all. I was looking forward to Congressmen's calls for investigations and expressions of outrage from anti-war leaders, but nothing like that happened. Was I naive to think my life had been in danger? Maybe syndicate members showed a better understanding of American opinion than I had, just by doing nothing; maybe they knew Vietnam corruption stories were old news, and therefore wouldn't jeopardize them. All I'd done was to achieve a new notoriety within

the U.S. embassy: the first time after the story ran that I phoned
the embassy spokesman, he responded to hearing my name by
yelling "Baloney!" Even my anonymous source was disappointed. One last time he picked me up at a corner and drove in circles, and when he finally stopped he proclaimed the story "a
bust." I thought I'd let him down. I noticed, though, that he
looked in his rearview mirror less often than before.

       And now I had visa troubles all over again. The day
after I filed the story, the South Vietnamese government refused
to renew my visa and press card, thus rendering my presence in
the country unauthorized. Not that the brass story provoked this
response: the government didn't react that quickly to invasions,
never mind foreign news dispatches. No, this was a tribute to my
earlier stories. What the government didn't do was expel me,
which would have earned it unfavorable publicity; whoever
made the decision must have hoped that with my visa status in
limbo, I would leave South Vietnam voluntarily. That suggested
a grievous misunderstanding of journalists: the part of me that
was resigned to leaving the country yearned to be expelled. I'd
play Br'er Rabbit up to the moment of my expulsion, pleading
"Please don't throw me in the briar patch" until the authorities
pushed me onto the plane and I leaped aboard, laughing. And
yet, I still wasn't sure I wanted to go. In the wake of the brass
story several people had come to me with tantalizing leads: if I
stayed, I could generate blockbuster stories without end. What
would I do without Vietnam?
       The day after I was notified that my visa wouldn't be
renewed, I met with Bui Bao Truc, the South Vietnamese government spokesman. Only a few years older than I was, Truc had
been on the job for only a few months, and still wasn't fit for it:
he'd apparently failed to cultivate the necessary ruthlessness, for
one thing. I walked into his room like a bull about to engage the
matador, wielding my pen and notebook in case he said anything I could use against him. He obliged. In a surprisingly soft

and quavering voice that matched his slight, bespectacled appearance, Truc said I'd written seven or eight objectionable stories, chiefly the ones I liked best. My offense, he said, was writing stories "which damaged the image of the Republic of Vietnam abroad."

I could hardly disagree. I said, "You mean you're not questioning my accuracy?"

Truc took the bait as if it were sirloin. "It's not a question of accuracy," he said. "I don't say you are right or wrong. I don't say you have fabricated stories. We can accept criticism but not insults. We ask you to be impartial and objective and neutral but you have not been."

Truc's mistake was to walk a middle line, trying to placate me instead of launching an all-out attack on my competence: governments often expelled foreign journalists for writing accurate but embarrassing stories, but I'd never before heard of one artless enough to admit that. Truc was conceding I'd written nothing he could call untrue. Did it bother him that I scribbled down everything he said?

The government wouldn't expel me, and I wouldn't leave: it was a stalemate. In the meantime McArthur played some of his embassy cards on my behalf, and Gibson tried to marshal American political pressure against the South Vietnamese government to prevent my expulsion. For a month I hung in limbo, unable to take a scheduled R & R because the government wouldn't have let me back in the country, yet advised by McArthur at first not to write anything, then later just not to write anything controversial. I wrote one piece about the train between Danang and Hue, another about the French colonial legacy in Vietnam, and fumed like a benched Reggie Jackson. Embassy officials said they were trying to help, but their enthusiasm was muted, to say the least. Once they told McArthur I'd get my new visa; when it failed to come, they said my situation was hopeless. McArthur consequently declared I ought to have a farewell dinner. I suspected him of shoving me out the door.

While biding my time I took a precautionary farewell trip to Quang Tri. If I was to be expelled, I wanted to see the province one last time, for it was there, more than a year earlier, that I'd spent my first anxious days in a combat zone. Since then the ARVN had recovered most of the terrain they'd lost, including the province capital, but that wasn't like saying they'd recaptured the town itself: under the onslaught of shells, the town had disappeared. I walked through it without recognizing a single landmark, for there no longer were any. Not one structure had escaped major damage. Some houses were collapsed like accordions. Fragments of buildings had merged with hulks of burnt-out tanks and jeeps. Odd-shaped plaster slabs that once were walls pointed into the air; one house still had a staircase intact, but it led up to nothing but blue sky. The roof of a Catholic church was shattered but the cross on top remained. Black twisted tree trunks and miles of trenches dug by the North Vietnamese lined the streets. The devastation was so vast that residents who'd returned to look for their belongings weren't sure where their houses had stood.

In the extremity of its desolation Quang Tri was fascinating. I poked through the ruins of a house and found a baby carriage, a bike chain, a Buddhist prayer book and candle holder, a twisted bed frame, a brassiere, a woman's shoe — what a rapid transformation these things had undergone, from household objects to artifacts of a lost civilization. In a row, apparently discovered by someone who'd combed the area before me, were human leg bones and a jawbone with two teeth attached. They probably were the remains of a North Vietnamese soldier, not a resident, but it hardly mattered: bleached white by the sun, they seemed the sort of thing archaeologists might discover at an ancient site.

I didn't want to leave. Quang Tri was perversely satisfying, as if without knowing it I'd been looking for the ultimate symbol of destruction and had finally found it. It was like touching the ocean floor. Here was war, holocaust, Armageddon, the logical end of the process. I took many photographs that day, but they all turned out the same: rubble.

After returning to Saigon I got a summons from the South Vietnamese immigration department. I drove to the appropriate government building and introduced myself. The sleepy clerk in front of me handed me an exit visa form and instructed me to sign it and pay four dollars. I concluded that I was being asked to assist the lumbering bureaucracy in its labor to expel me, and refused. The official insisted. I phoned McArthur and asked him what to do: he said pay. Too weary to resist both him and the government, I paid. On the visa form I wrote that I was applying for a visa extension, not an exit visa. By now the clerk was annoyed, and said this was invalid. The expulsion order arrived the next morning. I was given three days to leave the country.

From the moment a month earlier when I'd learned I might be expelled, the *Times* declined to run stories about my status, on the grounds that our only leverage against the South Vietnamese government was the threat of embarrassing it with stories once I was expelled. Now McArthur wrote one, citing Truc's admission that I wasn't charged with inaccuracy. Wire services also carried stories, while Truc continued to deny that I was being expelled. Curious whether he'd announce my expulsion at the afternoon press briefing, I decided to attend.

The first question was about my expulsion. True began calmly:

> We don't expel him. We just don't give him any
> press card any more,... because for the last three
> or four months he has been writing articles
> attacking us seriously.... Imagine that kind of
> thing happened in Hanoi. The correspondent
> like that would some night go out and just dis-
> appear. We don't do that.... He can be here —
> he can continue to be here as a civilian doing

any other thing, but we cannot help him — as
we can help you foreign correspondents doing
your job — any more. He could get help from
the other side.

I was fascinated. The government was not only claiming credit
for restraint in not imprisoning or killing me, but it was suggest-
ing that I aided the "other side," the Communists. A journalist
asked whether any of my stories were inaccurate.

> *Truc*: Well, I'm sorry but I don't have the articles
> here with me, but I have them downstairs and
> many of the articles proved to be inaccurate.
> *Journalist*: Can you give us some examples?
> *Truc*: Well, there are so many.
> *Journalist*: Just one then.
> *Truc*: But I'm afraid I don't have the answer
> right now. But you see that while he's in Saigon
> enjoying the security provided by the soldiers
> of the Republic of Vietnam, he attacks our sol-
> diers. We can't have that.... But we don't expel
> him.

Truc had lost his temper. He'd decided to accuse me of inaccuracies, but he hadn't bothered to devise a list of them. Now it was
his word under attack, not mine.

Suddenly Jim Bennett of ABC, a grizzled television
reporter who'd become strangely enraged when he found out
about my expulsion a few minutes earlier, erupted.

> *Bennett*: What do you call it then? Does he have
> three days or does he not have three days in
> which to get out of the country?
> *Truc*: Well, we don't order him to get out of
> Vietnam. We just take back his press card.
> *Bennett*: Can he stay beyond three days or must

he be out of the country by Monday?
Truc: Well, that is up to the immigration service.
But we don't make the decision.

At first Bennett sounded like a worthy defender, and I was glad
to have him on my side. Then he got frustrated: he had nowhere
to take his line of questioning.

    Bennett: Is this a provoked attack on the press
    in general or just on one person?

It was a "When-did-you-stop-beating-your-wife?" question, but
Truc, with his limited command of English, misunderstood.

    Truc: Just on one person. Not doing it —
    Bennett: You are then admitting you are making
    a provoked attack on one journalist.
    Truc: Well, we don't attack him first.

Bennett kept insisting that Truc cite my inaccuracies,
while Truc, increasingly frustrated, in one breath said he would,
and in another said he didn't have the examples with him. Other
journalists took up the questioning, even after Truc said he did-
n't want to talk about me any more. An aged Vietnamese
reporter who looked astonished by this rare display of temper in
the briefing room drew laughter when he asked Truc who everyone was talking about. When Truc oddly declined to say my
name, Bennett got on him for *that*. In desperation Truc tried the
offensive:

    Truc: Excuse me, sir, which agency do you work
    for?
    Bennett [angrily]: I work for ABC News. Jim
    Bennett. ABC News —
    Truc: Then do you have a press card? Do you
    have a press card?

> *Bennett*: Legitimately and in my pocket. Would
> you like to see it right now?
> *Truc*: Would you like to be seated please?
> *Bennett*: No, I don't want to be seated. Do I have
> to be seated?
> *Truc*: Yes, you do have to be seated!
> *Bennett* [sarcastically]: Is that a rule?

Again Bennett raised the question of the charges against me. This time Truc tried a different tack. "All right then," he said. "If Mr. Leslie asks me, then I'll answer him."

I obliged him. From the back of the room, where I was sitting, I said, "All right, I ask you then."

Truc pounced. "Do you have a press card? All newsmen coming here must have a press card. If you don't have a press card I ask you to leave the room immediately! Mr. Leslie, do you have a press card?"

In all the briefings I'd attended, nobody'd ever asked for press cards. Truc knew where mine was: he'd taken it from me a month earlier. I was amazed: he'd been fashioning this stratagem, this Catch-22 of a question, for the previous five minutes. I said I didn't have a press card.

Truc didn't hesitate. "Please leave the room," he said. "Thank you. Goodbye."

It was as close to victory as Truc got. Most of the journalists in the room laughed at his ploy. I stayed in my seat. And Bennett went right back on the attack, reminding Truc that he still hadn't answered the question. The two men sparred like arm-weary boxers near the end of the fifteenth round.

> *Truc*: I don't have to answer you.
> *Bennett*: No you don't.
> *Truc*: I don't have to answer you.
> *Bennett*: Or won't.
> *Truc*: I will not answer you.

Contrary to Truc's intention, the only subject he'd covered during his briefing was my expulsion. Now, in desperation, he passed the microphone to the government's foreign affairs spokesman and sat down.

Expecting more fireworks, the networks brought their cameras into the briefing room the next day. Truc foiled them: he didn't show up.

Two days after that I left the country, bound for Hong Kong. South Vietnamese police were at the airport to make sure I boarded my plane. Fortunately, customs officials didn't search my luggage, which contained one last batch of documents from Banks. I read in a Hong Kong newspaper that a few hours after I left, Truc charged me with "vilifying and degrading the South Vietnamese army" and "concocting a groundless article on the ill treatment of political prisoners." The only significant story of mine he didn't dispute was the brass story. On the contrary, he announced that the government was launching an investigation of brass smuggling. The head of the investigating team was to be Prime Minister Khiem.

DESCENT
Chapter

6

By granting me its backhanded form of acknowledgment called expulsion, the South Vietnamese government enhanced my career prospects, at the expense of exiling me from the one place in the world where I was sure I wanted to have a career. Cast out of Vietnam, I had to find another way to slake my mark. At first I thought that would be easy. *Give me more war*, I thought, and Gibson obliged: he sent me to Cambodia. For the time being — July, 1973 — Cambodia was a bigger story than Vietnam, so I concluded that in expelling me the South Vietnamese government had done me an even grander favor than I'd realized.

The war had spread to Cambodia three years earlier, when the prime minister, Gen. Lon Nol, overthrew Prince Norodom Sihanouk and established himself as president of the Khmer Republic, his creation. Whereas Sihanouk tolerated Vietnamese Communist sanctuaries on Cambodia's eastern border, Lon Nol and his new American allies were determined to drive them out. However, their efforts backfired, for Vietnamese weren't all that Phnom Penh troops (called FANK, for Forces Armées Nationales Khmer) encountered. The Khmer Rouge (literally, Red Cambodians), whose scraggly army constituted a minor irritant to Sihanouk while he was in power, now joined forces with the exiled monarch and flourished. The FANK suffered one devastating setback after another, and was exposed as a laughably inept army, whose soldiers were as likely to flee from battle as to fight. Lon Nol's deficiencies also became obvious: he was vain (he declared himself Marshal, and wore a six-star pin), isolated, and subject to delusion, such as that only Vietnamese, not Cambodians, opposed him. His regime was quickly mired in corruption, and his generals behaved as if the land their forces occupied comprised independent fiefdoms. On top of all this, Lon Nol suffered a stroke, which left him half-paralyzed. The war-weary U.S. Congress, taking advantage of Nixon's Watergate-induced weakness, had imposed an August 15 deadline on American military activity in Cambodia, and the Lon Nol government was considered unlikely to withstand Khmer Rouge attacks once American bombing ceased. I looked forward to adding another item to my checklist: I'd never seen a regime collapse before.

If Vietnam was an epic novel, obligatory and even ponderous, then Cambodia was poetic diversion. I'd been in Cambodia once before the war engulfed it, in December, 1968, when I was an English teacher on vacation from Hong Kong. I'd flown into Phnom Penh and boarded a limousine packed with tourists for a four-hour drive to the Angkor temples. As extraordinary as the temples were, I loved the drive more. The countryside looked preternatural. We passed sinewy, dark-skinned men working lush fields, bare-breasted women wearing bright sarongs, houses built on stilts. As dusk approached, we could see families sitting on the floors of the elevated houses, faces illuminated by golden lantern light. War was inconceivable here.

After a few days in Angkor, I contracted stomach flu, and took a plane back to Phnom Penh. The first available flight to Hong Kong was two days later, so I registered at the capital's best hotel, the Royale. The hotel was so swank I found it slightly intimidating. From a distance I caught sight of its gently sloping red tile roof and its colonnaded balconies, and I felt its aura of grace and permanence, so unlike the bland inconsequentiality of the city's newer commercial buildings. I was driven up a semi-circular driveway, past a garden with bright flowers that spelled out the hotel's name, and mounted the steps into the wood-paneled lobby. Casually dressed, like the college student I had ceased being only half a year earlier, I felt out of place in this monument to colonial splendor. For two days I took shelter in my room, recuperating and reading and surviving on room service, and looked down from my second-floor window to the pool. Westerners in bathing suits sat beneath canopies to shield themselves from the sun, occasionally commanding waiters wearing white jackets and severe expressions to fetch lemonades and pastel-colored drinks. A story I heard years later summed up the hotel's atmosphere in this era. Monsieur Lu, the gentle, rotund Sino-Khmer hotel manager, was said to have come rushing out of his office one evening after being informed that a European man and woman were swimming naked in the pool. "Please stop," he implored them, "there are foreign correspondents staying in this hotel."

Now it was the correspondents who swam nude in the pool. By the time I arrived, on the last day of July, the atmosphere at the hotel was bustling, even festive, reflecting the glee of a battalion or so of journalists who'd converged in hopes of covering a meaty crisis. They gathered information during the day and played at night: by ten or eleven p.m. the pool was filled with rollicking journalists, including a woman or two. The Dionysian aura permeated the entire hotel; not even the Cambodian roomboys, docile and reverent in their neat white uniforms, seemed to mind. I wasn't sure who was sleeping with whom, who was stoned on liquor, who on drugs, but I liked the good-natured nihilism of the place. Seen through the hotel's distorting filter, Cambodia appeared happy and tragic at the same time.

Compared to its pre-war condition, the hotel had turned dog-eared. In response to the demise of the monarchy, its name

had been changed to the "Phnom"; although the flowers that
spelled out "Royale" had been removed from the garden, the
offending word was still faintly visible in the grass, as if nature
itself deplored the coup. The hotel's only elevator no longer
worked, necessitating climbs up an elegant but creaky wooden
staircase whose floorboards already bore deep grooves made by
millions of footsteps. Only the lobby didn't acknowledge
Cambodia's changed circumstances: an advertisement for an
Eastern European airline in a lobby showcase must have been
placed there before the war began, for the airline stopped serving Phnom Penh when fighting broke out.

   Journalists, now the hotel's chief patrons, exemplified
its metamorphosis. The hotel was our coed dormitory, our dining hall, our press room, our rumor factory. Our rumpled countenances looked out from the restaurant by the pool; the guest
rooms were choked with our cameras, typewriters, short wave
radios, combat gear. Even our dissipations were on display. For
example, drugs: One of the hotel's largest suites had been con-
verted into the A.P. bureau, whose chief, a fat, loquacious
Englishman, kept a well-stocked bowl of marijuana on a prominently positioned table, and joints were passed around at the
pool as casually as cigarettes. Or sex: The aspiring siren Sarah
Webb Burrell, rumored to have been a call girl in Rome, now trying intermittently to catch on as a news photographer, boasted
that she'd slept with so many journalists at the hotel that the
mail clerk never knew which room to send her letters to. Yet
journalism was still our chief pursuit: throughout the day we
exchanged rumors, debated the significance of the latest military
and political developments, all while anxiously noting one
another's comings and goings, as someone's prolonged absence
conceivably meant he'd found a good story. I was particularly
interested in the whereabouts of the formidable Sydney
Schanberg, the New York *Times* reporter. Schanberg was the only
correspondent I knew who, in the interests of promoting exclusivity, unfailingly refused to discuss his stories until they'd been
published, and who, when covering combat on Cambodia's

treacherous roads, declined colleagues' company. Working alone, he left us to discover what he'd been doing by perusing the replays of his stories in the U.S. embassy reading room.

In a rare wistful moment, Schanberg once stepped out onto the balcony of his third floor suite, raised his arms, and shouted to the sunbathers surrounding the pool below, "My people! My people!" as if he were their supreme leader. Indeed, the setting inspired grandiose notions: Schanberg's balcony looked like a perfect spot from which to pontificate to assembled masses. The pool area looked like an inspired movie set, evocative of Fellini or some other connoisseur of the colorful and bizarre. It came alive at midday, when the hotel's patrons gathered around. Only the brave (and the intoxicated) dared actually swim: as Tony Clifton, a jocular Australian journalist, put it, the water was so thick "all it needs to make good French soup is croutons." Away from the pool, some of the swimmers were identifiable by eye patches they wore after contracting conjunctivitis in its murky waters.

Around the pool, middle-aged and elderly French men and women, the last vestiges of Phnom Penh's colonial presence, gossiped and sunbathed. They regarded Cambodians as children who would mature only by absorbing French culture, of which they themselves knew less than they pretended. Their snobbery was reflected in the words they used to beckon Cambodian servants: males were called "boys," females were "boyesses," and all lived in a "boyerie." The women took extravagant pains to retain their fading youthfulness, and looked correspondingly well-preserved. They basked in the sun, their faces covered with thick, expertly applied makeup and their fingernails with exotically colored polish, and discussed such subjects as their latest water-skiing expedition on the Mekong River and the inability of Cambodian seamstresses to copy Paris fashions.

A Frenchman in his early 20s who was fulfilling his national service obligation by teaching school sat in the shade of a palm tree smoking marijuana. A pot-bellied Swiss U.N. official expounded his elaborate theories on corruption and communism as he ate voluminous meals of cold cuts, French bread, and *salade verte*, while next to him his delicate French-speaking Cambodian mistress listened courteously. Prostitutes sat in one corner, trying to get the attention of potential customers, usually journalists. Swimming in the pool was a wonderfully proportioned nymphet from the lycée across the street, whose flirtatious behavior and tiny bikini provoked innumerable lustful speculations among the journalists. Sometimes a deaf Cambodian did irreverent mimes of Lon Nol, Sihanouk, and Nixon, as the waiters doubled over in laughter. Cambodian generals, in from the front for lunch with their wives or staff, ran up large bills which they then neglected to pay. A gold-toothed Cambodian who claimed to be a government official lurked near the bushes, hoping for reasons known only to him to pass on inaccurate tips to journalists. Each day trucks arrived with huge blocks of ice, which workmen slid along a cement path to the restaurant's ice box. When it rained, a hotel employee stood on duty with a large canvas umbrella to escort guests between the restaurant and hotel.

I stayed in Chambre 25, permanently rented by the *Times* for five dollars a day. The room was not air conditioned, which accounted for the bargain rate, but thanks to an overhead ceiling fan the heat was usually tolerable. The room offered such pleasing features as a balcony overlooking a garden filled with bougainvillea, a black-and-white checkered floor that was soothingly cool to walk on, and a four-legged bathtub. The musty items left behind by previous correspondents gave the room a moldering quality, as if some of them had not quite left. I felt the ghost of Arthur Dommen, a former *Times* correspondent who quit to study agriculture, still in the room, for I found his half-full pouch of pipe tobacco in the desk drawer. I also found military fatigues, numerous soap bars, a rusting can of French mosquito spray, and a tall stack of yellowed stationery with the letterhead, "Committee for the Safety of Foreign Correspondents in Cambodia." Dommen had formed the committee in the early months of the war, when some two dozen journalists either dis-

appeared from the roads outside Phnom Penh or were killed by
the Khmer Rouge, but the committee soon became moribund.
Now all that was left was the stationery.

The first Cambodian I got to know was Ang Kheao, the
Times' driver and interpreter, who'd been my guide during a
few   visits while I was stationed in Saigon. McArthur had spoken of him with affection, as if he were endearing, but I was surprised to find him cautious and aloof, almost formal, befitting
his age, which was close to 60. Invariably dressed in gray pleat-
ed slacks and a white shortsleeved shirt, Ang Kheao looked less
like a journalist's assistant than a school teacher, which he once
was; his appearance stood in prim contrast to that of the other
interpreters, all at least 30 years his junior, who typically wore
brightly colored shirts and dark sunglasses and looked like
American '50s rock-and-rollers. Informed by cable that I was
coming, Ang Kheao would meet me at the airport and deposit
me in the back seat of his Mercedes limousine, perhaps the
longest car in Phnom Penh. I couldn't understand why he owned
such a vehicle until he told me the story; then I suspected that
McArthur's fondness for him had something to do with pity.
Ang Kheao said he'd once won a scholarship to study English in
the United States, and indeed his English was excellent — this
fact alone distinguished him as a rare Cambodian. He worked
for the U.S. Information Service after he returned to Phnom
Penh, then turned to the more lucrative job of driving tourists
between Phnom Penh and Angkor — it's possible that back in
1968 I'd been one of his passengers. By 1969 the tourist trade had
grown so promising that he sent an order to Germany for the
limo, which could hold several more passengers than his previous car. Unfortunately, the war began a few weeks after the car
arrived. Tourism stopped, and Ang Kheao lost his livelihood. He
was left with two major assets, his command of English and his
car, both of which were in demand among the Western journalists who came to cover the war. Journalists were too unruly to

appeal to a man like Ang Kheao, but having little choice, he became a driver and interpreter for them.

Ang Kheao charged the going rate: ten dollars a day for driving in the city, twenty dollars a day for driving in the country, and forty dollars a day when the car was shot at. While on visits from Saigon I had no intention of paying the top rate, for my mission was to become familiar with the country, not to cover skirmishes. On my first visit I told Ang Kheao to drive me around the capital, and was pleased to find a city whose charm hadn't yet been dissipated by war. Its broad avenues were lined with trees and gardens, and at midday siesta time were practically free of traffic. Phnom Penh combined a pleasing concern for architecture and proportion, appropriate to a people who'd constructed Ankor Wat, with good natured Buddhistic tolerance: the result was a city that pleased the eye and soothed the mind. Not even the bizarre looked out of place: once I caught a glimpse of elephants padding down a main road, and was informed that they were the royal elephants, less easily exiled than the monarch himself.

The countryside around Phnom Penh was even more seductive, as villages filled me with a sense of repose. Shaded lanes, which Ang Kheao navigated in the long car with difficulty, led to Buddhist monasteries, and brightly tiled, spired temples appeared every few miles. Palm trees stood like exclamation points above the flat, lush landscape. The war seemed barely to have made an impact. In Vietnam, villages typically lined main roads, for peasants understood that roads were rarely bombed, but in Cambodia the villages, not the roads, seemed to have been built first, and appeared at regular intervals from the highway to the horizon. Even the army outposts, dainty rather than forbidding, reflected the war's unfamiliarity. Rural outposts in Vietnam interrupted their surroundings with brown splotches of sandbags, trenches, fortifications, but those I saw in Cambodia were green, gently rising mounds that didn't look capable of protecting against anything warlike. Vietnamese outposts were surrounded by menacing swirls of barbed wire, but in Cambodia barbed wire was used to make two neat rows of fencing around outpost perimeters — the wire looked capable of keeping out sheep but not the Khmer Rouge. Nor did Cambodian soldiers look imposing. They smiled broadly, something Vietnamese soldiers rarely did, and they carried their rifles without the cocksureness that Vietnamese displayed. Part of the trouble was simply physiognomy. With their high-cheekboned, angular features, Vietnamese faces conveyed dignity and decorum, while Cambodians' faces, all soft curves and roundnesses, suggested warmth and openness. No wonder Cambodian soldiers were reputed not to fight: they appeared suited not for combat but for sitting under the gloriously colored milkfruit or kapok or mango trees that Ang Kheao and I drove by.

Now the countryside was no longer accessible: the Khmer Rouge not only occupied most of it, but they'd cut most of the main roads from Phnom Penh, and an estimated 15,000 to 20,000 Khmer Rouge soldiers had massed within 25 miles of the capital. Most of us expected the Khmer Rouge to attack Phnom Penh soon after the bombing halt, a prospect the Americans were trying to ward off with last-ditch B-52 and tactical air assaults on positions close enough to the city to rattle windows at the Phnom. In case those blasts weren't unnerving enough, the Khmer Rouge periodically set off plastique and grenade explosions inside the city's movie theaters, yet such was the fatalism of the populace that movie attendance remained high. One of Lon Nol's disillusioned pilots even bombed the marshal's palace, but, typical of the Phnom Penh air force, missed the target.

For all that, it was hard to detect a crisis atmosphere at the FANK press information office, where military briefings were conducted, after a fashion. The colonel in charge, the marvelously and all-too-accurately named Am Rong, usually didn't even bother to attend; he just posted a note on a bulletin board, written in French, on which appeared vague references to armed conflict. At other times Am Rong was accompanied by his translator, Major Chhang Song, who despite his rank was only in his 20s. Chhang Song had earned his position on the strength of his English, which he'd perfected while matriculating at some university in the American South. He enjoyed displaying his knowledge of American culture to journalists, and sometimes introduced Am Rong as if he were Ed McMahon to the colonel's Johnny Carson: "And now, he-e-e-e-ere's Am Rong!" When Am Rong found out what Chhang Song was up to, Chhang Song was briefly demoted. But Chhang Song had the right idea about the briefings: their function was less the transmittal of military information than amusement. An outdoor bar, in fact, was located a few yards from the information office: the briefings were excuses for drinks.

In the face of that, who could take the collapse of Phnom Penh seriously? The crisis didn't frighten me, partly because the U.S. government promised to evacuate the press corps if events turned dire, partly because the downfall of the Khmer Republic was still abstract, close to unimaginable. Nevertheless, appearing with three other journalists on a discussion of the Cambodia situation for BBC radio, I predicted that Lon Nol would fall soon after the American bombing halt — we all did. It was odd to be speaking through a technology which reached many millions of people to predict Lon Nol's collapse, which no amount of technology, however vastly applied, seemed capable of preventing. Why was one task simple and the other impossible?

At 4:30 a.m. on August 6, an American B-52 crew committed a monumental error: it made a direct hit on Neak Leung, a town controlled by the Lon Nol regime. Word of the bombing reached the Phnom Penh press corps a few hours after the event, followed quickly by rumors that it had caused hundreds of civilian casualties and destroyed much of the town. With the bombing halt only nine days away, the debacle seemed especially poignant, and strengthened the arguments of those who'd

favored stopping the bombing long before. It made sense to try
to rush to Neak Leung immediately, particularly because U.S.
embassy officials were refusing to provide any information
about the accident, but the problems of getting there seemed
insurmountable. Neak Leung was only 40 miles southeast of the
capital, abutting the Mekong River, but the Khmer Rouge
blocked the road there, so that land transport was impossible,
and they occupied both river banks along the way, rendering a
boat trip exceedingly risky. I assumed that by going into Viet
Cong territory, I'd developed a reputation for bravado, and now
I wanted to defend it — the trouble was that I had no desire to
visit Neak Leung. Even in the unlikely event that a boat captain
could be convinced to go there, I told myself, a journalist would
still need an interpreter willing to risk his life, and Ang Kheao,
no daredevil, would certainly refuse. Was the lack of an interpreter a sufficient excuse?

I spent the day fretting. I was torn between leaving the
story to the wire services — they'd broken the news, after all—
and finding an angle, any angle, so that I could write about it.
But without going to Neak Leung, I had no information to justify a story — the U.S. embassy wouldn't even confirm that the
accident had taken place. I haltingly opted for finishing work on
another piece I'd started two days earlier.

Late that night several of us were chatting by the pool
when a call came from the U.S. embassy press spokesman. He
said that Col. David H. E. Opfer, the embassy air attaché, would
stop by the hotel in fifteen minutes to answer questions about
Neak Leung. This was bizarre. By remaining silent all day, then
convening an eleven p.m. poolside briefing on fifteen minutes'
notice, the embassy seemed to be trying to release as little information as it could to as few journalists as possible. Opfer himself
did nothing to dispel such suspicions: his mission seemed to be
to bat down estimates of 300 or more casualties that were already
circulating. Opfer, who'd gone by helicopter to Neak Leung that
morning and spent three hours there, called such estimates
"inflated," but he provided no statistics of his own. Pressed for a

figure, he said he thought the bombing caused perhaps 150 casualties, including 25 to 75 people killed, and "minimal" damage to
the town. The survivors, he said, "were sad, but they accepted
the fact that this is war."

    At that moment a voice rang out from behind us — it
was Schanberg, who'd just arrived. "I talked to a man in the hospital today who lost his legs," he bellowed, "and he didn't think
damage was 'minimal'!" So Schanberg had spent the day interviewing the wounded survivors who'd been transported to
Phnom Penh hospitals — that was what *I* should have done.
Schanberg took over the briefing. While the rest of us sat, he
paced back and forth, challenging every one of Opfer's claims,
displaying as much interest in lecturing Opfer as in asking him
questions. Opfer clearly was in no position to fight back: he was
the embassy's fall guy, sent over to put the best face on a disaster. Schanberg alone seemed to have the information to expose
Opfer's evasions, but the venom in his attack suggested he was
after bigger prey; as he interrogated Opfer, his white-flecked
beard seemed to bristle, and his eyes, relentlessly on the move
even in times of relative serenity, now flashed with anger. He
didn't appear simply interested in setting the record straight
about Neak Leung; he was intent on showing that Opfer was
barbarous, as if by doing so he could prove that the American
role in Cambodia was, too. Schanberg's magisterial confidence
filled me with envy, assuaged only by a suspicion breaching the
edges of my awareness that his performance was overkill. After
all, Neak Leung offered easy outrage because the victims were
on the wrong side, and Opfer was an inviting, defenseless target.
Schanberg's cross-examination went on for fifteen minutes
before the briefing ended.

    The next day the embassy announced revised casualty
figures. Far from Opfer's claim, the embassy said 137 people
were killed and 268 were wounded; 81 of the dead and 150 of the
wounded were civilians. One last time I surveyed the Phnom
Penh docks, hoping not to find a boat captain prepared to go to
Neak Leung, trying to satisfy myself that a journey there was

impossible. After a cursory search I felt reasonably certain that this was the case, and hurriedly left the scene, to avoid the risk of learning otherwise. Unfortunately, this tactic failed to deceive its intended target — me — for I spent the rest of the day wondering whether I might have found transportation to Neak Leung if my search had been more earnest.

Then that night a rumor spread, and soon it was confirmed: Schanberg and Dith Pran, his interpreter, had made the river journey that day, and returned with the sole eyewitness account of the bombing error's consequences. Schanberg had outperformed me; I felt shown up. I cheered up slightly when I heard that the New York *Times* ran Schanberg's story on an inside page, but I was nevertheless disturbed. Why had I been unwilling to go?

A few days later, driving down one of the main roads from Phnom Penh, Ang Kheao and I ran into a battle just three miles from the capital. The Khmer Rouge had just bitten off a few more miles of highway, and the FANK were trying to push them back. This sort of combat occurred frequently, and was generally inconsequential: if the Khmer Rouge stood their ground now, they might still decide to peel back during the night, or the FANK might cede the terrain now only to attack with a larger unit tomorrow — the front line here was as variable as the notorious moods of the exiled Prince Sihanouk.

I knew better than to risk my life for this. Instead, I stood two hundred yards behind the front line and peered down the road: it was like trying to watch a Cubs game on a rooftop across the street from Wrigley Field. Sometimes I caught sight of zigzag streaks of tracer rounds ricocheting in trees and white puffs of smoke demarcating mortar explosions. The sound of rifle fire was almost constant, until my ear heard the noise not as individual shots but as harsh waves, the aural equivalent of a pointillist painting — how could any soldier motivate himself to walk into that? Or any journalist — certainly this skirmish justi fied no risk. Yet some of my colleagues were at the front — an ambulance rushed by me, bearing a wounded journalist back to Phnom Penh, and by the time the fighting ended, an hour or two after it started, three more journalists were injured. Peter Arnett, an A.P. correspondent who'd won a Pulitzer Prize for his reporting from Vietnam, lurched out of the battle zone, sweaty and wild-eyed, with two cameras slung around his neck that he bore with as much bravado as weapons, and I thought of the Pulitzer I hoped to win for my Vietnam reporting. If I won it, I wondered, would I be satisfied, or would I, like him, forever feel compelled to prove I'd earned it?

As the August 15 bombing deadline approached, tension in Phnom Penh increased. Each day the airport was filled with wealthy Cambodians who paid bribes for exit visas and were leaving the country with as many personal belongings as they could manage. One day leaflets instructing residents on what to do when "the armed forces of the National Liberation of Cambodia enter Phnom Penh" appeared on the streets; the most ominous of the eight points it contained warned against giving refuge to Lon Nol's soldiers, or else "your life will be in danger." We all assumed we'd be evacuated before the Khmer Rouge were close to carrying out such threats, and indeed American officials alluded to an evacuation plan to be put in effect if the Lon Nol government collapsed. Non-American journalists, however, were told they didn't qualify for the evacuation and were urged to leave the country immediately. Most assumed embassy officials were bluffing, and stayed on.

My chief concern was figuring out how to file stories from Phnom Penh. I considered the local telegraph office unreliable, and in any event I hated to submit my stories to the unpredictable government censors who passed judgment on our stories before they were cabled. As a result, I double-filed — whenever I heard of a colleague leaving for Bangkok or Saigon, I gave him a second copy of my story to file at his destination. That way, I hoped, at least one complete version would reach Los Angeles. Now, faced with the possibility of an impending break-down in communications, we asked U.S. embassy officials to let us use their circuit if needed. They responded in the begrudging manner that characterized most of their interactions with the press, agreeing only to transmit a daily pool report of a few hundred words. The mere existence of the contingency plans implied that a cataclysm was near. Still, as imminent as a Khmer Rouge victory might be, the prospect seemed absurd, unreal. Food in the restaurants was still plentiful, and the hotel clerks continued to accept our personal checks. Did they know something we didn't?

On the eve of the bombing halt I visited In Tam, a political rival of Lon Nol who nevertheless became the marshal's prime minister, then discovered that he'd been given the job only because it commanded no authority. In Tam even behaved as if he were powerless: I was touched just by my ease in seeing him. I rang the bell at his residence and was led to an outdoor reception area where I joined a few Cambodians awaiting him. Together we listened to the rumble of distant air strikes, a sound which would disappear from Cambodia in half a day. After finishing his dinner, bald, graying In Tam shambled out. He wore sandals, which he slipped on and off while we talked, khaki pants, and a khaki shirt open at the collar. "We thank the American people for having helped us until now, for saving the situation," he said. "Without the United States, North Vietnam would have swallowed up little Cambodia." This was the Cambodian style: even in his abjection In Tam didn't denounce the U.S. for stopping the bombing. Although he still purveyed the hollow myth that his government's chief adversaries were North Vietnamese, not fellow Cambodians, I couldn't help feeling sympathy for him.

August 15 was anti-climactic. Far from preparing for an attack, the Khmer Rouge had eased pressure on Phnom Penh in

previous days, and FANK troops managed to loosen the enemy
noose around the capital. At 10:45 a.m. I was standing in a rice
field ten miles west of Phnom Penh when I saw two Phantom
jets dive and drop their bombs in the distance: they were the last
American bombers I saw in Cambodia. The Cambodians within
my field of vision failed to acknowledge the milestone. A woman
in a rice paddy performed the delicate maneuver of bathing
while keeping her sarong wrapped around her. I asked a peasant
what he thought of the bombing's end, and he said, "I have no
idea."

The military situation didn't change appreciably on the
15th, nor on the 16th or 17th — the only noticeable difference, in
fact, was that air strikes no longer interrupted our sleep. We figured that the Khmer Rouge were just resting, preparing for an
all-out assault on the capital. Still, they didn't have much time:
the rainy season, already building towards its end-of-the-year
crescendo, would bog them down before long.

I didn't mind waiting. Most Saigon journalists regarded
Cambodia as a step towards heaven, and looked forward to visits there as if they were holidays; even now, with a crisis looming, at times it seemed to me I was on vacation. Phnom Penh
was, among other things, a drug haven, where marijuana was on
sale in the central market and opium was provided at a den
famous throughout Indochina. The den, the only one in Asia I
ever heard of that catered specifically to Westerners, lured journalists, old French plantation owners, even a few reckless diplomats. It's indicative of journalists' priorities that despite being
professionally dedicated to uncovering whatever was illicit or
covert, none of us ever wrote about the place: if we had, it would
have ceased to exist.

I visited the den every week or two, attracted less by the
opium than by the den's cozy aura. It was located in a decep-
tively large house in a residential district a couple of miles from
the hotel. We entered through a side door, whispered *"bonjour"*

to Chantal, the Sino-Khmer proprietress, and undressed and put on sarongs, Cambodia's native costume. Chantal insisted that we all whisper because she was in constant fear of being arrested; her patrons considered her paranoid, citing as an example her decision to protect her wealth by investing it in diamonds which she had surgically embedded in her arm. The rear of the house was divided into several cubicles, each big enough for four or five people. We entered our assigned room and lay on straw mats. The sound of cicadas and croaking frogs outside mingled with the whines of a Cambodian opera on Chantal's radio. Eventually she appeared with the pipe, which she prepared in the flame of a kerosene lamp. Printed on the lamp's chimney was the word "Howdy" — the name of a local soft drink. The chimney had once been the upper two-thirds of a soda bottle; the bottom had been lopped off, and the remaining piece fit the lamp perfectly. In such manner were objects continually transformed in Southeast Asia.

I loved the idea of smoking opium. The act hinted of the illicit, of boldness and transcendence. It mocked my eighth grade science teacher, who said only drug addicts did anything so depraved; it mocked staid Gibson, Richard Nixon, the entire earthbound Establishment. At the same time, I was wary, for opium was, after all, a poison. Addicts consumed up to a hundred pipes of opium a day, and some aficionados among my colleagues smoked as many as ten, but two or three was ample for me — I wanted to be able to work the next day. In her clipped, heavily accented French, Chantal expressed scorn at my inability to consume the opium pipe's contents in one breath, as experienced smokers did. Then she retired to the front of the house and called in Arem, her young maid, to give us massages. Arem was not adept; she sat on her haunches, kneading my calves, until she fell asleep. After awakening with a start, she began again, and repeated the cycle two or three times before completing the massage. We lay on our mats, sipping Cokes, discussing the war, love affairs, the mysteries of Indochina. The opium made me feel warm and lithe, but it left my head clear: I didn't feel high, just inordinately comfortable. At the end of the evening, Chantal reappeared and toted up what each visitor owed her. For a few pipes, a massage, and soft drinks, the price was a couple of dollars.

By the time we left Chantal's, at eleven or midnight, the curfew had long since commenced. Our Western faces were our passports, giving us free passage through the police checkpoints, and we rode back to the hotel through deserted streets silvery with moonlight. On those nights, suspended in the half-sleep that opium addicts know well, my dreams were vivid. Once, for instance, I imagined myself in a luxuriant jungle reminiscent of Henri Rousseau; the palm fronds glistened with dew, and the tigers smiled.

Without American bombers the war returned to Cambodian proportions. It was as if we'd gotten it all wrong, as if the big powers' weaponry and preoccupation with geopolitics had obscured the modesty of the enterprise, so low-key it almost didn't deserve the title of war, so bizarre it sometimes seemed that Sgt. Bilko's platoon was fighting the Keystone Cops. One morning I went looking for combat. I drove down Route 4, one of the main roads from Phnom Penh, and after fifteen miles thought I'd located not war exactly but the promise of it. A lieutenant at a FANK command post told me that a battalion of FANK troops eight miles away had been surrounded and besieged by the Khmer Rouge for more than a week; the physical condition of the surrounded men was presumed to be worsening, for only one of three attempts at dropping food supplies to them had succeeded. Now FANK planners had decided to send a brigade to rescue them. I waited and waited for the action to begin, until finally the lieutenant informed me that there would be no operation after all. "The troops are very tired," he said. "We've had a lot of killed and wounded. We are taking a break today. Tomorrow we start." Around him soldiers dozed in hammocks.

I came back to the command post the next morning. By then another development had complicated the operation: before dawn the Khmer Rouge had cut Route 4 between the command post and one of the FANK brigade's forward units. This meant that before the brigade tried to rescue the besieged battalion, it would have to fight its way down the highway just to reunite with its own isolated unit.

By 10 a.m. about twenty armored personnel carriers and as many trucks loaded with soldiers were massed near the command post, but the operation didn't start: the APCs had no ammunition. General Ith Suong, the division commander, arrived at noon and berated his officers. "I told you yesterday to get ammunition," he said. "Why didn't you let me know last night that you didn't have any?" He instructed his logistics officer to go back to Phnom Penh to get it.

The ammunition arrived two hours later. At last the APCs and trucks churned their way down the road. Rifle and machine gun fire ripped the surrounding foliage. Using an American tactic called "reconnaissance by fire," FANK troops shot without actually seeing Khmer Rouge soldiers, without knowing whether they were causing any casualties. It was a tactic suited to the Americans, whose ammunition was plentiful, but now that supplies were limited, it was wasteful.

I tagged along behind the attacking soldiers. After taking cover at the base of a ridge, I noticed that a teenaged soldier next to me was wearing, of all things, a Mao button, the sort of button worn in China to indicate veneration for Communist Party Chairman Mao Tse-tung. I was astonished, for Mao wasn't exactly a hero in Phnom Penh. The soldier said he found it on the road that morning. Perhaps he thought of it as a pretty bauble: informed that the button indicated support for the Communists, the soldier giggled but continued to wear it.

As I walked back from the front, I passed a command post that Ith Suong had set up in the shell of a destroyed house. From there the sounds from the front suggested a momentous battle unfolding, but the general was oblivious: he lay stretched out on a lounge chair. I asked him for an interview, but he replied in French, "For the moment, excuse me — I am sick." A subordinate officer said he had a fever.

At least he wasn't inebriated, like the soldier I spotted next, staggering back from the front line. "There were hundreds of enemy!" he said with a drunk's slurred words and sweeping hand motions. "I don't know where they were shooting from!"

An officer told him, "You're drunk. Why do you stay here? I told you to go. Why don't you show some respect for me?" The soldier shuffled off.

Soon a man with curly hair almost a foot long was driven up to Ith Suong's command post in a jeep. Long hair was as unusual in the Cambodian army as it was in the American one, a fact reflected in the slack-jawed gapes of FANK soldiers, but this man was no hippie — he was a battalion commander. Another officer explained: "His grandfather and father did this, too. He believes that if he cuts his hair, he'll be in danger" — it was the Cambodian version of the myth of Samson.

More and more soldiers straggled back from the front line, as the battalion failed to break through to its forward element. An officer said something about trying again the next day, but by now no one even mentioned the surrounded battalion a few more miles down the road.

Still the Khmer Rouge didn't attack Phnom Penh — three weeks after the bombing halt it was clear they wouldn't attack until the rainy season ended in December. Perhaps the bombing before the August 15 deadline had been effective; in any event, the Khmer Rouge apparently had exhausted themselves before then. We'd all miscalculated: the regime would last at least through another rainy season.

Part of the reason we misjudged the Khmer Rouge was that we had virtually nothing to go on: the Khmer Rouge were so murkily perceived that U.S. embassy officials weren't even sure of the names of their leaders. Their composition was so vague I referred to them in stories as "Communist-led insurgents" instead of simply "Communists," as it was likely that some factions within them didn't embrace Communism. The turgid rhetoric which issued forth daily from the Khmer Rouge clandestine radio station implied that the leaders were firm Marxists, bloodthirsty at that, whose first official action upon taking power would be to execute the "seven traitors"— the seven men at the top of the Phnom Penh regime, starting with Lon Nol. This suggestion of Khmer Rouge ruthlessness was reinforced by the experience of Western journalists who'd accidentally crossed into their territory — the only ones to survive had been fortunate enough to fall into the hands of North Vietnamese troops. On the other hand, some officials in the Lon Nol government regarded the prospect of a Khmer Rouge victory with equanimity, as if the Khmer Rouge were just enlightened social democrats put off by Lon Nol's corruption. On my way to an interview with a Phnom Penh cabinet minister, I was amazed when the minister's aide stopped me to avow that his regime deserved to collapse, and that he didn't fear a Khmer Rouge victory — he compared them to French Resistance fighters during World War II. Who knew? Certainly not our editors, at the very least. A newsmagazine reporter received a cable asking for a photograph of a Cambodian village being overrun by the Khmer Rouge — he passed the cable around and we laughed. No such picture had been taken in the course of the war, since anyone who got that close to the Khmer Rouge faced execution for his efforts. The photographers in Phnom Penh were crazy, but not that crazy.

Instead of the Battle of Phnom Penh, we got the Battle of Kampong Cham, a dress rehearsal. Situated beside the Mekong River 50 miles northeast of the capital, Kampong Cham was the third largest city in Cambodia, but its fate would hardly determine the course of the war. From a military perspective, its most interesting attribute was that its physical layout was similar to

Phnom Penh's: both cities were bounded by lakes to the north
and south, the Mekong River to the east, and an airport a few
miles to the west. Furthermore, just as in Phnom Penh, the
Khmer Rouge controlled the terrain outside Kampong Cham
and were attacking Lon Nol's men entrenched inside it. This
gave rise to the suggestion among diplomats that the Khmer
Rouge were practicing for an assault on Phnom Penh a few
months hence. The battle, however, was not going as the Khmer
Rouge must have expected: with both sides having committed a
roughly equal number of troops, from 6,500 to 8,000 men each,
the FANK soldiers were holding onto the town. The various military attachés in Phnom Penh thought that perhaps the Khmer
Rouge had set up a "meat grinder," a battle whose purpose was
simply to kill large numbers of FANK troops. With characteristic
swagger and lack of judgment, the Australian military attaché,
who'd earlier predicted the Khmer Rouge assault on Phnom
Penh that hadn't materialized, proclaimed, "The reinforcements
will never come back."

Most of us considered the battle big stuff — we had to.
Having predicted the siege of Phnom Penh for so long, we felt
relieved to bear tidings of some kind of large-scale combat, even
if the arena was substantially less significant than the capital.
Once more, the question was how to cover the story, but as with
Neak Leung, means of travel were few and precarious. I thought
I should try to go to Kampong Cham, if only to atone for what I
perceived as my failure to reach Neak Leung, but I wasn't at all
sure that the story was worth the trouble. Had anyone in the U.S.
heard of Kampong Cham? Was I wise to risk death in a battle for
the third largest city in the second largest country in Indochina,
a region which in its entirety was barely larger than Texas?
Would my editors even play the story on the front page? I knew
the answer to all these questions almost certainly was no, but I
felt compelled to try to get to Kampong Cham nevertheless. All
too mindful of the acclaim that followed my journey into Viet
Cong territory, I felt like a boxer who has just won the title only
to discover that defending it is harder than winning it. My Viet

Cong coup created the impression that I was audacious; didn't I therefore have to display audacity every time an important story broke, regardless of the risk?

The only ways to get to Kampong Cham were by helicopter or river boat; going by land was out of the question. Barry Hillenbrand, a *Time* reporter, was the first to pull off the feat, apparently by using connections within the FANK to obtain helicopter transport there and back. He looked very pleased with himself when he returned, but the most noteworthy aspect of his achievement was not what he reported, but simply that he'd made the trip. I didn't mind too much: if I reached Kampong Cham in the next couple of days, my story would appear before the next issue of *Time* was published.

There was more pressure on Ron Moreau, who'd flown in from Saigon to cover the story: he felt he at least had to equal the coverage of his main competition, *Time*. Ron, a *Newsweek* stringer named Beth Becker, and I decided to go to Kampong Cham together. I understood perfectly well that Ron and Beth were more gung-ho than I was. I figured they'd work for me, in a sense: they'd supply the enthusiasm I lacked. Together we searched the Phnom Penh docks for a naval vessel bound for Kampong Cham, and had no trouble finding one: a World War II-style LST loaded with soldiers was leaving within half an hour. FANK ships were off-limits to journalists, so we took care to avoid the gaze of officers on the bank, and sneaked aboard.

Three Westerners couldn't easily hide on a vessel packed with Cambodian soldiers, and the ship's captain quickly discovered us. Instead of ejecting us, however, he extended a welcome. I deduced from his manner — economical in word and motion, dignified, calm — that he'd seen too much dying to care about petty rules. Now our passage was assured, but the longer we talked with the captain, the less I wanted to go. Points along both banks of the Mekong were controlled by the Khmer Rouge, who would undoubtedly fire at us. The captain pointed to dents made by Khmer Rouge M-60 rounds the day before, when the LST returned from Kampong Cham. Three men were wounded in that attack, he said. I thought we'd be lucky to make the passage upriver with as few casualties, for the ship struck me as a distressingly vulnerable target. I looked for a spot where I'd feel safe, but I couldn't find any. Soldiers were even sitting on ammunition boxes, which were scattered helter-skelter around the ship. I couldn't stop imagining a Khmer Rouge shell landing on the deck. In that case, I thought, we'd all be killed.

The poor soldiers didn't even have proper equipment. Their uniforms were tattered, few wore boots, and fewer had helmets. Given their perilous circumstances, I expected them to be contemplative, even mournful, just as I was, in acknowledgment of the reality that some soon would die. On the contrary, these men acted blithely, even inanely. One kept saying to us, over and over again, *"Excusez-moi, monsieur"* — it was the only phrase he knew in a foreign language. Another frequently requested to have his picture taken. We obliged him a couple of times, then grew weary of him. I searched for some acknowledgment from Ron or Beth that they were as prepared to walk off the LST as I was, but though they admitted fear, their determination to go was unshaken. How could I leave if they were courageous enough to stay?

Worse, as the day wore on and the ten-minute wait stretched to several hours, the soldiers began to celebrate, with an intensity that horrified me. They weren't celebrating anything in particular — they were just in a boisterous mood. Many got drunk. Two men made a joke of playing catch with a hand grenade. One pranced about the ship like a wild animal, his head covered with a dragon-like mask. In the center of the deck a man played a harmonica, and another fashioned a six-foot-long one-stringed instrument and plucked it as if it were a bass violin. A dozen soldiers danced to the music, so frenetically that the scene looked like some ancient instinctual ritual. While onlooking soldiers giggled delightedly, the dancers became sexually suggestive. They bumped and grinded, and two ended by by embracing and, amid hollers, kissing.

The soldiers might as well have been from another planet for all the connection I felt to them. Were they noble and fearless, spitting in death's eye, or were they just trying to take their minds off the fate awaiting them? And why was I the only one on the ship feeling dread, the same dread I'd experienced in Dong Ha a year and a half earlier? I thought I'd outgrown that feeling, but here it was again, an old and unwanted companion. It was older than Dong Ha, older, in fact, than my stay in Indochina: it brought me back twenty years, to the hospital where my parents had deposited me without explanation when I had polio. Then, as now, I'd felt trapped, surrounded by strangers in frenzied, death-haunted motion. The captain hauled up the landing platform, and we prepared to embark. Then, unexpectedly, I was granted a reprieve, as someone had discovered a mechanical problem. We were all sent off the ship. We'd try again tomorrow.

I shouldn't have returned the next day, but I was too ashamed of my fear to admit it. Instead, I clung to the faint hope that we'd find the LST permanently incapacitated. No such luck: when we returned to the docks, the ship was deemed fit, and we reboarded without difficulty. The soldiers still exuded anarchy, but this time there was no delay. It wasn't until we were moments from departure that I knew I couldn't go through with the journey — I stood up and said I wanted to debark. A Cambodian officer on shore realized I'd sneaked aboard, and asked angrily whether any other journalists were with me. Ron and Beth glared at me, then reluctantly stepped out from their hiding places. The officer ordered them to join me on the bank. They were furious with me, and I couldn't blame them, but their anger couldn't touch the awareness I'd forced on myself: I was no daredevil after all.

I understand now that there is another way of looking at my failure of nerve, which is that whatever lessons of passage awaited discovery on that LST, I'd already derived from my trip to Viet Cong territory; this journey promised to be only an echo of that more momentous one. At the time, however, I could find no consolation for my behavior, and for the next few days I mourned. What did I have to offer my profession if not a willingness to take risks? I wrote a story about the soldiers' antics on the ship, and sent it to Los Angeles accompanied by this spare, forlorn message: "As is obvious from piece, I did not make it to Kampong Cham, and prospects now appear all but nil."

I was wrong; we all got to Kampong Cham two days later anyway. By then the Phnom Penh regime felt certain of victory, and arranged a helicopter flight for about twenty of us to show off the success to the world. There was no longer a question of exclusivity: we all tied for second, behind Hillenbrand.

Kampong Cham didn't look much different from other cities once war had churned through them. It reeked of death. We saw bloated bodies, leveled residential blocks, charred ruins. Near our helicopter pad, waiting to be evacuated, a few soldiers lay dazed on blood-soaked stretchers, and a little girl, too weak to brush away the flies dining on her wounds, lay on the ground. All the wounded were bound for hospitals in Phnom Penh, but even though we had room on our helicopter, none came with us. Instead, a few uninjured civilians did. Just before we left Kampong Cham, we saw them giving money to Am Rong.

Until now I'd gotten by on the illusion that Cambodia was an extension of Vietnam, with an equivalent lode of intensity and front page stories. Once the Battle of Kampong Cham ended, however, the hollowness of that conceit was revealed. To my astonishment, the discovery disturbed me less than I expected, for it was accompanied by a compensating realization: what Cambodia lacked in worldwide significance, it made up for in the pleasure it afforded me. War or no, I was beginning to like the place. I took a quick jaunt to Bangkok, and found myself looking forward to returning to Phnom Penh. When I returned, even the hotel roomboys, beguilingly awkward in their white uniforms and hopelessly worn-out European shoes, looked happy to see me. The sun still shone, the bougainvillea still bloomed, and the Khmer Rouge offensive was still just the Australian military attaché's mean-spirited fantasy. Maybe the FANK would repel the Khmer Rouge forever; maybe the two armies were both muddled, too weak to knock each other out. I was surprised at how much this prospect pleased me.

With Cambodia returned to its customary news status, subordinate to Vietnam, the press corps was whittled down to the hardcore few who permanently resided in Phnom Penh. Their eccentricities were so pronounced I felt uneasy about being associated with them; even going at half-speed, I thought I deserved to be identified with the comparatively more wholesome types in Saigon, who subscribed to the reassuring credo that stories alone bestowed meaning. By contrast, to some Phnom Penh journalists, stories were a permanent sidelight — the peculiar appeal of Cambodia came first. It wasn't just the easy availability of drugs, though that was part of it; the journalists shared a lethal attraction to Cambodia, as if they walked close to the abyss, dared to look into it, connected with the idea of entropy which Cambodia embodied. Most of them weren't particularly on a quest for acclaim, and some held a tenuous grip even on survival. I once heard Cambodia compared with Haiti, and though I doubted the two countries really had much in common, in one sense they seemed to: Haiti meant voodoo, and Cambodia was a voodoo land, a step beyond Vietnam into the unknown, a zone where not just religion but spirituality and even spirits still reigned, where soldiers entered battle clutching Buddha-like amulets in their mouths to ward off danger, and where astrologers had great influence, over Lon Nol as much as anyone else. It was a country where combatants ate enemy corpses to gain their foes' strength, and where, on a memorable night a couple of years earlier, FANK troops in Phnom Penh fired thousands and thousands of rifle shots at no apparent target — the abruptly awakened residents were terrified until they realized that the soldiers were aiming straight up, trying to shoot down the moon. It was Buddha-consciousness gone amok, chaos with a difference. There was an anarchy of voodoo abroad in Cambodia.

Even then, in the era before "Cambodian auto-genocide" was a phrase that carried weight, it seemed to some of us that Cambodian civilization was near the end of the line. Cambodia had reached its apex in the thirteenth century with the construction of the Angkor temples, but the enterprise was so vast and costly that the country never regained its economic bearings. Some historians believed that only the advent of French colonialism in the nineteenth century prevented the collapse of Khmer society and its absorption into some more energetic culture such as Vietnam's. Now that the French and their handpicked successor, Prince Sihanouk, were gone, it appeared that the disintegration was again gathering momentum, a fact reflected in the decreasing authority of the central government and a mysterious halt in Cambodia's population growth.

Appropriately, the resident journalist in some ways most in tune with Cambodia was Denis Cameron, whom Nick Proffitt casually called "Mr. Death." This appellation alluded to something more profound than Cameron's gaunt, Reaper-like appearance; the country's decay seemed to set off sympathetic vibrations within him. An expert freelance photographer and cameraman, he divided his time between Vietnam and Cambodia, even though he would have made much more money if he'd stayed in Vietnam. He didn't seem particularly interested in money, however: Cambodia had an overriding claim on him. Like so many other Westerners beguiled by the country, he seemed to regard himself as a protector of the innocent Cambodians, and took in two homeless Khmer children. Still, having made this gesture in the direction of fatherhood, again and again he streaked in the other direction, by placing himself in situations of extreme danger, as if courting death. Perhaps because his connection with darkness was so resonant, he understood long before the rest of us that the Khmer Rouge were monsters. When he expressed such views, I tuned him out, and not just because he sounded then like a garden-variety anti-

Communist: it seemed to me that he enjoyed the idea of Khmer Rouge loathsomeness.

Even Cameron's sense of humor tended towards the mordant. A heavy pot smoker, he was fond of hosting large dinners whose main course, couscous, was laced with the stuff. The meals were legendary among journalists throughout Indochina, but not to Richard Moose, the U.S. Senate Foreign Relations Committee staff member, and his colleague, Jim Lowenstein; having received an invitation from Cameron during one of their Southeast Asia swings, they unknowingly consumed their entrées and then fell sick. Once the dinner's key ingredient was revealed to them, they became furious with Cameron.

Their anger paled besides that of the First Secretary of the Burmese Embassy in Phnom Penh, whose 19-year-old daughter Cameron secretly married, to the astonishment of us all. The diplomat's response was to whisk his daughter back to a secret location in Rangoon, where he presumed Cameron would never find her. Cameron made several trips to Rangoon to fetch her, and when these failed he concocted elaborate plots, some involving rugged journeys through the Burmese jungle, and then he lost interest. The girl eventually managed to leave Burma on her own, but by this time Cameron would have nothing to do with her, even though their brief union had produced an infant son. Instead, he took up with a Dutch woman whose most notable feature was a ring she wore depicting a couple having sex.

Cameron wasn't even the most erratic personality among Phnom Penh's journalists; that distinction belonged to Al Rockoff. An Army photographer in Vietnam, Rockoff decided to try freelancing and moved to Phnom Penh instead of coming home when his tour was over. He dressed like a hippie GI, which perhaps described what he'd been. His hair was parted down the middle and tied with a rubber band in back. He seemed to have only one shirt, a green army T-shirt, which he wore along with fatigue pants or cut-off jeans. Just after he received one of his several wounds, this one in his leg, the cut-offs left visible his scar, unbandaged though unhealed, and the fly or two that occasionally alit on it.

When not taking pictures, Rockoff sat by the pool, smoking grass and scowling. He was as close to being constantly stoned as anyone I ever met: he once announced that he was going to cut down on marijuana consumption, and then explained that this meant he wouldn't smoke more than one joint per day. Even that regimen   didn't last long. Alerted by the slow, dreary monotone he spoke in, some people thought the marijuana had permanently harmed him. Maybe it had, for he seemed barely alive. He spoke infrequently, and when he did, it was usually to register a complaint or an accusation. He was convinced, for example, that the waiters at the Phnom continually cheated him, and made fusses over his restaurant bills so regularly that some colleagues refused to sit with him.

I thought surely that Rockoff's rigid, deadpan manner was a put-on, a Buster Keaton imitation, but I understand now that I was wrong: Rockoff was dangerously paranoid. Alone among journalists I knew, he even armed himself: to the distress of Monsieur Lu, the hotel manager, he kept a grenade in his room. Monsieur Lu asked him a couple of times to remove it from the hotel, but Rockoff didn't respond. Next Monsieur Lu tried writing a letter. Rockoff was sufficiently perplexed or amused — I couldn't tell which — to show the document around. The neatly hand-written missive read as follows:

> Dear Mr. Rockoff:
>   I have asked the room boy about the
> hand grenade and he said it is still in your
> room. Will you please remove it as quickly as
> possible? It's dangerous!
>   L.

When Rockoff still did not remove the grenade, Monsieur Lu took unilateral action. A few days after Rockoff received the letter, Beth Becker told me she saw two roomboys gingerly carrying a grenade down the stairs, through the lobby, and out of the hotel.

Rockoff's chief asset as a photographer seemed to be his doggedness in battle. He barely scraped together a living by selling combat pictures to the wire services. The only thing I knew about his technique was based on a complaint voiced by Philip Jones Griffiths, one of the best photographers to cover the war. Griffiths said that on the one occasion he and Rockoff went to the front together, Rockoff watched Griffiths shoot a picture, then stood in the same spot, used the same lens, and pointed his camera in the same direction to take *his* picture — it was the photographic version of plagiarism. Still, I doubt Rockoff was interested in becoming a great photographer. Photography was simply the trade he'd learned in the army, instead of auto mechanics or mail sorting. What drew him to Phnom Penh was the latitude the place gave to aberrant behavior. He'd found a nest: he was local color, a character. I thought even that was more than he'd ever aspired to be.

No matter how long they'd been in Phnom Penh, the regulars all looked as if they'd been in Cambodia too long, as if the country had subverted their ambition or diverted it into unalloyed obsession. Unlike Vietnam, Cambodia was more often journalists' dead end than their proving ground. James Fenton, for example, was an eccentric Englishman who wrote essays for the *New Statesman* while wandering through Asia. Once he reached Cambodia, however, he ceased wandering: he took up residence in Phnom Penh (for a time living in a hotel room with a monkey), acquired an extra job as a stringer so he'd have enough money to live, and sent whimsical, brilliant dispatches back to London. When the war ended, he abandoned journalism for poetry: indeed, he eventually became one of Britain's leading poets, whose lofty reputation was based partially on poems about Cambodia.

Fenton's frequent reporting partner was a Tasmanian named Neil Davis, another gentle, talented man whose head was turned by Cambodia. Like Cameron, he probably would have benefited professionally by staying in Vietnam, but he couldn't leave Cambodia alone — the country was all but his second home. In some sense Davis was Cameron's double, his obverse, attracted not to Cambodia's morbidity but to its grace. Soft-spoken, looking much younger than his 40-odd years, he had more Cambodian friends than any other journalist in Phnom Penh, and was deeply distressed by the country's tribulations. A skilled cameraman and reporter, he had an unerring military instinct that enabled him again and again to perceive danger just in time to avoid it, but not before he'd obtained fine combat footage. Davis survived the Indochina conflict despite taking innumerable risks: years later, he was killed in the streets of Bangkok while covering a Thai coup attempt that was extinguished in a day.

Many of the other regulars were on their first reporting jobs. Sarah Webb Burrell, whose tiny Betty Boop voice was in comic contradiction to her lust-provoking appearance, had the most dubious credentials of all. She'd arrived in Phnom Penh as the girlfriend of a *Time* magazine photographer. Then, before he left for a brief trip to Saigon, he loaned her a camera so that she could learn photography. A profession wasn't all she pursued, however; when he returned, he learned that she'd bedded some of his colleagues, and indicated his displeasure by tossing the loaned camera into the pool, much to the glee of media onlookers. This deterred Sarah neither from photography nor promiscuity: she became a noted late-night nude swimmer, a juggler of journalistic paramours, and a published photographer (whose work, not coincidentally, appeared chiefly in her bedpartners' publications).

Presiding over us all was Schanberg, the press corps' paragon and yet its biggest exception. Schanberg was perhaps the only journalist in Phnom Penh who was neither a backsliding veteran nor a beginner, the only one riding the crest of his talent and career. In his late 30s, he'd already been narrowly passed over, in many people's view unjustly, for a Pulitzer Prize for his reporting during the 1971 India-Pakistan war; now he was assumed to be on the Pulitzer's trail once more. He was intense, volatile, unscrupulous, obsessed with documenting what he considered to be America's evil foreign policy in Cambodia. His pieces earned him the wrath of U.S. embassy officials, who frequently denounced him to the rest of us, yet he somehow continued turning out stories whose sources could only have been employed inside the embassy. His preoccupation with American policy, in fact, was what separated him from the rest of us, more than his ambition or talent did: unlike most of us, he never talked about Cambodia's charms, as if he hadn't noticed them, and his stories focused on the American role in Cambodia, not the country itself. It was as if he lacked a feel for Cambodia, as if he were too hard and the country too soft. I perceived the blind spot, but I didn't think it mattered: I was in awe of Schanberg. In his persistence and courage, his sense of mission, he was who I hoped to be.

For a time I had an American companion among the hotel's boarders. I loved her room, homey and feminine and filled with plants, in contrast to my much starker one. I got accustomed to Tonle Sap, the resident gecko, so named by us because its usual hiding place was behind a wall map of Cambodia, approximately at the spot where the great expanse of the Tonle Sap Lake appeared. The gecko earned its keep: about the only time we saw it was when it darted out from behind the map to consume a small insect. We acquired a black kitten found on a battlefield, and called it Front Line; it lived up to its name by racing ferociously around the room and caroming off walls. After it got older and calmed down, we renamed it Desk Job. As the rainy season took hold, I found it increasingly easy to stop working in mid-afternoon, then spend the rest of the day amid the gecko, the cat, the plants, and my companion, smoking dope, talking, and listening to the distant melodic street sounds that wafted up to the room.

Sometimes we got stoned and went on long pedicab

rides through Phnom Penh, allowing the emanations of the capital to wash over us. After leaving the hotel we went down a broad green esplanade, passing a musty French library, the decaying Cercle Sportif, and the residence of the French embassy first secretary, who could sometimes be heard assuaging his tensions in sessions of classical piano. Eventually we reached a hillock, or "phnom," from which the capital derived its name. Dating from the fifteenth century, it rose symmetrically to a point perhaps a hundred feet above the surrounding terrain. On top was a Buddhist temple where sensuous relief sculpture of dancing girls loomed out of stone; a staircase bounded by sculptured nagas, or serpents, led to the ground below. We caught glimpses of Buddhist monks padding around the temple, then continued on to the river bank and the royal palace, which, though unoccupied, was still the locale for daily rehearsals of the Cambodian royal ballet. Pedalled down wide avenues surrounded by graceful buildings and flowering trees, beneath magnificent clouds whose rain bathed the city once a day, I had no eyes for conflict. The women wore bright sarongs; the monks were gentle and quaint; my driver sang to himself. I'd turned a corner away from war.

LANDING
Chapter

7

My tour was over. After two years in Indochina, I left Phnom Penh in mid-December, bound for a home leave in the U.S. and eventual reassignment. I was as excited as any GI short-timer: I was returning to the World. Colleagues experienced in home leaves warned me that Indochina was the last subject most Americans wanted to talk about, that I'd be disappointed if I imagined people wanted to hear my tales — I believed these admonitions, but I was too haunted to heed them. What experience in the staid States could compare with mine? Wasn't I a war hero, or, more precisely (and better still), an anti-war hero? Besides, I had expectations of recognition: Gibson told me he was nominating me for a Pulitzer.

I felt deflated as soon as I arrived home. Los Angeles looked dim. Nothing moved, except in a predictable way; the city, the whole country, was impossibly tidy and drab. No matter whom I met, I wanted to explain that I'd-been-wounded-gone-into-Viet-Cong-territory-been-expelled-from-Vietnam, but I could see the boredom in my listeners' eyes after a sentence or two. How could the war be *boring*? To me, everything else was: the war had settled over my mind like lava, and nothing else would grow.

Gibson and I agreed on my next assignment, New Delhi,

but since the bureau there wouldn't need a replacement for six months, I was sent to Washington in the interim; the twenty-plus reporters in the bureau there needed reinforcements to cover two big stories, Watergate and the energy crisis. *Good*, I thought, *I like crises*.

Washington reporters were as consumed by Watergate as I'd been by Indochina, but I couldn't match their enthusiasm — I had trouble believing in the direness of any crisis in which no one died and whose principal actors wore coats and ties. I tried to get excited about my assignment, the energy crisis, but by then it was technicians' fodder, featuring discussions of the contrasting properties of petroleum, coal, and nuclear reactors: as long as I covered it I felt as if I had a cold, and yearned for the chance to write about what I saw with my eyes. The war was still my reference point, my glory, yet my new colleagues behaved as if Indochina were nearly off the planet. I thought they were as provincial as the Chinese emperors who believed they surveyed the world from its exact center.

My award nominations comprised my silent rejoinder: few of the bureau reporters gave evidence of having read my Indochina stories, or any Indochina stories for that matter, but I thought they'd take notice if I won an award. I did better than that: I won two. Gibson called to say I'd won a citation from a foreign correspondents' club, and soon afterwards I received a letter saying I'd won an award for foreign reporting given by a journalism society. Of the three prizes I'd been nominated for, only the big one, the Pulitzer, remained to be announced.

At the journalism society's banquet I wore a tag that said in big red letters above my name, "WINNER." As much as I appreciated being so considered, I couldn't get used to the idea: I felt defanged, co-opted, officially approved but secretly scorned. The dinner was held in Williamsburg, Virginia, on premises evoking American colonial life by way of Howard Johnson's Motor Inns, fife-and-drum corps mixed with modern plumbing, and I suspected that I was somehow being sanitized, just as Williamsburg had been. I'd won an award for stories about a war, after all, yet here everyone was so cheerful that conflict itself seemed discredited. I gave a short talk about my most notable war experiences, then sat down to a black-tie dinner with a table full of Virginians. They treated me with exquisite delicacy — in deference to me, one man referred to the "N.L.F." instead of the "Viet Cong" for what I was certain was the first time in his life — but I felt merely patronized. It was the old story about not wanting to be a member of any club misguided enough to include me: I was sure my dining companions were hawks.

The event's organizers kept reminding us that at the awards ceremony we winners were to take our awards in our left hand while shaking the presenter's hand with our right — they seemed to look on us as precocious children who might not be able to perform both tasks at once. Yet I couldn't deny that receiving the award was pleasurable. When it was my turn, a hostess led me across a darkened stage, a spotlight was focused on me, and the audience applauded, while my stories were flashed on a screen behind me — it was like winning an Oscar. Once the awards were handed out, all the recipients were gathered on the stage and given a standing ovation. By then I thought the organizers understood journalists rather well.

That night, lodged in a Williamsburg hotel room, my date and I took LSD. The drug induced the euphoria that the awards ceremony failed to. The day's events now struck us as hilarious, and we gave in to fits of laughter. We would have spent the entire night laughing, except that at 2 a.m. someone in the next room pounded on our wall. I envisioned this headline— "AWARD WINNER NABBED IN DRUG RAID" — and even though I was genuinely fearful, it took us hours to stop giggling over that. Even as we checked out of the hotel the next morning, we couldn't contain our laughter, but no one seemed to notice, and we left unimpeded. We drove back to Washington while still on LSD.

The big one, the Pulitzer, was announced a week later. On that day, a Monday, I discreetly scanned the bureau wire service teletype machine again and again — I must have read the wire half a dozen times in two hours. When the winner's name appeared there, I stared at it longingly, trying to imagine a typo. Then I returned to my desk. *I will never be fulfilled,* the voice said. A colleague told me she was sorry I hadn't won. I said I really hadn't expected to.

Just before departing for India, in late June, I returned to Los Angeles for a short visit home. On my second day there my father, after playing tennis at his club, lay down to rest on a locker room bench, something he'd never done before. He came home, asked the maid to make him lunch, and turned on the television in his bedroom. The jolt came a few minutes later. The maid found him on the floor next to his chair, unconscious. She awoke my mother, who sought out the household's long-time boarder, a nurse. The nurse applied artificial respiration. I was playing tennis at a friend's house. I got a phone call from my sister's husband saying that my father was seriously ill, and that I should return home immediately. Driving home, I felt nothing. I entered the house, went upstairs, and found paramedics violently pushing on my father's chest to get his heart started. Despite the commotion, my father even now was by himself, for my mother, leery as always of emergency, of need, stayed in the refuge of her separate bedroom. I watched from the doorway for perhaps a minute, and then I went into my room to change clothes. By the time I'd finished, my father had been borne into an ambulance and taken to the hospital. The maid asked if she could eat my father's salad.

I drove my mother to the hospital. The nurse at the front desk wouldn't give us any news; she just ushered us into an empty waiting room. A few minutes later the family doctor walked in. "He's gone," the doctor said. Then he offered us tranquilizers. My mother took one. Neither of us cried. My mother talked briefly with the doctor about the cause of death — a heart attack — and then we left.

As we walked to the car, my mother said, "You don't care, do you?" It hadn't taken her long to unsheathe her knives, but the malice in her question was less apparent to me then than my conviction that I must be guilty of something. But what? Long before my father died, continents, planets, galaxies already separated him from me; his death only made the condition permanent. Nothing had changed: I'd been grieving for as long as I could remember. I didn't answer my mother. I didn't know what to say.

People kept offering me consolation in the days that followed, but I thought I didn't need it: to me it was just one more death. At a memorial gathering for my father, his law partner eulogized him. The partner said that considering my father's fastidiousness, it was appropriate that he died on June 30, the last day of the fiscal year.

The Subcontinent was my new configuration of extremes, my peacetime equivalent of Indochina. I was adrift in a sea of calamity: drought, floods, famine, and disease were my staples. In India people stole postage stamps off unmailed letters, and children were maimed to make them more effective beggars. It didn't take long to find my journalistic coordinates: interviews with mothers holding starving babies in their arms got good play, stories about the population growth that caused the starvation didn't. Very few stories made the front page: the conventional wisdom was that Americans weren't interested in the Subcontinent. The connection I'd felt to my readers, tenuous in Indochina, now seemed entirely severed: I sent my accounts of suffering into the ether, and they rebounded on me. The sensation wasn't entirely uncomfortable. India swallowed me up in its maternal embrace, until, fetus-like, I began to doubt that any other bond was vital. At night I retreated to my bedroom and my stash of hashish.

I followed the war through the newspapers. The two American-backed regimes clung to power just as before, earnestly in Thieu's case, haphazardly in Lon Nol's. Then, on the first day of 1975, the Khmer Rouge launched a new offensive, and within weeks the collapse of Lon Nol's government appeared imminent. Phnom Penh itself became perilous: in the first two months of the offensive the Khmer Rouge fired a thousand rockets into the city, causing 750 casualties and disrupting resupply operations at the airport. The papers said everything was in short supply: ammunition for the soldiers, blood for the wounded, food for the swollen populace. Sometimes, imagining the drama in Phnom Penh and the trove of front page stories I'd find there, I thought of volunteering to return, but I always decided not to: I'd gotten accustomed to not being shot at.

At four o'clock in the morning of March 6, the phone at my New Delhi bedside rang. I was half-asleep when I answered, but once I realized Gibson was on the line I got wide awake: I knew immediately why he was calling. For once he skipped asking me the time, a subject of unceasing interest to him in previous conversations because the difference between Los Angeles and New Delhi time, eleven and a half hours, perplexed him. McArthur was in a Saigon hospital with a perforated ulcer, Gibson said; he therefore wanted me to take McArthur's place in Phnom Penh. Gibson didn't quite order me to go — he said that since I was no longer stationed in a war zone I could refuse — but his request drove a wedge through my ambivalence. For a few seconds I lay in the darkness, wincing at the realization that I'd soon be under the rockets. I tried to console myself with the thought that I'd nearly volunteered for this. Then I said, "Okay, I'll go."

Once that was settled, Gibson wanted off the phone: I had to think fast to remember the questions I needed to ask him. First, considering that the Khmer Rouge were likely to capture Phnom Penh, how long did he want me to stay there, and under what circumstances should I leave? Gibson said I should depart in the final American evacuation; on the grounds that remaining would be too risky, he forbade me from sticking around to witness the first days of Khmer Rouge rule. It wasn't quite what I wanted to hear, as I would have preferred making the decision on my own, but I figured now wasn't the time to object.

Second, since commercial flights into Phnom Penh had just been suspended, how did he suggest I get there? The question seemed to annoy him. He answered blithely that I should take an American military flight from Thailand. Didn't he know that journalists hadn't been allowed on such flights for years? Oh well — I'd get to Phnom Penh somehow.

Third, considering that recent fighting had already once forced the temporary closure of Cambodia's communications facilities, did Gibson have any ideas on how I could file stories? He didn't see any problem there, either — he said I should just give my copy to the Reuters correspondent in Phnom Penh. He was alluding to the *Times'* arrangement with the Reuters news agency, by which Reuters bureaus around the world transmitted *Times* stories to Los Angeles, but he'd apparently forgotten that the agreement didn't apply to Phnom Penh, where Reuters reporters faced the same obstacles the rest of us did. My suspicions were confirmed: Gibson hadn't been following events in Cambodia. Once I arrived in Phnom Penh, I'd have left any realm that *Times* editors understood. I got off the phone and went back to bed, but I didn't sleep soundly again for weeks.

A day later I was in Bangkok, trying to find a plane that would take me to Phnom Penh. The only commercial aircraft still flying there belonged to Air Cambodge, the national airline, and its last scheduled flight had been cancelled because of shelling at Pochentong, the airport outside Phnom Penh. Airline officials held out hope that the next day's flight would proceed, but that struck me as implausible: I couldn't imagine FANK troops pushing the Khmer Rouge out of shelling range of the airport in twenty-four hours, or twenty-four days for that matter. Nevertheless, I gathered supplies for the intended journey — my hastily assembled assortment included film, notebooks, peanut butter and jelly, *pâté de foie*, and candles — and appeared at the Bangkok airport the next morning.

I didn't really expect to leave Bangkok: I counted on being able to cable Gibson that night that all routes to Phnom Penh were blocked. Just as I thought, the flight was delayed — I waited in the airport for one hour, two hours, three hours past the scheduled departure time. An airline employee said the Khmer Rouge were shelling the runway, and I relaxed — faced with that prospect, surely no plane would take off. Then, just as I was contemplating which Bangkok hotel to register in that night, the flight was announced. I couldn't believe it. Even as I walked through customs, I assumed there'd been a mistake, and listened for an announcement rescinding it. I listened until I was inside the airplane and we were on our way to Phnom Penh.

Considering my uneasiness, the flight wasn't all that bad. The plane was mostly empty, as many more people wished to get out of Cambodia than into it. I recognized a few journalists, and figured the other passengers were war profiteers — who else would board such a flight? After all, at the end of it waited the Khmer Rouge, whose rockets and artillery in the past two months had struck one plane as it was landing, nearly hit another, and killed an airport worker. The closer we got to Phnom Penh, the more nervous I became. Pochentong was a few miles outside Phnom Penh; government troops controlled the road between the airport and the city limits, but all the surrounding terrain belonged to the Khmer Rouge. Since an ordinary descent would have taken the plane low over Khmer Rouge territory, exposing it to fire, instead it began its descent while directly over the capital. The plane hurtled downward on a nearly vertical trajectory, as the pilot dipped one wing, then the other — it was called the "falling leaf" approach. We bounced jarringly on the runway, then quickly stopped. In place of the usual end-of-flight speech, the stewardess wished us good luck — such generosity of spirit came easily to her, as she was flying back to Bangkok.

We hurried out of the plane, donned helmets and flak jackets handed to us by an attendant, and boarded a bus — in a reversal of the usual procedure, we were to be driven into the city before going through immigration. To save time, the driver had left the bus' engine idling, but then he got into a heated conversation with an airport worker, and we ended up waiting on the tarmac after all. Despite everything, I was amused; I kept thinking, "How Cambodian!" The airport looked deserted; the only people there were essential to getting planes into the air, and they spent much of their time in bunkers. At last we got started. The bus hurtled down the highway at breakneck speed, and didn't slow down until we were out of the rocket zone. By then we were nearly inside the city limits.

I felt odd walking back into the Phnom's lobby, an outsider in a place that felt more intimate to me than my family home. Yet there were Schanberg and Rockoff and Cameron and Davis and Fenton, all right where I'd left them, still playing the parts my mind had cast for them the previous year and more. They greeted me almost without surprise, as if I'd been expected back: the collapse of Phnom Penh was our reunion. It wasn't just *our* reunion: the crisis had attracted Indochina hands from Saigon, Bangkok, Vientiane, Hong Kong, New Delhi, London, New York, wherever they happened to be biding their time. Every generation of Vietnam correspondents was represented, going back to the early '60s; somebody even figured out that the entire U.P.I. Saigon bureau of 1966 was reunited, its members now employed by disparate news organizations. The presence of so many familiar faces was calming, but it was a newcomer, an Australian named Anthony Paul, who focused my mind on the inevitability of upheaval. Paul was gathering information for a planned book about "the success of the evacuation" and its "hero," U.S. Ambassador John Gunther Dean. When I heard that, I was apoplectic. "What if the evacuation isn't successful?" I asked him. "What if Dean is no hero?" In that case, he said, he wouldn't write a book.

        Hardly any of the diplomats I knew were still around, as
most of the embassies had closed down or cut their staffs to the
bone. My companion was gone, too — for old time's sake I
peeked in her room, but without the plants and wall map and
Tonle Sap and Front Line/Desk Job it just startled me with its
bleakness. So did the rest of the hotel — it looked like an old-
time movie star who'd turned so dowdy that makeup only high-
lighted her aged features. The phones had been removed from
the rooms and the air conditioners might as well have been: fuel
was in such short supply that electric power flowed only for a
few hours every other day. Water was rationed, too: if I wanted
a bath when I came back from the dusty roads in the late afternoon, I had to leave the bathtub taps open in the morning and
entrust the roomboys with closing them after the water started
flowing at midday. Hot water was out of the question.
        The *Times* had given up its permanent room, so I select-
ed a bigger one on the next-to-top floor. Once I settled in it, I
worried that a rocket would burst through the roof and kill me
as I lay in bed. Only the roomboys seemed unpreoccupied with
dire imaginings. When they saw me for the first time in fifteen
months, they smiled, and took up looking after me with their
usual befuddled charm.

        Am Rong had become a general, but Chhang Song, his
erstwhile Ed McMahon, topped him: Chhang Song was now Lon
Nol's information minister. I heard this whimsical piece of news
in Bangkok, and got it confirmed from Chhang Song himself on
my first night back, after I spotted him holding forth with a few
colleagues by the pool. Appearances suggested that despite his
promotion, Chhang Song hadn't changed: he was, for one thing,
inebriated, and for another, disarmingly blunt. His assessment of
the Khmer Rouge offensive was hard to dispute: "We are," he

said, "really in for the shit." Expletives out of the mouths of government spokesmen were rare, but what Chhang Song offered
next was rarer still: he said offhandedly that we could see the
marshal the next morning. Considering Lon Nol's reclusiveness,
recently more pronounced, the invitation induced visions of
front-page stories in all of us, but it was extended with one large
catch: we would be allowed to observe Lon Nol but not talk to
him, for Chhang Song said the marshal would fire him if we
asked questions.

I suspected a practical joke, particularly after Chhang
Song said we'd have to be at the palace at 6 a.m., but he was true
to his word. At a few minutes after six he led half a dozen of us
into Chamcar Mon Palace, where Lon Nol lived. The word
"palace" seemed inappropriate, for unlike the unoccupied royal
palace a few blocks away, the blandly functional Chamcar Mon
didn't aspire to artfulness; the closest thing to art I saw was a calendar on the wall of the visitors' room where we waited for Lon
Nol. Published by the FANK's psychological warfare department, the calendar was a kind of forecast, something close to
official prophecy. It contained a page for each month of the year,
and on each page was an illustration of the event predicted for
the month. Up to July, the forecasts were bleak: the Khmer Rouge
were depicted raping, killing infants, burning women at the
stake. Things looked up in August, when angry Cambodians
were shown chasing away Khmer Rouge troops while triumphantly waving a Khmer Republic flag, but in September the
Khmer Rouge again were shown committing atrocities, this time
by slowly bleeding Buddhist monks to death — apparently not
even the FANK's own sage could imagine a victory without set-
backs along the way. By October the FANK achieved dominance,
as the Khmer Rouge were again depicted fleeing, and in
November Cambodians cheered as a dove of peace appeared.
Final victory came in December, when a triumphant Lon Nol
held up a book emblazoned with the catch-all phrase he'd
devised for his personal philosophy, "Neo-Khmerism."

The calendar set the theme for our visit to the palace:

delusion. Here, where Lon Nol lived like a hermit, everything suggested that the war was going well. The palace was the only place in Phnom Penh exempt from rationing of electricity: even the visitors' room was air conditioned. And while soldiers at the front were short of everything from helmets to weapons, the troops guarding the palace were conspicuously spiffy: they sported not just complete uniforms but holstered pistols and shiny boots. I spotted five generals on the grounds, including the notorious Ith Suong, the man I'd observed a year and a half earlier resting on a lounge chair while his troops tried to rescue a besieged battalion. Now Ith Suong was in charge of protecting the palace, a disturbing omen indeed. "The situation has ameliorated a little bit," he said. "The enemy cannot reach its objective. It can fire rockets, that's all." Welcome to the palace of wishful thinking.

After a half-hour wait, we were led to a garden where Lon Nol strolled with his wife, two small daughters, and about ten soldiers. We were being granted a privilege of sorts, yet the experience induced squeamishness, the kind that is inspired by seeing people in awkward circumstances, trying to preserve their dignity. The fenced-in garden contained rabbits, turkeys, ducks, monkeys, and three caged ocelot kittens, but no animal there was more a prisoner than Lon Nol himself. His residence was his bunker: it was covered with sandbags, to protect him from dissident FANK pilots, two of whom had already tried to bomb him, as much as from Khmer Rouge shells. Still partially crippled by his stroke, he walked haltingly, leaning heavily on a cane that bore his six-star insignia. He acknowledged us as he left the garden. "I wish you a nice morning," he said in French. "Thank you," we all said.

After we left the palace, I learned of a rumor that had circulated in Phnom Penh the previous day. According to it, Lon Nol and other government leaders had secretly boarded a caravan of black cars, driven to the airport, and fled the country in the same Air Cambodge plane I'd arrived on. To Western observers the rumor wasn't believable, but its existence showed how jittery Phnom Penh residents had become. Moreover, the rumor seemed to explain the motive for Lon Nol's publicized stroll, as it proved he was still in the country.

I hated being a potential rocket victim. I knew the odds of being harmed by one were incalculably small, particularly since by the time I arrived the Khmer Rouge had shifted the focus of rocket attacks from the city to the airport, but logical considerations couldn't erase my dread. I hated knowing that at any moment I could be struck down, eating or sleeping or conducting an interview.

I felt least frightened in the daytime: the idea of being hit by a rocket seemed implausible as long as I was on the move. The most frequently rocketed sites were the areas surrounding the U.S. embassy, Lon Nol's palace, and the residence of Long Boret, In Tam's successor as prime minister. I didn't linger in any of these zones. When I had to visit the U.S. embassy, my driver — I'd fired Ang Kheao and replaced him with a younger, less cautious man — dropped me there and picked me up at a designated time; understandably, he wasn't keen on waiting out in front. I felt truly safe only when I was indoors, on the bottom floor of a building several stories high. By that criterion the safest place in the capital was the Phnom's lobby, where I stopped to take deep breaths.

The fear touched me with all its force only at night, when the curfewed city was unnaturally still, when even the cicadas ceased their shrill vibrations, and I lay in bed listening to the all-too-audible sounds of combat wafting in from the front. I couldn't stop thinking about being killed by a rocket as I slept. Most rockets fired into Phnom Penh were shot from the north; since my room faced south I was well-protected. I still worried. Since I was on the top floor, a rocket could crash through the roof and kill me. After a few nights I switched rooms, but I still couldn't shake my dread. The new room, a floor beneath the old one, was unquestionably safer, but it still had one tiny drawback, in the form of a large balcony just outside it. It was barely conceivable that a rocket from the north could clear the hotel's sloping roof and strike the balcony, sending fragments through the window into my room. I knew the odds against this were a million to one, a billion to one, but I couldn't dispel my fear: the long odds only made the prospect of my death more poignant. On my second night back I heard rockets whistling overhead, then exploding somewhere in the city. Every night afterwards I smoked a joint before going to bed: it was my fortification against fear. Stoned, I was on another plane, where sensation alone justified existence, where loneliness and sorrow and fear commingled and were rendered glorious. I was scared but I was throbbing again; I was back to running on full throttle.

What grip did death hold on me? When I was in college, I became infatuated with a Wellesley student whose boyfriend had just died in a hiking accident. I went with her to a movie, and when someone in the film was killed she covered her eyes. I knew she was envisioning her boyfriend's death, and I believed at that moment that I loved her. Many years passed before I understood that what attracted me was her connection to death — for some reason death mesmerized me long before I reached Indochina. Why, it was a man's death that enabled me to go to Indochina, and then I went there and hovered around death. I even met my wife at a death-and-dying workshop, where I heard of her near-death experience. The drama of dying contained something I needed to feel whole. Here, in Phnom Penh, I experienced its force as exhilaration. Maybe it was good that Gibson had summoned me from New Delhi, for in truth I could hardly remember the place.

Three days after I got back to Phnom Penh, Lon Nol went on the radio to announce that he'd fired the FANK commander-in-chief, Gen. Sosthene Fernandez. That day I'd already written a piece about the military situation, so now I wrote a new story and instructed the editors to run it in place of my earlier one, which I said I'd revise for use later in the week. I added a note warning the editors not to use an A.P. report that Prime Minister Long Boret had resigned, for I felt certain the story was wrong, as it indeed turned out to be. Two days later I saw my story in a press survey transmitted by the State Department to the U.S. embassy in Phnom Penh. To my astonishment, the story's lead was that Long Boret had resigned, and didn't even attribute the information to the A.P. I figured I knew what had happened: the deskmen hadn't received my second story, and instead they ran the A.P. story under my byline. I was incensed. Not only was the practice of running wire service material under a staff reporter's byline unethical, but the mistake complicated my news gathering task by damaging my reputation among embassy officials who saw the playback. I complained in a cable to L.A. that the error "makes [the] paper and me look bad." Gibson's assistant, who led the day-to-day foreign desk operation, had this to say in reply:

> IF EMBASSY WAS SO DAMNED EFFICIENT ON PLAYBACK OF YOUR ORIGINAL FERNANDEZ [STORY] WHICH APPEARED ONLY IN REGULAR EDITION THEY OBVIOUSLY NOT SO EFFICIENT IN PLAYING BACK YOUR WRITETHROUGH BASED ON LON NOL BROADCAST WHICH APPEARED IN MAKEOVER AND ALL SUBSEQUENT EDITIONS STOP

I felt a bit relieved, for at least the erroneous Long Boret information did not survive later editions, but my anger at the paper did not subside. Gibson's assistant made it sound as if the State Department was remiss for playing back an early edition. He didn't even respond to my chief complaint, about carrying a wire service story under my byline. I thought of the word Gibson once cast at me: unprofessional.

Sarah Webb Burrell, everyone's lover in '73, returned a few days after I did. This time she even had credentials of a sort: she'd somehow arranged to do stories for the New York *Daily News*. It didn't take her long to understand that she'd horribly misjudged the situation. I saw her a few hours after she arrived, sitting on the hotel's back steps, cheerlessly staring out at the pool, having just digested the realization that nude frolicking there had become inappropriate. She said, "It's not going to be fun this time, is it?" It was a statement, not a question.

The evidence was everywhere. The regime's currency was so inflated we had to carry great wads of bills just to make minor purchases. While I was absent from Cambodia, the black market exchange rate rose from 400 to 2,000 riels per dollar; the largest bill in circulation, a 500-riel note, was worth a quarter. People stapled ten of the notes together and exchanged the clumps as three-dollar bills; the chief disadvantage, aside from the bulk, was that each note had to be counted, in case somebody had ripped one out before passing on the stapled wad.

The sense of impending disaster permeated even the colonial sanctuary of the hotel. A prostitute who usually appeared at the hotel only at night, on business, showed up in daytime with her malnourished baby, and induced an American TV network cameraman to take up a collection on her behalf: he and a reporter got into a loud argument when the reporter declined to contribute. The restaurant menu shrank as one key recipe ingredient after another became unavailable, and for some reason breakfast was no longer served by the pool. Now the only place for it was a sweltering banquet room off the lobby, where we sat sweating and grumbling about the service. Conversation revolved around one subject: the potential permutations of collapse. Would FANK troops turn on foreigners as the end approached? Would non-Americans be included in the American evacuation? Would the Khmer Rouge takeover be peaceful or bloody, and should we stay to cover it? The tension affected us in different ways. One reporter kept mumbling darkly that he was certain the U.S. embassy would exclude all journalists from the evacuation. Another got so paranoid he begged his employer to let him leave Cambodia immediately. Permission was granted, but the man still couldn't shake off his glimpse into the abyss, and soon afterwards quit journalism altogether.

Only the French behaved as if nothing had changed: they still made their Sunday pilgrimages to the pool. Aware that their elevated status would vanish if they returned to France, they'd clung to Cambodia, first when independence took away their legally mandated superiority, then when war deprived them of many of their remaining pleasures, and now it was too late to leave, for they had no place else to go. On my first Sunday back, as I looked out at the French sunbathers, all trim and manicured and greased for the sun, I was struck by how dignified they were, and how ludicrous. It occurred to me that 1953, when France ceded independence to Cambodia, didn't mark the end of the colonial era; this year, 1975, did.

The military situation grew dire. The Khmer Rouge cut the Mekong River and all overland routes to the capital. The only remaining means of supplying the city was by air. Cargo planes bearing desperately needed shipments of ammunition, rice, and petroleum were making 40 to 50 flights to Pochentong daily, but the airlift was constantly disrupted by Khmer Rouge fire. During a two-day period in late March, rockets killed five Cambodian airport workers and wounded 35. Even with the shipments, the FANK was plagued by shortages. Soldiers complained of being hungry. Blood was so precious that military doctors gave transfusions of a pint or less to patients who normally would have received two quarts; the doctors effectively decided which of the patients would live. On top of all this, the Lon Nol regime faced the likelihood that the U.S. Congress would reject a request by President Ford for more military aid for Cambodia. Such a development would almost certainly cause the FANK to run out of ammunition within months, and even more significantly, would signal the end of American support for the Lon Nol regime.

The end was coming, but when? I kept thinking about August 1973, when we'd all predicted a collapse that never came. I was determined not to make that mistake again, and grew cautious. The fighting "could easily continue for weeks or months," I wrote in late March. In fact, the evacuation was two and a half weeks away.

Some FANK soldiers refused to fight. I found about 60 of them huddled about a mile from the front line on Route 5, the road that ran north from Phnom Penh along the Mekong River. They looked scruffy and forlorn and a little wild-eyed. Most had been wounded and released from the hospital: one walked on a crutch, and several had visible scars. Still, from the FANK command's point of view they were fit enough to fire a rifle, so they'd been sent back to combat. The trouble was that they hadn't been paid since they were wounded. They were supposed to have received their salaries and food rations in the hospital, but when they were discharged they were told to collect at the front. They went to the front, and their paymaster said their money was back in Phnom Penh. Some of them had gone back and forth several times, but they still hadn't been paid. It was conceivable that the military bureaucracy had failed to catch up with the men, but it was far more likely that some officer had pocketed their pay. Even so, the men weren't charging anyone with corruption — they just wanted what was owed them. The demand was noteworthy in its modesty: their salary was less than ten dollars a month, and their food ration, consisting solely of rice, was miniscule. One man said, "If we are regularly paid and have enough rice, we can fight bravely." The question I asked myself was, "Why do they still want to fight?"

Route 5 was so dicey that I rarely drove closer to the

front than the spot where the recalcitrant soldiers gathered. One journalist who knew Route 5's dangers intimately was Rockoff: during my long absence from Phnom Penh, he'd been seriously wounded there. Shrapnel hit him near his heart, and, as legend had it, he survived only because a Swedish medical team whose chief had just read a book on emergency heart surgery happened to be nearby. Rockoff was evacuated from Cambodia in a U.S. Air Force medical plane and taken to the Philippines, where he mended. Crazed man that he was, he came back to Phnom Penh as soon as he could, wheezing from lung damage. He still hadn't learned his lesson: one day, standing around the pool, he announced that he was going after combat photos on Route 5. Somebody said he was crazy, that he could easily be killed there. "It wouldn't be the first time," Rockoff said.

My most immediate concern was making sure the paper received my stories. I didn't trust the Phnom Penh telegraph office, with its antiquated equipment and torpid employees, and whenever possible I double-filed, also sending my stories by a second route, usually via Saigon or Bangkok. I asked the deskmen in L.A. to send me confirmations when they received my stories, but they failed to acknowledge three of my first four stories. *I am living under the rockets,* I thought, *watching a civilization unravel, and the least my editors can do is rouse themselves to write me two or three informative lines on those occasions when I write them a story.* I was sure they didn't care. After a week in Phnom Penh I sent this cable:

THIS IS URGENT REQUEST FOR ACKNOWL-
EDGMENT BY YOU OF STORIES RECEIVED
AND AT WHAT TIME. LACK OF CABLE IN
THIS SITUATION CAUSES GREAT UNCER-
TAINTY, AS I DO NOT KNOW WHETHER TO
REPEAT INFORMATION PREVIOUSLY FILED
BASED ON ASSUMPTION YOU DIDN'T

RECEIVE PREVIOUS STORY. BECAUSE OF
CRUSH OF JOURNALISTS HERE, FILING
FROM PHNOM PENH TAKES UP TO FOUR
HOURS WAITING AT TELEGRAPH OFFICE
TO ENSURE STORY HANDLED PROPERLY
AND EVEN THEN NO CERTAINTY YOU'LL
RECEIVE IT...

I had more problems than the ones I mentioned. The difficulty of filing began with the act of writing the story. Because power flowed for only a few hours every other day, it was necessary to work in candlelight much of the time. The only way I could see adequately was to put candles on either side of my typewriter; sometimes, engrossed in writing, I'd knock over a candle with the typewriter carriage, and I had to move quickly to avert a fire.

Equally annoying, the Phnom Penh telegraph office, reflecting the principle that the amount of paperwork a government generates is in inverse proportion to its legitimacy, required that all stories be filed in quadruplicate. Since I wanted one for myself, I made five copies. Writing became a physical feat, requiring punching my typewriter keys hard enough to make an impression through nine sheets of paper, including carbons. It was wasted effort, of course: whoever in the government got the third and fourth copies couldn't possibly have deciphered the faint markings gracing those wispy onionskins. The cable operators fortunately used the originals, which were readable; that, however, didn't ensure that stories would be transmitted accurately, as a disgruntled *Times* editor informed me by cable. He said my pieces were arriving in Los Angeles without punctuation: the cable operators weren't bothering to include it. Thereafter I wrote it out: cma for comma, stop for period, query for question mark, para for paragraph. By the time I finished writing a story I was so giddy I could *talk* with punctuation included: "I need to go to the telegraph office stop where the hell is the driver query."

At the telegraph office, journalists had started paying bribes to the operators to guarantee priority transmission for their dispatches. Schanberg was assumed to have initiated the practice, and others mimicked it out of necessity. Soon the payments became self-defeating: not only did the cost escalate, but they bought nothing, since everyone was making them. Worried that my stories wouldn't get transmitted, I sometimes waited hours at the cable office, hovering over the operators, until the deed was done. As the efficacy of the bribes declined, some journalists got fed up, and denounced Schanberg. He finally agreed to curb the practice, but by then we were all reluctant to stop paying the cable operators out of fear that they'd grown accustomed to the bribes and might not send our stories without them. With a logic borne of Western largesse, we decided to keep making the payments, only now we wouldn't use them to get a story transmitted ahead of a colleague's. After a brief negotiation with the cable operators, we agreed on an amount that each news organization should pay weekly, based on its average cable wordage — the amounts ranged from $35 to $70 per organization, and totaled $350.

I was designated to deliver the first week's sum to the telegraph office. The dollar amount represented no hardship for the organizations involved, but it represented a great mass of Cambodian currency: 1,400 five-hundred-riel notes, to be exact. I gathered them in a leather satchel, and, as I sat in the back of a taxi with the loot, imagined myself a gangster making a delivery. I dumped the satchel's contents onto a desk at the telegraph office, and the manager's eyes gleamed. It took twenty minutes for him and his assistants to count it all. The system lasted a couple of weeks.

Late at night we met at the pool to listen to the BBC worldwide news service on our shortwave radios. For a while Cambodia dominated the broadcasts, and then, all of a sudden, it didn't. The news was still about collapse, but no longer the

Khmer Republic's: the South Vietnamese regime was crumbling, too. One night the North Vietnamese were said to be close to capturing a province capital in the Central Highlands; four days later the South Vietnamese were abandoning all of the Central Highlands; the day after that, thousands of refugees were fleeing the Highlands before the Communists got there. Within two more days, ARVN troops had abandoned ten provinces, and in less than another week, Hue was under Communist control. By the end of March the Communists entered Danang, precipitating more panic. The Communists' path south was clear. This was going to be the last offensive, and it would end in Saigon.

With no other allegiance than to the big story, some journalists abandoned Phnom Penh for Saigon. I might have, too, had I not been persona non grata in Saigon, but I didn't feel envious of my departing colleagues. I was a member of the aberrant Phnom Penh press corps now, one of the semi-loonies; somehow my fate and Cambodia's felt intertwined. I regretted the Thieu regime's impending demise, but not out of any attachment to Thieu or Vietnam: it meant that even in its death throes Cambodia would get second billing.

Schanberg was in a ferocious mood most of the time. The man considered most likely to emerge from the ashes of the Cambodian war with a Pulitzer, he perhaps had more reason to regret Vietnam's emergence as a rival story than the rest of us. In addition, he couldn't have been pleased that the New York *Times* sent two correspondents to supplement his coverage. One of them, Joe Lelyveld, possessed journalistic credentials as impressive as Schanberg's, while the other, David Andelman, was new to both Indochina and foreign correspondence. Schanberg reserved his wrath for Andelman. He denounced Andelman to the rest of us, and strove to shut him out of coverage. It was startling to see Schanberg using up so much emotion on him, for he was no threat to Schanberg. Andelman appeared gaunt underneath his fresh safari suit and thick black-rimmed glasses, was full of facial twitches and inconsequential boasts, and clung to his New York *Times* identity like a life buoy. Backing up Schanberg hadn't been Andelman's idea: he was supposed to be stationed in Saigon, but when the Lon Nol regime began to totter, he was diverted to Phnom Penh. It was indicative of Andelman's haplessness that his belongings, which he'd put in a sea shipment, continued on their way to Saigon; when South Vietnam showed signs of following Lon Nol in collapse, Andelman realized he'd probably never see the shipment again.

Soon after I arrived, I attended a U.S. embassy briefing at which Andelman represented the New York *Times*. That fact didn't seem notable until a few minutes into the briefing, when the embassy press attaché interrupted to say he'd just spoken to Schanberg on the phone, and Schanberg wanted Andelman to leave the room immediately. We surmised that the attaché had informed Andelman of the briefing but not Schanberg; either Andelman kept the information to himself or wasn't able to notify Schanberg in time. Now Andelman slunk out of the briefing room, humiliated. Several minutes later Schanberg appeared. The briefing didn't recover. Schanberg was as manic as if he'd been taking uppers: he dominated the briefing, virtually took it over. He asked questions and then answered them before the briefer had a chance, and rephrased other journalists' questions instead of letting the briefer respond. The session ended desultorily, once we grew tired of listening to Schanberg interview himself.

They must have been hard days for Schanberg. He had just written what some considered a sensational story saying that a year earlier Henry Kissinger rejected a proposal by John Gunther Dean, the U.S. Ambassador, to make diplomatic contacts with the Khmer Rouge; now some colleagues were saying Schanberg got the story by violating ground rules in an interview with Dean. In addition, Martin Woollacott was infuriated with Schanberg for breaking *Woollacott's* ground rules. Woollacott said he interviewed a senior U.S. embassy official who denounced the American policy of supporting the Lon Nol

regime and thus prolonging the war. Surprised by the out-
burst, Woollacott sought out Schanberg to find out what
Schanberg made of it. Before telling Schanberg what the official said, Woollacott exacted a pledge from Schanberg not to
use the information in a story. Schanberg then did exactly
what Woollacott said he pledged not to: he wrote a story
about it, scooping Woollacott. As if all this was not enough,
rumors were circulating to the effect that late each night
Pran, Schanberg's interpreter, brought copies of other journalists' stories from the cable office to Schanberg's room,
where Schanberg checked them to make sure he'd omitted
nothing vital from his own dispatches. In the middle of
everything Schanberg took off to spend a week with his family in Bangkok.

I was willing to overlook Schanberg's ethical short-
comings. I thought they were peccadilloes, justified by the
importance of publishing the truth about Cambodia in the
most important newspaper in the world. True, Schanberg
was abrasive, aggressive, insensitive, but those were precisely the qualities that seemed to make him a superlative
reporter — I worried that I lacked them. In a letter from
Phnom Penh, I wrote, "How can you think of yourself as the
best when Schanberg has the story covered from every angle,
swallowed up?"

The pressure on Lon Nol to resign intensified. The
idea, promulgated by the regime's foreign backers including
the United States, was that if Lon Nol left the scene, the
Khmer Rouge might be moved to end the war by negotiation
instead of military conquest: it represented the Phnom Penh
side's last display of wishful thinking. The biggest problem
with it was that the regime had no collateral with which to
negotiate; it couldn't threaten the Khmer Rouge by saying,
"If you don't come to terms, we'll fight on," because the U.S.

Congress was poised to cut off its military supplies. Besides, the Khmer Rouge showed no interest in halting combat before they achieved total victory; they wouldn't meet with the Lon Nol side, let alone discuss terms. One by one the regime's last supporters abandoned it. The British and Australians closed their embassies, and the French at last evacuated most of their citizens and nearly all their staff. Among Cambodia's Asian allies, the Indonesians and Malaysians closed their missions, and the Thai embassy reduced its staff to one person. Even the U.S., the regime's sponsor, cut its embassy staff to one-fourth its previous size and began burning documents.

Lon Nol still wouldn't resign: his pridefulness was in inverse proportion to the respect he commanded. Finally he hit upon a solution of sorts: he would leave the country "temporarily," still acknowledged as the President of the Khmer Republic, on the pretext that he was getting medical treatment abroad. At noon on April 1, while a military honor guard saluted and a band played, a tearful Lon Nol and his wife boarded a helicopter inside the palace grounds and flew to the Phnom Penh airport; from there, Air Cambodge's sole jet took the couple to Bangkok, where they got a connecting flight to Bali. Most people in the capital didn't even know of Lon Nol's departure until a few minutes after he boarded his helicopter, when a taped announcement was played on the radio. The marshal said he would return to Cambodia "when my health improves or when the situation in the country requires my presence to continue the common struggle for the freedom of the people," but nobody was holding his breath for Lon Nol's return. I peered in vain over a palace gate to see Lon Nol's departure. Across the street, at a food stand, a grinning soldier played a guitar, and three children danced.

That afternoon a Cambodian-speaking colleague and I drove out towards the front to see if Lon Nol's departure had any impact on his troops. A mile behind the front line we struck up a conversation with a soldier repairing an armored personnel carrier. We asked him what effect he thought Lon Nol's departure would have on the course of the war.

"That means there will be peace — a ceasefire."

"Who will ceasefire?"

"Both sides. We soldiers will join hands together in solidarity."

Then, having completed his repair, he climbed in his APC and headed back to the front.

I still hadn't decided whether I'd leave in the American evacuation. True, Gibson had ordered me to go, but he'd certainly print my stories from Khmer Rouge-held Phnom Penh. Staying would prove that I was brave; it would atone for my failures of nerve in 1973, when I'd failed to go to Neak Leung and Kampong Cham. Still, I didn't feel comfortable with the choice: unlike my journey to Viet Cong territory, when I'd chosen the time and the place, this time I'd choose nothing, I'd be at the mercy of the Khmer Rouge. "Sure you ought to stay," said Denis Cameron over lunch, "if you don't mind not just being killed but being dismembered." Those words clarified my choice, for I never thought seriously about staying again.

Lon Nol's successor, a brittle reed of a man named Saukham Khoy, appeared so delicate I took pity on him the first time I talked with him, which was on the day after I found out Lon Nol was leaving the country. A few other journalists and I waited on the dirt road in front of his house until he let us in: I had the feeling he didn't realize he could turn down our interview requests. This was no case of the man seeking the job: Saukham Khoy was anything but ambitious, and his ascension perfectly illustrated the vacuum of political leadership that Lon Nol left behind. Sixty years old, he was apparently educated in the manners of French colonialism, for he still confronted Westerners including journalists half his age with an attitude that smacked suspiciously of awe. Khoy became the regime's interim president because he was president of the Cambodian Senate, and the holder of that position was designated by the Khmer Republic's Constitution to assume power when the national president resigned or left the country — it was the first time since the Constitution's creation five years earlier that so much attention was paid to that frail document.

During our interview Khoy offered the opinion that even if the U.S. Congress rejected additional aid for Cambodia, surely "President Ford wouldn't let Phnom Penh be occupied by the Khmer Rouge." He didn't even know that American law now prohibited Ford from using U.S. military forces in Indochina. When we told him that, he was surprised, but he quickly thought of an idea: Ford "could send troops to Phnom Penh and then resign 60 days later. If I were the President, I would do that to save American honor. American power — with F-4 Phantoms, B-52s, the Seventh Fleet, the marines — it is to save the honor of America." Khoy would soon be educated in American priorities.

Maybe he was by the second time I saw him, a week later. By then the U.S. embassy had reduced its staff, and Cambodian embassy employees were being given the option of moving with their families to Thailand. Khoy tried to sound unconcerned. "That is their affair," he said. "It doesn't bother me." Nobody believed him, of course. His response to a question about how much he enjoyed his new job was more revealing. "The work is very hard, intellectually and physically," he said. Pressed to say whether he liked being President, he shook his head and said softly, "No."

Before the war Cambodia was a rice-exporting nation. Now, with vast tracts of agricultural land lying fallow and Phnom Penh's population swollen to four times its pre-war size, not even the American airlift could stave off the starvation of thousands of Cambodians. The starvation story was a crucial element in the demise of the Lon Nol regime, even if it did not strike editors with the same urgency as the battle for Phnom Penh. I waited until I'd covered the important facets of the military and political situation, and then I took it on.

Just outside a medical clinic whose head doctor I intended to interview, I was caught in a crowd of hundreds of destitute mothers and their starving children. When the mothers saw me, they assumed that because I was a Westerner I might be able to help them, and they tried to get my attention by displaying their children's maladies. One woman pointed to a swelling on her child's head; another waved her infant's matchstick limbs. I wished to be invisible. For a moment I feared that the women would think of my enclave of comfort at the Phnom, and vent their indignation at me, but all they did was display their pitiableness: they lacked the imagination necessary for anger, or maybe just the strength.

The clinic's interior was no refuge. It had one examination table for the facility's four doctors. The head doctor sat at a desk and examined babies while their mothers held them. One mother was giving her starving infant tea from a bottle because she couldn't afford milk and was too under-nourished to nurse. A doctor was giving a glucose transfusion to a skeletal infant girl; the procedure would stave off her death for a little while. The infant's mother said she would have come to the clinic earlier, but she lacked the bus fare. No words could soften the pathos.

The clinic's doctors suspected they were witnessing the demise of a generation, for malnutrition was so widespread that even the children who survived the famine were likely to suffer brain damage. "I'm lucky if I see one child in a day who has the weight of an American child of the same age," said a British doctor at the clinic. "If I find one, I usually take it around and show everybody."

The doctors turned away almost as many patients as they treated, and lacked food and medicine for the children they did treat. Even those who on the clinic's recommendation gained admittance to a local hospital weren't faring well: in one pediatric ward, 45 percent of the patients had died in the previous three weeks. "The greatest pediatrician," a distraught Swiss doctor said, "would be the man who is able to stop the war."

I cannot claim to have been deeply affected by the starvation, at last not then: in order to be suffering's medium, I couldn't let suffering claim me. The choice wasn't conscious: my mind was like   photographic paper, absorbing impressions but not allowing them to surface until immersed in a solution of appropriate ingredients. In my case the immersion didn't take place until years afterward, and the chief ingredient was my willingness to hold the images I'd retained up to the light. Then I was horrified by such notions as that Cambodian parents had been forced to starve their weakest offspring so that their other children would stand a chance of survival, and at last I grieved, and wondered why I'd endured being death's witness.

What I did at the time was to retreat to my hotel room; despite the depredations it had endured, it was still my haven. The room contained an air conditioner, whose use had precluded any need for screens to keep out insects. Now, however, with the power shortage rendering the air conditioner useless, I slept with the windows open, and was beset by mosquitoes. One morning I bought a mosquito net and asked my roomboy to install it. Held in place by freshly whittled twigs tied to the bedposts, it was already in place when I returned the same afternoon.

A few nights later, trying to light a joint, I accidentally set the mosquito net on fire. It was the quickest I have ever gotten out of bed. I put the flames out with a pillow, and resigned myself to sleeping with a foot-wide hole in the top of the net. I didn't mention the accident to the roomboy, but when I came back from my reporting chores the next day, he'd already repaired it, with a great mass of white tape that made the net look like one more war casualty.

Phnom Penh was so tightly besieged that we could eat our breakfasts, check all four fronts by car, and be back at the hotel before lunch. One morning Lew Simons, the Washington *Post* correspondent, toured the fronts, found them all quiet, and then stopped at the telegraph office in the center of Phnom Penh to see if he'd received any cables. One from his editor awaited him. It said:

LEAVE PHNOM PENH IMMEDIATELY AND TAKE FENTON WITH YOU IF YOU CAN REUTERS SAYS COMMUNIST TROOPS HAVE PENETRATED CITY AND THAI PREMIER SAYS IT HAS FALLEN GOD BE WITH YOU

For a second Lew thought the cable might be right. He looked around the telegraph office to make sure the Khmer Rouge hadn't seized it without his noticing. Then he got a telephone line through to Washington and explained that Reuters and the Thai premier were wrong, not the first time for either, that the capital was tranquil, and that the cable was at least inordinately premature. Lew's editor said in that case he could stay.

Lew showed us the cable at lunch. We laughed. It confirmed our estimations of how little editors knew. Only Fenton, who'd become a *Post* stringer months earlier, was disturbed by the cable: he couldn't get over those eerie words, "If you can."

I thought Lew's cable was ridiculous, but all the same I missed getting one like it: I thought, at least Lew's editors care about him. At about the same time as Lew received his cable, I got one saying:

> ...APPRECIATE CONTINUING FLOW OF
> COLOR PIECES GIVING US SOUND FEEL
> AND FLAVOR OF CITY THAT SEEMS TO
> BE DYING AS ENEMY PRESSES IN
> AROUND IT AND FOREIGN DIPLOMAT-
> IC MISSIONS DESERT THE SHIP STOP
> THERE CONTINUING MARKET HERE
> FOR STORIES TELLING US HOW THE
> CAMBODIAN MILITARY IS REACTING
> DASH FOR INSTANCE AYEPEE
> [Associated Press] REPORTED TODAY
> THAT 300 SOLDIERS SIMPLY WALKED
> AWAY FROM KEY POINT IN PHNOM
> PENH DEFENSIVE PERIMETER REFUS-
> ING TO FIGHT DASH HOW ARE PEOPLE
> GETTING FOOD AND FUEL ARE MAR-
> KETS OPERATING HOW IS DISTRIBU-
> TION OF UNISTATES AIRLIFTED SUP-

PLIES BEING HANDLED HOW IS AVER-
AGE MAN IN STREET VIEWING POSSI-
BLE FALL OF CITY DASH IS HE AFRAID
OF COMMIE RETRIBUTION DEATH OR
WHAT/HOW ARE PEOPLE COPING
WITH DAILY JOBS/HOW ARE HOSPI-
TALS COPING WITH SICK AND WOUND-
ED AND SIMILAR TO GIVE US HUMAN
TOUCH OF CITY UNDER SIEGE...

I'd already written about most of the topics the cable listed—
hadn't my editors been reading my stories? Somehow when
they described Cambodia it sounded routine, like an inflation story: they understood what a "city under siege" was,
but they didn't understand Cambodia. It seemed to me that
we were all invisible: me, the Phnom Penh press corps,
Cambodia itself. Even Henry Kissinger overlooked
Cambodia: he busied himself with Middle East negotiations,
and left it to a deputy to make pronouncements on such a tri-
fling subject as Cambodia. In a press conference in early
April, Kissinger didn't mention the country once.

Cambodia's invisibility had become indistinguishable from my own. I was choking on frustration, for it was no
longer tinged with the consolation of the war's exhilarating
novelty, as it had been during my first few months in
Vietnam. Since then, I'd achieved something, I thought; I'd
played by the rules of the craft and been acknowledged, yet
nothing had changed. The copy editors still sleepwalked,
and my words had as little impact as ever. And because I
wasn't overcoming my frustration, I knew that I must be
falling back: it felt like defeat, everything did. I wasn't yet
ready to acknowledge what was truly slipping away from
me, that what I was losing, ever so slowly, was my ambition.
It was another fissure in my obsession, which I did not perceive until the entire edifice collapsed.

More FANK soldiers refused to fight. A group of them had just been brought back to Phnom Penh after enduring the longest siege anywhere since World War II. From May, 1974, until January, 1975, they were among 10,000 soldiers and civilians in the town of Kampong Seila, which was surrounded by the Khmer Rouge and entirely dependent on air drops. More than a thousand of the surrounded people were killed, and food was so scarce that in order to survive some soldiers resorted to eating the remains of dead Khmer Rouge soldiers. Both sides in the Cambodian war occasionally practiced ritual cannibalism, for some Khmers believed that in consuming their vanquished enemy they took on his strength, but this was the first time I'd heard of cannibalism compelled by hunger. Kampong Seila lost its tactical significance when the 1975 offensive began, but FANK commanders decided to continue defending the town on the grounds that it had become an all-too-rare symbol of FANK courageousness — from then on the soldiers essentially risked death in order to play their part as symbols. Finally, as the situation around Phnom Penh grew desperate, the soldiers were extracted from Kampong Seila by helicopter and returned to the capital. Most of them hadn't been paid in at least four months, but they weren't given a leave or even their salaries — they were just ordered to fight on the capital's northwest front. They refused.

I went to see them three days after they returned to Phnom Penh; they were at a camp five miles outside the city. They were surly, almost menacing, and I put my questions to them delicately. Our conversation revolved around corruption. One soldier said it was twice as hard to fight corruption inside the Kampong Seila perimeter as Khmer Rouge troops outside it. Another one said: "Our commander had wine and pork and chicken while we ate grasshoppers. He could use wine to wash his face. He had three or four girls with him. But if a soldier was sick and wanted to go to the hospital in Phnom Penh, he had to pay a 10,000- to 15,000-riel [$5 to $10] bribe to get a helicopter ride."

The men said some of their officers charged them for the food dropped from American planes into the defense perimeter — many of them left Kampong Seila owing the government money. To some the ultimate indignity was the promotion a few months earlier of Kampong Seila's commander from lieutenant colonel to brigadier general. "How did our commander get promoted to general when he took all our money?" asked a soldier. "We want justice, we want fairness." A soldier yelled, "We don't care about the situation in Phnom Penh. We want the money, we want clothes, then we'll go to fight."

I asked the soldiers whether they'd eaten other men, and as soon as they said yes I changed the subject — I didn't want to be their next meal. Nor did I stick around the camp long. I returned to Phnom Penh, conducted two unrelated interviews, and had lunch at the hotel. Then I realized that in my haste I'd neglected to ask the soldiers for information I needed to round out my story.

I went back that afternoon. As soon as I arrived, I knew something was wrong. At least a hundred Cambodians were clustered around the entrance, and two soldiers with rifles said they had orders to keep journalists out. My interpreter approached some soldiers in the crowd for an explanation. A few minutes later he returned, looking incredulous. Some soldiers had just killed and eaten their paymaster, he said. I thought I hadn't heard correctly, and kept asking, "They ate him?" The interpreter nodded yes. The paymaster had arrived at the camp a few minutes after we left that morning, and told the soldiers they were being moved to the front line. They said they wouldn't go unless they were paid, so the paymaster told them they'd get their money at the front. The soldiers refused to move. One told the paymaster, "You can kill me, but I won't go." The paymaster was pensive for a few minutes. Then he drew his pistol and fired it repeatedly at the men's battalion commander, a captain. The bullets missed the commander, but struck nearby soldiers: one was killed instantly and four were wounded. The other soldiers chased the paymaster, shot him, and then ate his lungs, liver, heart, biceps, and calves.

How could the paymaster have shot at the captain? — that was tantamount to committing suicide. And how could the paymaster's own men have eaten him? I wanted to talk to the soldiers who'd taken part, but I didn't feel like walking past the guards, daring them to shoot me. Just as I was contemplating what to do, Lew Simons drove by, and seeing the crowd, stopped his car. My disappointment over losing an exclusive was more than tempered by the sight of a familiar face. I told Lew what had happened. A former Marine, he called the guards' bluff by walking by them. When they didn't react, I joined him.

A few soldiers acted as our escorts: they must have been involved in the killing, for they seemed emboldened, as if proud of their deed. We were shown the paymaster's records, which were strewn on the ground, and then, 25 yards further on, his corpse. All I could see were enormous red welts where the missing organs had been, undefined raw human matter, as if the only thing beneath a man's skin was potential wound. One of the soldiers stuck a cigarette into the paymaster's open mouth, and villagers who'd gathered around laughed. I was ready to believe that Cambodians were primitives, barbarians, nothing more. I talked to a soldier who boasted that he ate the paymaster's lungs. Remorse was non-existent: he even told me his name.

I went back to the hotel. For hours I sat at the typewriter, struggling to write my lead. From a journalist's perspective, I suppose, I never did get it right: I couldn't bring myself to mention cannibalism until the second paragraph. The first paragraph was my warning.

The FANK command did nothing to discipline the soldiers — it just paid them. That happened the next day, by which time cannibalism was the main topic of conversation at the hotel. By then we'd absorbed the incident and used it to reinforce our jauntiness: as we ate lunch, we discussed the relative culinary merits of human lungs,   livers, hearts, biceps and calves. The consensus was that all these organs tasted rich but stringy.

In South Vietnam, the inhabitants of Danang had panicked before the North Vietnamese advance and fled in total disarray, hanging from helicopter skids or on over-loaded vessels that soon sank, but in Phnom Penh panic was impossible to locate, as if the prospect of collapse was an illusion. The Khmer Rouge had almost entirely ceased training rockets on the city now, and the days were relentlessly sunny: if you focused your mind adroitly enough, the idea that the war could go on forever sounded almost plausible.

One day the hotel clerk gave me a slip of paper that had a Los Angeles phone number written on it and the words, "Call back." I went over to the cable office, the only place in Phnom Penh from which overseas calls could be made, and put the call through, and found myself talking to a Los Angeles radio station. The line was clearer than it usu-ally was during local Phnom Penh calls. A man with a boom-ing voice, the kind that registers on the spectrum that has announcer at one end and "radio personality" on the other, asked how it felt to live in a surrounded city whose defenses were crumbling. He sounded so pleased by Phnom Penh's debacle that I got annoyed: I said that calm prevailed, that the city's defenses hadn't yet disintegrated. He sounded disappointed. He asked me a few more questions, then tried the first one again, as if he were giving me a last chance to be dramatic. I couldn't indulge him. Indeed, talking to him was enough to make me wonder whether Phnom Penh was surrounded after all. If it was, I thought, why did the man on the other end sound so cheerful, and how could I speak so effortlessly to him across 6,000 miles?

At the same time, even the U.S. embassy had stopped pretending that the Khmer Republic might survive: it put out word that if we knew of any Cambodians who wanted to leave the country before the regime collapsed, we ought to inform the press attaché, who'd arrange for their departure within two days. The offer was gracious but ill-considered, I thought: unless the Khmer Rouge committed mass carnage, a proposition I still thought unlikely, most Cambodians would be better off staying in their own country. Nevertheless, I passed the offer on to my interpreter. The next day he told me that he, his wife, and his eleven children wanted to accept. I said I thought he was making a mistake, that exiles led enormously difficult lives, but that if he wanted to leave, I'd arrange for it. He said he'd give the decision more thought. The next day he told me he'd changed his mind: he and his family would stay. The subject never came up again.

Sitting around a lunch table with Schanberg, I proposed studding a news dispatch with the word "help" every tenth word, to see what effect it would have on the foreign desk. It wasn't a clever idea: I expressed it chiefly to end a conversational lull, yet it surely signified slightly more than that. Schanberg answered quickly, as if he'd already thought of doing that. "They'd pull you right out of here" was about what he said.

By April 10, even Saukham Khoy couldn't keep his head buried in the sand any longer. On that day the Khmer Rouge drove two FANK battalions off the east bank of the Mekong River, which meant that only the river separated the Khmer Rouge from Phnom Penh. In desperation Khoy offered the job of prime minister to Chau Sau, a Sihanouk-era cabinet minister who was acquainted with some of the Khmer Rouge leaders. The purpose of the gambit was to give Chau Sau a chance to negotiate with the Khmer Rouge, but of course the idea was absurd: poised for military victory, the Khmer Rouge wouldn't settle for anything less now. Lew Simons and I heard about Khoy's offer and located Chau Sau for an interview; he gave us details on his talks with Khoy which provided the basis for our stories that evening.

Still the urgency of the situation found no reflection in the streets. Here was a country enmeshed in a bloody five-year civil war, yet I could instantly get an interview with the regime's probable new prime minister — Chau Sau didn't even have a bodyguard. Half the people were afraid but had no antidote for their fear, and the other half didn't know enough to be afraid.

That morning as I made a tour of the capital's southern front, I found the wife of a FANK soldier standing inside a shack gently rocking her fifteen-day-old baby. The woman and child were only a few hundred yards behind the precarious front line, but the mother professed no worry about her infant's safety. "I'm not afraid because this is a strong position," she said. From what source did she derive her serenity? Had she somehow transcended fear or was she just unaware? I thought I understood Cambodians at least a little, but now I wondered if I knew them at all.

On another front, a mile behind the line, I spotted five soldiers dancing to celebrate the Cambodian New Year. The soldiers probably saw me in the distance, but if so, they didn't care. They were walking towards a stream where several teenaged girls were wading. One of the soldiers pounded a drum made of plastic stretched over the open end of an artillery tube. The stream and the banks were glistening greens and golds, and the girls' sarongs were vermilion. The soldiers gyrated around the girls: it was a mating dance. The soldiers splashed the girls; the girls splashed back. First one girl got dunked, then one soldier; eventually everybody was soaked. Everyone giggled. Here the Khmer Rouge were no menace; here they didn't even exist. In the middle of war, near its point of greatest intensity, the warriors themselves were playing. What secret reserve did they draw upon?

That night I lay in bed, listening to the combat; for the first time it was so close to the hotel that I could hear soldiers yelling to one another as they fought. Was it possible that the Khmer Rouge had finally penetrated the city? *No,* I told myself, we'll be evacuated before then. Just then I felt a presence on the balcony. I tiptoed to the window and looked out. It was one of the roomboys, smoking a cigarette. He saw me, and said softly, *"J'ai peur."* I am afraid. Then, as if he considered his confession a professional lapse, he asked me if I'd been awakened by mosquitoes and offered to spray the room.

Two days earlier fighting had broken out near the cable transmitting center just outside Phnom Penh: our stories were delayed for several hours, and we were on notice that the facility might close down at any time. As a precaution, I began filing twice a day. So much was happening that I was reporting with a shovel, gathering huge lumps of information and packing them into one all-purpose story after another.

President Ford delivered the first and most significant shock of April 11. Appearing on American television, he was presumably spending all of his political capital to argue in favor of aid for the tottering regimes in South Vietnam and Cambodia. The speech came on Voice of America as we sat down to breakfast at the Phnom; we ate while we listened on our shortwave radios. And listened and listened, more and more uncomfortably — Ford spoke in detail about the prospect of collapse in South Vietnam, but he hardly mentioned Cambodia. When he finally got around to it, we were astonished, for instead of delivering the expected plea for aid, all Ford said was that "it may be soon too late" to help the Khmer Republic. At first I assumed there'd been a mistake: he must have overlooked the appropriate passage. I rushed to the embassy for a clarification, but by the time I got there, I understood: the United States was abandoning the Khmer Republic, without even sending public regrets. It was such an odd sensation: I stood in the U.S. embassy and felt betrayed.

Still the streets were quiet, as if the entire city had been anesthetized. I felt like the possessor of an awful secret: I was Paul Revere, or Cassandra. The juggernaut was coming, and all I could do was watch.

Chau Sau told Lew Simons and me that on Friday morning Saukham Khoy was going to meet with him at Chamcar Mon Palace, almost certainly to ask him to form a new government. Lew and I went to the palace to wait for word. Until Schanberg joined us at the gate, the two of us thought we might be the only journalists in Phnom Penh who knew about the meeting. Even then, we weren't sure Schanberg knew; trying to protect our exclusives, we talked with him about everything except the reason why the three of us were there. Suddenly the gate swung open and Chau Sau drove past. Simons and I jumped into a car to follow him; then Schanberg got in his car and joined the chase. He more than chased — his driver passed us, caught up with

Chau Sau, and drove the Khmer Republic's Prime Minister-apparent off the road, all so that Schanberg could ask Chau Sau a question. As I watched the maneuver, something snapped. For once, instead of doing something I'd dreamed of doing but didn't dare, Schanberg had done what I had no desire to — he'd crossed a boundary into a zone of indecency. The seeds of self-forgiveness were spawned in that moment of insight. I'd been under Schanberg's spell, under journalism's spell, and now both looked exposed, tainted. Some things were more important than exclusives after all.

Chau Sau was livid. He got out of his car just long enough to tell us he'd speak with us at his destination. There he confirmed that Saukham Khoy had asked him to form a government; he said he hadn't decided whether to accept. Of course, it didn't really matter: considering Ford's speech, which Chau Sau said he hadn't heard, Chau Sau would have to hurry to form a government before the Khmer Rouge rendered the task unnecessary.

Several of us got an interview with Saukham Khoy that afternoon. He understood the significance of Ford's speech, though he wasn't up to coping with it: he was threatening to seek aid from the Soviet Union, as if a chance existed that the Soviet Union would respond. "We could change our politics," he said. "We could become socialist, we could join the Soviet bloc, and then the Soviet Union might help us." The leader of a regime founded to resist Communism was proposing to embrace Communism in order to survive.

At the end of the interview he had one question for us: "When the American embassy pulls out, will journalists go, too?" A few seconds passed before anyone answered: nobody in the room had the heart to say yes.

Word that the evacuation was imminent came that evening. To prevent panic from spreading among

Cambodians, the actual message was only to meet at the Phnom dining room at 7 a.m. for an important announcement. Nobody expected a practice run. All I could think of was getting out. I'd had enough, not just of Phnom Penh but of war and journalism. I was so ready to leave I paid my hotel bill that night — since I periodically brought my bill up to date, the hotel clerks suspected nothing. As it turned out, my check was never cashed.

The next morning I was up long before the designated time. At 7 we got the official word: the evacuation was on. We were given two hours to pack and gather at the embassy. I didn't know what to do with all the time — I could have been at the embassy in five minutes if that had been necessary. A long line of journalists formed at the front desk: the clerks were shocked when they realized what was happening. For a moment I wished I hadn't paid my bill the night before: I wanted someone to say goodbye to. I waited in the lobby until I could think of no more reason to stay, and then I walked out of the hotel alone.

My interpreter was waiting for me in his car. He drove me through Phnom Penh for the last time, and then he stopped in front of the embassy. I paid him, as usual in U.S. dollars, and looked at him for the last time, shook his hand, and said good-bye.

The streets of Phnom Penh were still calm; it was the U.S. embassy that had changed. It was barricaded, and marine guards stationed at the entrance wore helmets and flak jackets and carried M-16s — it was as if the Americans, not the Cambodians, had panicked. Once past the embassy gate, I walked into an argument between the deputy ambassador and Ed Bradley, a CBS correspondent. Uncertain whether the evacuation would take place, CBS had scheduled a flight into the Phnom Penh airport to pick up film, but now the airport was closed, and the diplomat was infuriated at this inadvertent violation of the embassy plan. The veins on his neck reddened and he screamed, "Now just don't interfere with our plans! We're responsible for a lot of lives!" Then he got in a car and drove off.

The oddest thing about the scene was that while the two men were arguing, Schanberg hovered over the two men, furiously scribbling down the conversation. Following his lead, I started taking notes, too, but I didn't have my heart in it the way he did. Standing a few yards from the three of them, I didn't know whether to focus my attention on the enraged official or the journalist arguing with him or the other journalist covering the dispute. I'd lost the point. I felt as if I were watching the news on television, as if I were watching someone else watching the news on television.

I entered the building and ran into John Gunther Dean, the ambassador; he looked like Nixon in defeat, trying to pretend he'd forged a victory. Journalists were allowed in only a small portion of the embassy, so Dean could have avoided us if he'd wished; instead, he seemed to want our attention. The most noteworthy thing he said was that he'd had two hours sleep in two days; perhaps unfairly, I thought he was laying the foundation for the assertion that he was extraordinarily valiant. (Where was Anthony Paul, Dean's aspiring hagiographer, now that the ambassador needed him?) He wore an eerie smile and, as he talked, reached over and fastened the next-to-top button on my shirt, then a button on my pocket. I was too intrigued to object.

I went back outside and found Doug Sapper, an ex-Green Beret who'd been working on the airlift at the airport. While we all avoided the airport because of the danger, Sapper spent day after day there: he liked the risk. Now he was carrying a rifle. "I think we have abandoned our responsibilities to these people," he said, and walked off. Did he think he'd hold off the Khmer Rouge by himself?

Saukham Khoy and his family were chauffeured through the gate in an embassy car: so the man who the pre-

vious day had bemoaned the Americans' lack of support for
his regime was leaving with them. A cameraman began film-
ing him; embarrassed for Khoy, an American official tried to
block the camera's view. Khoy looked ashamed. He said he
was going "on a mission to Bangkok for several days to try
to contact" the Khmer Rouge, then would return to Phnom
Penh. Nobody believed him, of course; he would have been
better off saying nothing.

I wanted the evacuation to begin, and, so that I
wouldn't regret missing the Khmer Rouge victory, I wanted
every journalist in Phnom Penh to leave with me. I wanted to
roll Cambodia up like a wall map and take it on my helicopter; then I'd hide it, so that I'd never have to think about
it again. I'd been one of the first evacuees to arrive at the
embassy; once inside, I kept looking to see who else had
come, but I never saw Schanberg's face, or Rockoff's, or
Cameron's. I'd expected Schanberg to stay, and Rockoff's
remaining was no surprise, but when I realized Cameron
wasn't coming, I was baffled — the man who'd scared me off
by predicting Khmer Rouge mutilation was staying himself.
For a moment I felt deceived, but then I thought I understood. Cameron's motive might not be journalistic; rather, it
was "Mr. Death"'s last chance to die.

By the time the operation started, something like 300
people were there, mostly American diplomats plus the press
corps, American and foreign, and a surprising number of
Cambodian families. The Cambodians were agitated and
tearful. They were leaving their homeland on an hour's
notice, probably never to return, and now, as if to underline
the rupture, they'd learned along with the rest of us that all
they could take with them was one bag small enough to
carry on their laps. Apprized of this new rule, I cheerfully
sacrificed my typewriter.

The evacuation began promptly at nine. We were led
out a back door, past trash cans aflame with embassy docu-

ments, and into trucks. The truck I boarded was covered, but the one behind ours was a flat-bed: for all their fear of Cambodian rioting, the evacuation's planners had over-looked the point that nothing announced our departure as vividly as all those somber Western faces staring out from the flat-bed truck. A few pedestrians who noticed the trucks pointed at us, but most Cambodians barely looked up. Nobody betrayed the slightest sign of hostility. The only hint of violence came from an American diplomat in our truck who showed us a pistol he carried underneath his coat.

The trucks stopped at a soccer field. We waited. Helicopters appeared in the sky, and raised huge clouds of dust as they landed. As soon as they touched down, 350 marines charged out and trotted to the edges of the field. Now at last the evacuation got the attention of a substantial number of Cambodians: hundreds of them, mostly children, many shirtless, ran to the field to see what the commotion was about. As I boarded a helicopter, I strained for my last sight of Phnom Penh: brandishing rifles, the marines stood hunched over the children, who were nevertheless smiling and waving goodbye. I didn't think we deserved the grace with which they reacted to our flight.

Phnom Penh's defenses collapsed five days later. The first stories out of the capital were cheery, implying something like a Khmer Rouge victory celebration in Phnom Penh. One report said that when Khmer Rouge soldiers entered the city, Rockoff was perched on one of their jeeps. Then the tone of the stories changed: first came references to Khmer Rouge brutality, then the forced dispersal of the city's two million residents into the countryside. Then the stories stopped. We learned later that in an effort to eradicate all bourgeois influences from Cambodia, the Khmer Rouge had emptied all cities of their inhabitants. That was the beginning of a four-year-long reign of terror, during which one or two or three million of Cambodia's seven million citizens were killed or died of starvation.

Our evacuation helicopters took us to an American carrier in the Gulf of Thailand. We passed a day aboard the ship, writing our last stories and then cooling out. I felt as if I'd been thrown from fourth gear into neutral. I circulated aimlessly around the ship, and engaged in long conversations about Cambodia: we were already nostalgic. Tony Paul said he wouldn't be writing a book about the evacuation after all — it had been too successful. I saw Saukham Khoy in the mess hall and considered interviewing him one last time, but he looked stricken with shame, and I left him alone. That night I watched a dreadful movie, the kind that assumes nothing is more hilarious than a roundhouse punch. What interested me was that when the Americans in the audience laughed, the Cambodians were silent, and when the Cambodians laughed the Americans were silent. When I returned to my sleeping quarters, I found some Cambodians gathered in a circle on the floor, gambling their riels as if the currency still had value.

We were flown to a base near Bangkok the next day. In Bangkok I checked into a hotel and tried sleeping it off, but all I could think of was Cambodia. I felt incomplete, as if I'd left significant membrane there, so I decided to go back one last time.

James Fenton and Neil Davis had once visited a temple called Preah Vihear, which rested atop a promontory jutting across the Thai border into Cambodia. The temple was of historical interest because it predated the more famous structures at Angkor, but what gave it immediate relevance was that during the war FANK troops had manned a fortress there. The three of us figured that the soldiers might still be there: the only way Khmer Rouge troops could reach Preah Vihear was by crossing first into Thai territory, something Thai troops were likely to resist. Five days after the fall of Phnom Penh, we set off to visit what conceivably was the last FANK outpost in Cambodia.

The journey consisted of a ten-hour train ride from Bangkok and a two-hour drive over an unpaved road. We bribed some Thai soldiers so that we could cross the border, and then we walked down a long stone staircase to a ravine. From there on, the land was Cambodian: it sloped gently upwards toward the majestic temple at its crest. Beyond it was a 1,500-foot cliff and the plain below. We caught sight of a tattered Khmer Republic flag waving above the temple: we'd guessed right.

If there is a time between the surrender of a man's brain to death and his body's receipt of the message, the scene on that salient represented it. Preah Vihear's inhabitants — 130 soldiers, 10 monks, some roosters and cats — wandered aimlessly around the grounds. The place was an armed camp, yet it looked ethereal. Weapons lay on the ground as if deprived of all menace, as if they'd been deflated, and the temple looming in the background gave the area a mythic quality, a hint of what Cambodia once was.

We encountered a lieutenant who wore, of all things, a tiny metal likeness of a dove on a chain around his neck. Neil asked him what the dove meant. The lieutenant said, "It's a symbol of peace, but now there is no peace. Why?" Neil tried to draw him out, but he was incoherent.

After a while we found the troops' commander, Lt. Seng Rean. He looked crazed. "The marshal [Lon Nol] is lost," he said. "Phnom Penh has disappeared. So now we don't know what to do. I know nothing. I've lost all radio contacts.... I can't stay here, but behind us is Thailand and in front of us are the Khmer Rouge. What can I do?"

Neil asked why he didn't surrender. "When the Khmer Rouge come here, they will kill everyone," Seng Rean said. "I would surrender if the Khmer Rouge were of good heart, but they aren't. I wait only for the day of death which approaches. My head is spinning like a crazy person's." Then, saying he had to get back to work, he excused himself.

We walked up the slope towards the temple. It had yielded some ground to the requirements of modern warfare. Bunkers had been dug along the main pathway through the complex, saplings had been planted and demarcated by half-buried whiskey bottles, and, a few feet from the edge of the cliff, a mortar tube had been set up and ammunition neatly stacked. I looked down to the throbbing plain a quarter of a mile below, layers of green fading into the misty horizon. Down there the carnage had just begun. For the last time I felt the exquisite bittersweet tug of the abyss, and then I backed away. On our way back down the hill, we found Seng Rean asleep in a cot, his boots lined up beside him.

EPILOGUE

As I conceive it now, my path through Indochina resembled the flight of an airplane: in my first few months in Vietnam I went down a runway, preparing for takeoff, and then, as I amassed experience, I ascended and finally soared; once I was expelled from Vietnam and resettled in Cambodia, I started to descend, and touched ground again on the day I left Phnom Penh. My path afterwards traced a mirror image of that Indochina arc: engulfed in sadness, I sank into ocean waters just as deeply as I'd previously soared through the air, and then slowly, over years, rose towards the surface.

At first I kept moving. After Cambodia I covered the Communist takeover in Laos, Indira Gandhi's imprisonment of tens of thousands of political opponents in India, Franco's death in Spain, Mao's death in China, until I ran out of momentum, like a ball rolled uphill. Each crisis held my attention less than the preceding one, for none of them measured up to the war. In my last tour I covered China from across the border in Hong Kong: that's what I'd been hired to do, of course, back before I went to Vietnam, before my real life began, but now the assignment had lost even the suggestion of allure. Hong Kong was Asia's mercantile capital, where passion was taboo except in pursuit of money. Each day I read the dreadful bombastic outpourings of the New

China News Agency, the Chinese government's chief propaganda organ, and tried to extrapolate from minute shifts of wording what grand developments might be transpiring 1500 miles away in Beijing. I attended diplomats' wearisome parties, I listened to the speculations of professional "China-watchers," and I never stopped feeling that I'd died and gone to a soulless and eventless purgatory. Journalism was falling away from me now. When Mao died, I seemed to be the only journalist in Hong Kong not delighted by the prospect of a big story. Instead, six months later, I quit my job.

On the day before I left Hong Kong I brought a few cases of empty soda bottles back to the market where I'd bought them. The checkout girl wouldn't give me the six dollars and change the bottles were worth in deposit, however; the store's policy, she said, was to deduct the amount from other purchases. I explained that because I was leaving the colony I had no use for groceries, but she refused to yield. I talked to her manager, reminding him that I'd patronized the market for nearly a year, but he, too, insisted on the policy. I became irate. Here was the embodiment of Hong Kong's cold esteem for money and its contempt for relationship. I felt a year's worth, a career's worth, a lifetime's worth of anger awaken inside me. I told the manager, a diminutive, concave-chested Chinese, that until he gave me my money I intended to follow within a foot of him, and then I did exactly that, shouting all the while that he was a thief, that I wanted my money. Together we lurched up and down the food aisles, the wild-eyed American hovering over the increasingly agitated and indignant Chinese. The market's customers, chiefly British matrons, looked at me in amazement, then drew away as if they'd concluded that I was deranged. When the manager ordered me to leave the store, I grabbed him by the front of his shirt, and was astonished by the violence of my act. The manager screamed that he was going to call the police, and I knew that I'd followed my tactic for as long as I cared to. I left — first the store, then the colony, Asia, my job. In five years as a foreign correspondent I had never stopped feeling invisible.

I found an apartment overlooking L.A.'s Sunset Strip, and, having settled into it, ceased moving. In the evenings music from the night clubs would drift up to me, and I'd feel the sensual energy from the street below, a faint iteration of the heat from the Saigon pavement that had once aroused me, but Sunset didn't tempt me; nothing did. I'd wake up in the morning and read the *Times*, paying particular attention to my ex-colleagues' peregrinations, imagining them writing their stories, guessing who their sources were. Part of me was ready to rejoin them, but I knew that if I did that, I'd be moving backward; I just didn't know where forward was. I'd finish reading the paper with regret, dreading the empty day ahead of me, and then I'd slowly gather myself, and try in vain to write, and then, sooner or later, I'd start to mourn. From a wellspring I didn't know I possessed, I'd cry, and wonder at my luckless fate, and cry some more.

I thought the world had betrayed me. Only a few years earlier, seemingly randomly, I'd been cast into a world of unimagined vibrancy: I'd savored the lurid astonishments of battle and the mysteries of uncharted hidden zones. Now, just as arbitrarily, the world denied me its vitality: no government spokesman denounced me, not even an editor awoke me with a phone call in the middle of the night. No matter how I tried, I couldn't regain my former ground: the door that had opened so mysteriously in 1971 was now slammed shut. I stirred through the war's embers that were lodged in my memory, uncertain whether I should try to extinguish them or feel grateful that they still burned. Deprived of the war, I didn't know why I lived.

Now at least my shrunken circumstances reflected my sense of self: I think that was the beginning of authenticity. I started to work at understanding myself. I read Eastern philosophy, and discovered in my esteem for it a new explanation for my attraction to Asia. I attended workshops designed to expose underlying feelings that influence behavior; I tried yoga, meditation, and kept a journal. I embraced therapy, and, after years of searching, found counsel that I considered wise. It seemed to me that I was looking through a telescope, constantly turning its lens, until my psychic topography came into sharper and sharper focus. One by one I removed the strands of my confusion that stretched like a cobweb across my field of awareness, until my anguish gradually eased.

I married, in the process acquiring two stepchildren, and eventually we had a daughter of our own. Outwardly, my life had become tranquil, but something continued to elude me. I still succumbed to depression, I still longed for excitement. Periodically I'd take a stab at getting another job as a foreign correspondent, but after a while I knew I'd been out of the business too long to have a serious chance. I talked of moving the family to Asia, and once went so far as to get a visa to India so that I could make an exploratory trip there. My mark remained, as fiercely opaque as ever.

My mother inadvertently helped me, by telling me for the first time the story of my birth. We were in a restaurant in Beverly Hills, and both of us had imbibed a drink or two. She slipped the information in among her more customary tales, the sort that meandered endlessly through the follies of everyone she'd ever known, from my father, a frequent fall guy, to the various famous people she'd brushed up against. I'd heard innumerable times how as a college freshman she'd dressed up as a child for an intelligence exam, and thus managed to convince the test's administrator that he was face-to-face with an 8-year old girl whose IQ was above 200; about how my father once had the chance to represent an unknown singer named Elvis Presley but turned him down on the grounds that his music was ghastly; and about how various giants of the movie industry,had sufficiently dubious morals (but the excellent taste) to proposition my mother.

I was so used to these narratives that when she launched into them in the restaurant I reflexively stopped listening, except in the way a new mother sleeps through loud noises but awakens instantly to her infant's faint cries: a tiny, alert part of my brain scanned my mother's words for anything unusual while I diverted myself with the menu and my plans for the next day. Suddenly I thought I heard her say that because she suffered from constant abdominal pain after the birth of my sister and then endured a miscarriage, she was afraid I'd be stillborn — so afraid, in fact, that just before my birth she blindfolded herself and stopped up her ears. She got my attention with that. Thus she failed to hear my first cries, she said; she learned that the delivery was successful from her doctor, who proclaimed my gender by announcing triumphantly, "Biggest penis I ever saw!" Laughing coquettishly, my mother ended the story there, as if its point were the doctor's naughtiness, while I sat stunned, trying to be sure I'd heard her say that she prepared for my birth by stifling her senses. I swam back desperately, through the drinks, my daydreams, my numbness, to check her words, and then I saw that they rang true. Somewhere deep inside her, my mother knew she was telling not a joke but a horror story, and she knew what lesson I'd derive from it. I realized then that I began my life the way I'd experienced so much of it: alone, groping for union; my life's task was connection. Frightened of fleshly matter and insulated from all emotion, my mother didn't participate in my birth but rather waited passively, sadly, for it to end. Even at the moment of my first breaths, the paths we traveled failed to merge. I was primed for the mark at birth.

Fifteen years after leaving Indochina, I finally surfaced— I know the exact day and hour. It had been two years since I'd last talked to my wise adviser, and now I told her I wanted to see her one more time, in order to talk about the mark. I was so certain the meeting would be important that I taped our conversation, something I'd never done before, and afterwards I transcribed the words, and read them over and over. It wasn't words, however, that comprised my epiphany, but instead a vision, a series of visions. I saw the four-year-old who, close to death in a hospital, found no acknowledgment of his plight in the comportment of those closest to him. I saw the refugee camp woman who turned down Gibson's hundred dollars, the underground survivors of three months of shelling in Quang Tri, the prisoners in the Quang Ngai hospital ward, the starving children and their mothers in Phnom Penh— all voiceless victims in extreme circumstances, just as I'd been. One version of what I'd been doing in Indochina, I realized, was giving expression to their suffering, making the connection that had been thwarted when I was in the hospital. I could feel an excitement welling up in me: I was tantalizingly close to the ocean's surface now, close enough to see the light rippling across it and to imagine the air coursing through my lungs, and I was frightened that I could not travel the last few yards upwards. Then, a moment later, at five minutes before the hour, I saw the tiger cage prisoners' atrophied legs, and realized with a start that they resembled my polio-ridden leg, and I saw the men's smiling faces, and I understood that they knew the answer to the question I'd been asking all my life. They were wiser versions of me, who, like me, had looked into death's abyss, but had leaped across it, to freedom. Amazed and joyful, I wept. At last I understood that in Indochina I found myself.

ACKNOWLEDGMENTS

This book began modestly, as an essay about the hotel where I lived for six months while covering the war in Cambodia. The essay never felt complete, however; by the time I'd taken up all the issues I intended to raise in it, I understood that I was writing a book. I was accustomed to writing newspaper and magazine stories, but the idea of producing a book-length manuscript was daunting. That I carried on through seven drafts, written intermittently over a dozen years, is in great part attributable to the advice and encouragement I received from many people. Among those who read partial or complete drafts and offered valued assurances were Jill Bobrow, Bill Steadman, Jonathan Sanger, David Elliott, Mai Elliott, Nancy Daniels, Michael Daniels, Sylvia Wernick, Lester Wernick, Bob Kriegel, Marilyn Kriegel, Judy Johnstone, Hansine Goran, David Sibbet, Jerri Holmes, Susan Goldthwaite, Diane Huffman, Fred Huffman, Philip Jones Griffiths, Peter Sandmann, Pauline Tesler, Anna Hawken, and David Greenway. Thaisa Frank, Naomi Lowinsky, C.E. Poverman, and the late Helen MacAvity all provided invaluable critiques of the text. With passion and forcefulness, Nancy Haugen prodded me towards insights that were essential to the book's development. Mary Mackey's enthusiasm at a pivotal time impelled the book towards production. Aleen Leslie provided indispensable material resources including a word processor on which I wrote early drafts. The devotion and resourcefulness that John Oakes and Daniel Simon have displayed while shepherding the book to publication has been particularly heartening; I feel fortunate to have found publishers of such uncommon energy and decency. Most sustaining of all has been my wife Leslie, who late each afternoon graciously put aside whatever she was doing while I read aloud to her my day's production of words; then she'd offer both criticism and crucial encouragement. It is a testament to her extraordinary generosity that although I reacted badly to much of her criticism and felt that I could not receive enough of her praise, she did not tire of the project or of me.

December, 1994

GLOSSARY

ARVN — Army of the Republic of Vietnam

COMUSMACV — Commander, United States Military Assistance Command, Vietnam.

CORDS — Civilian Operations Revolutionary Development Support, an American program to promote rural development in South Vietnam.

COSVN — Communist Office for South Vietnam, the Viet Cong's headquarters, located across the South Vietnamese border in Cambodia through much of the war. Also, Nick Proffitt's dog.

FANK — Forces Armées Nationales Khmer, the army of the Khmer Republic led by Marshal Lon No1.

GVN — Government of Vietnam, the regime of South Vietnam.

HES — Hamlet Evaluation System, the computerized system by which American officials attempted to assess the political leaning of every district in South Vietnam.

I Corps — Pronounced "eye-core," and also known as "Military Region One," the furthest north of the four military regions in South Vietnam. It extended southward from the Demilitarized Zone through Quang Tri, Hue, and Danang.

JUSPAO — Joint United States Public Affairs Office, where foreign journalists in South Vietnam received American military accreditation.

Khmer Rouge — the "Red Cambodians," who overthrew the Khmer Republic in April, 1975.

MACV — (United States) Military Assistance Command, Vietnam, pronounced "mackvee."

National Liberation Front — the Communist force opposing the American-supported regime of Nguyen Van Thieu in South Vietnam. See "Viet Cong."

PSA — Province Senior Adviser, the highest-ranking civilian American official stationed in a province of South Vietnam.

RVN — Republic of Vietnam, the official name for the South Vietnamese governmental unit.

USAID — United States Agency for International Development.

Viet Cong — The phrase coined by the Americans to refer to the Vietnamese Communist forces who opposed them. They themselves preferred the term "National Liberation Front," but I have used "Viet Cong" throughout the book because it is more familiar to Western readers.

VNAF — Vietnamese Air Force, the air force of the Republic of Vietnam.

INDEX